PREHISTORIC SETTLEMENT PATTERNS
in the
NEW WORLD

VIKING FUND

PUBLICATIONS IN ANTHROPOLOGY

Number Twenty-Three

PREHISTORIC SETTLEMENT PATTERNS

in the

NEW WORLD

Edited by

GORDON R. WILLEY

GREENWOOD PRESS, PUBLISHERS
WESTPORT, CONNECTICUT

Library of Congress Cataloging in Publication Data
Main entry under title:

Prehistoric settlement patterns in the New World.

    Reprint. Originally published: New York : Wenner-Gren
Foundation for Anthropological Research, 1956. (Viking
Fund publications in anthropology ; no. 23)
    Bibliography: p.
    1. Indians--Antiquities--Addresses, essays, lectures.
2. Land settlement patterns, Prehistoric--America--
Addresses, essays, lectures. 3. Cities and towns,
Ruined, extinct, etc.--America--Addresses, essays,
lectures. 4. America--Antiquities--Addresses, essays,
lectures. I. Willey, Gordon Randolph, 1913-
II. Series: Viking Fund publications in anthropology
no. 23.

E53.P73 1981   970.01   81-13233
ISBN 0-313-23223-7 (lib. bdg.)   AACR2

S. L. WASHBURN

UNIVERSITY OF CHICAGO

Editor

Reprinted with the permission of The Wenner-Gren
Foundation for Anthropological Research, Inc.

Reprinted in 1981 by Greenwood Press,
A division of Congressional Information Service, Inc.
88 Post Road West, Westport, Connecticut 06881

Printed in the United States of America

10 9 8 7 6 5 4 3 2 1

PREFACE

THIS volume of essays on prehistoric settlement patterns in the New World had its origins in a symposium at the annual meeting of the American Anthropological Association held at Detroit in December, 1954, entitled "Settlements and Society: A Symposium in Archeological Inference." The original panel consisted of Emil W. Haury, W. H. Sears, Betty Meggers and Clifford Evans, Jr., E. M. Shook and Tatiana Proskouriakoff, and Alfred Kidder II and Evon Z. Vogt as discussant. The present editor served as chairman. As a result of the considerable interest in the symposium offerings, plans to publish these, along with other similar articles, were projected at that time. In organizing the volume, the authors of the five area papers given at Detroit were asked to make only minor changes or revisions in their original twenty-minute presentations. In keeping with this, the additional invited contributors were requested to limit their writings to a comparable length. In some cases this limit was exceeded; but, for the most part, the essays are brief summary reviews. Except for the initial symposium papers and the article by Douglas W. Schwartz (which was read at another session of the Detroit meetings), the manuscripts were submitted between April and June, 1955. Evon Z. Vogt revised and expanded his appraisal at this time.

G. R. W.

CONTENTS

INTRODUCTION 1
By Gordon R. Willey

SPECULATIONS ON PREHISTORIC SETTLEMENT PATTERNS IN THE SOUTHWEST 3
By Emil W. Haury

TYPES OF VILLAGE-PLAN LAYOUTS IN THE SOUTHWEST 11
By Erik K. Reed

SOME DISTRIBUTIONS OF SETTLEMENT PATTERNS IN THE PUEBLO SOUTHWEST . . . 18
By Fred Wendorf

DEMOGRAPHIC CHANGES IN THE EARLY PERIODS OF COHONINA PREHISTORY 26
By Douglas W. Schwartz

CALIFORNIA SETTLEMENT PATTERNS 32
By Robert F. Heizer and Martin A. Baumhoff

SETTLEMENT PATTERNS IN EASTERN UNITED STATES 45
By William H. Sears

SETTLEMENT PATTERNS IN THE LOWER MISSISSIPPI VALLEY 52
By Stephen Williams

PREHISTORIC SETTLEMENT PATTERNS IN THE NORTHERN MISSISSIPPI VALLEY AND THE
UPPER GREAT LAKES 63
By James B. Griffin

PREHISTORIC SETTLEMENT PATTERNS IN NORTHEASTERN NORTH AMERICA 72
By William A. Ritchie

CHANGING SETTLEMENT PATTERNS IN THE GREAT PLAINS 81
By Waldo R. Wedel

SETTLEMENT PATTERNS IN MESO-AMERICA AND THE SEQUENCE IN THE GUATEMALAN
HIGHLANDS 93
By Edwin M. Shook and Tatiana Proskouriakoff

SETTLEMENT PATTERNS IN THE GUATEMALAN HIGHLANDS: PAST AND PRESENT . . 101
By Stephan F. de Borhegyi

PROBLEMS CONCERNING PREHISTORIC SETTLEMENT PATTERNS IN THE MAYA LOWLANDS 107
By Gordon R. Willey

THE CENTRAL MEXICAN SYMBIOTIC REGION: A STUDY IN PREHISTORIC SETTLEMENT
PATTERNS 115
By William T. Sanders

SETTLEMENT PATTERNS IN NORTH-CENTRAL MEXICO 128
By J. Charles Kelley

CONTENTS

PREHISTORIC SETTLEMENT PATTERNS ON THE NORTHEASTERN PERIPHERY OF MESO-
AMERICA 140
  By Richard S. MacNeish

SETTLEMENT PATTERNS—PERU 148
  By Alfred Kidder II

THE RECONSTRUCTION OF SETTLEMENT PATTERN IN THE SOUTH AMERICAN TROPICAL
FOREST 156
  By Betty J. Meggers and Clifford Evans, Jr.

SETTLEMENT PATTERNS IN THE CARIBBEAN AREA 165
  By Irving Rouse

AN APPRAISAL OF "PREHISTORIC SETTLEMENT PATTERNS IN THE NEW WORLD" . . . 173
  By Evon Z. Vogt

BIBLIOGRAPHY 183

INTRODUCTION

By GORDON R. WILLEY

IN SETTLEMENT, man inscribes upon the landscape certain modes of his existence. These settlement arrangements relate to the adjustments of man and culture to environment and to the organization of society in the broadest sense. Viewed archeologically, settlement patterns are, like any prehistoric residue, the incomplete and fragmentary oddments of something that was once vital and whole. Nevertheless, settlements are a more direct reflection of social and economic activities than are most other aspects of material culture available to the archeologist. Because of this, settlement investigations offer a strategic meeting ground for archeology and ethnology. It is no accident that Strong's (1935, pp. 271–300) summary of prehistoric-to-historic culture sequences and development in Nebraska makes frequent reference to village patterns or that Steward's (1937) analysis of the ecological aspects of ancient-to-modern southwestern society relies heavily upon archeological settlement data in conjunction with ethnography.

An interest in settlement patterns is by no means new to American archeology. Site plans, survey maps, and site descriptions in archeological monographs testify to this. It is true that there have been few studies in which prehistoric settlement has been a major theme or in which a region has been treated from this point of view; but this has not been for lack of interest on the part of archeologists. Time, money, and the combined labors of many people are necessary to produce sufficient data to make settlement analyses possible in any area; and, as all archeologists will attest, such information, even in the best-documented situations, is still relatively meager. American archeological research has, however, reached a point at which attention can be turned to settlement problems. In many localities a beginning can be and has been made, as the following essays demonstrate.

Let it be made clear that there is no "settlement-pattern approach" to archeology. An awareness of settlement data simply extends the net of archeological interest to take in a larger and legitimate part of the record. The grouping of dwellings, one to another, is as important as the potsherd refuse within these houses. Like most archeological facts, those of settlement are robbed of much of their importance when considered in isolation.

Any number of different approaches to various problems may begin with the factual data of prehistoric settlement. These varied orientations and interests are exemplified in the following papers, whose authors were invited to participate with no conditions other than that they give some attention to the nature of prehistoric settlements in their areas throughout known archeological time.

The purpose of this volume of essays is to place on record what is known about prehistoric settlement patterns in several American areas. As such, the book is intended to provide basic source material as well as to indicate problems that will be incentives for future research. We hope that it will be a reference not only for the archeologist but also for the ethnologist. Aside from the primary requisite of the interest of the writer in the topic, participants were invited in order to give an approximate coverage of the New World. Those areas where archeological research is well advanced were given some priority in emphasis, but there are notable exceptions and omissions. The Arctic—which could well be examined in its history of settlement—is one of these, and there are others for which I can plead only happenstance and limitations of space. It should be noted that the final essay—an appraisal of the others—is the work of Evon Z. Vogt. It seemed fitting that an American ethnologist should have his say on what the archeologists have done and are trying to do in the interpretation of aboriginal settlement patterns in the New World; for, in the long run, only the joint and concerted effort of archeology and ethnology can bring full meaning out of the subject.

SPECULATIONS ON PREHISTORIC SETTLEMENT PATTERNS IN THE SOUTHWEST

By EMIL W. HAURY

THE archeological literature of the Southwest of the United States is astonishingly unproductive on the general problem of settlement patterns and interpretations of settlement data in cultural terms. This is all the more surprising for an area that has been studied so intensively for so many years and where existing groups provide living models of what went before. The main efforts at extracting sociopolitical factors from archeological data have been made by ethnologists, though there are a few notable exceptions (Martin and Rinaldo, 1950). Obviously, what is needed is the formulation of problems and the invention of procedures for gathering and studying comparable data. This will mean a shift in emphasis from historical to functional research and a more intensive dependence upon the work of the ethnologist, at least for the interpretive basis of certain aspects of Southwestern prehistory. The works of V. Mindeleff (1891), Fewkes (1900), C. Mindeleff (1900), Kroeber (1917), Strong (1927), Hawley (1937), Steward (1937), Parsons (1939), Eggan (1950), and others could be consulted with profit by the archeologist as a point of departure in the development of this problem.

Specifically oriented studies of two categories might be undertaken. First, environmental research, focusing on the forces at work, land forms, changes through recent times, the nature and amount of resources, etc. Hack's analysis (1942) of Hopi Indian physical environment has superbly demonstrated what can be done along this line, how an exposed, wind-swept desert actually is superior to other nearby areas for primitive agriculture because of a permanent ground-water supply and its greater resistance to the effect of climatic change resulting from a peculiar combination of exposure, duning of sand, and little arroyo-cutting. Second, parts of the Southwest must be understood by intensive investigation of the human adaptation to the land on the order of Willey's (1953) Virú Valley studies. Two threads in such studies must be interwoven—the historical and the functional—as either one by itself will not do. After these regional studies are viewed against one another, generalities may emerge. The trend in Southwest research, happily, is in this direction, as witness Peabody Museum's early work at Awatovi and presently in western New Mexico, the Chicago Natural History Museum's endeavors near Reserve, New Mexico, and the University of Arizona's excavations on the San Carlos Indian Reservation.

We are, as yet, ignorant about the nature of settlements of Early Man. The existence of the elephant hunters (Clovis) and bison hunters (Folsom) is known chiefly, though not exclusively, through widely scattered "kill" sites. Mobility, demanded by a hunting economy, suggests small, loosely knit family, or at the most band, units. Formal structures of a shallow-pit nature are known within the first millennium B.C., possibly coincident with the advent of agriculture, but before the arrival of pottery in the Southwest. The archeological record shows that this stationary existence, related to an improved food supply, was also characterized by larger and more population groups than was the case earlier. Fixed village life, with some grouping of families and possibly a kin-determined headman implied, probably came into being no more than four thousand years ago among the people of the Cochise culture.

We have, of course, numerous site reports encompassing the last two thousand years which show the nature of the individual houses, their arrangement with respect to one another, and their relation to buildings other than domestic units for the three of the Southwest's chief physiographic provinces, namely, the northern plateau, the central mountains, and the southern desert. With these as a starting point, a few problems can be formulated. The physiographic differences themselves, impressive to the modern traveler, have frequently been cited as the prime reason for cultural differences. This has led to the correlation of the Anasazi with the plateau province on an early time level, later extending over into the mountain zone; Mogollon with the mountain region; and the Hohokam with the desert. But no one, to my knowledge, has attempted seriously to single out the factors, ecological or cultural, which explain why this is so. By size, by climatic and altitudinal extremes, by accessibility, and by archeological resources, the Southwest would appear to be an ideal test area for some "grass-roots" studies along this line. In this connection a desirable starting point would be a study of the distribution of species of wild food and the influence of spotty rainfall on food supplies, apart from those produced by agriculture, following Steward's analysis (1938) of the Basin-Plateau region.

The dispersal of sedentary people over the ground in the Southwest, regardless of the physiographic province, was determined, first of all, by water. This, of course, is generally true, but the aridity of the area concerned imposed greater limits on the location of settlements than was the case in better-watered regions. In other words, habitation depended acutely on the conditions of physiography, exemplified especially by the Hopi (Hack, 1942). It stands to reason that limited water sources or those with a slow recharge would allow a wide dispersal of small groups; but, with town development, larger water reserves were necessary, and the number of possibilities was at once limited to settlement along living streams, near permanent springs, and where the water table could be tapped by shallow wells. Mesa Verde, Chaco Canyon, the Hopi country, the Rio Grande, the Gila River and its upper tributaries, and the White Mountains were such areas.

The second requisite for an agricultural people was land, present in the instances mentioned, but each area required special agricultural techniques to make the land produce. This is a problem which has not been adequately explored.

Both these factors—water and land—tended to anchor people to one spot. It should be observed that land as such need not keep an agricultural people rooted, as is illustrated by the Papago. The degree of permanence appears to be dependent on the extent to which natural foods supplemented the foods grown. An awareness of this element is essential in assessing settlement patterns archeologically. On the whole, however, Southwestern societies maintained a high degree of permanence, which shaped the effects of both internal and external cultural forces.

Before about A.D. 700 the villages of the Anasazi, Mogollon, and Hohokam were not greatly different, being composed of independent dwelling units arranged in clusters without formal order, strategically located with respect to water and arable land, and usually on high ground. When seen in plan only and without consideration of differences in structural details and materials, the village pattern was essentially uniform in spite of sharp environmental differences. The subsequent divergences, culminating in such concentrations as in Chaco Canyon, Mesa Verde, and the Gila Valley, came within documented archeological time, and these trends are traceable in some cases to existing people. Hence the opportunity to recapture social, political, and religious elements would appear to exist. What factors there were or by what strange coincidence a common force was operative up to a certain time, less so afterward, has no immediate answer, though I suspect it lies in the non-material aspects of the societies.

In my opinion one of the greatest achievements of the Indians of the Southwest was the development of the pueblo type of domestic architecture. This employed the principles of joining room to room, of one wall serving two rooms, and of going upward more than one story, with the roofs supported by the walls and the houses often arranged around plazas. Early explanations held that the limited environment of cliff recesses and caves caused buildings to be put hard by one another and one on top of another so as to accommodate the maximum number of people. This supposition will not stand much scrutiny. It would not be difficult to show that the cliff house was the exception, that infinitely more compact buildings were in the open, where the same restrictions did not hold. Furthermore, the best evidence for the origin of pueblo architecture exists in open sites rather than in caves. Some other explanation must be sought.

Obviously, two conditions were needed for this achievement. The first was environmental: the existence of building stone, clay, and structural wood. All these were to be had in unlimited quantities in almost all parts of the plateau and mountain zones. But abundance did not assure use. Another condition had to be operative, and that was internal or within the social environment. The explanation, perhaps naïvely sought by a "dirt" archeologist, lies in the kinship organization of the modern western pueblos.

Using Eggan's study (1950) of western pueblos as the starting point, we see that the Hopi, Zuni, Acoma, and Laguna present a remarkably uniform architectural adjustment to the environment and that the territory encompassed by these villages lies close to the heart of the area where, long ago, pueblo architecture arose. In the modern villages the outward appearance often reflects the internal organization of the occupants (Eggan, 1950, p. 3). For our purposes it is important to note that among the Hopi, as an example, the primary local organization is the extended family, based on matrilocal residence, the members occupying a series of *adjoining* rooms, which are used in common. These groups Eggan refers to as the "household" (1950, pp. 29–30), and the unity of the group is retained in the face of divisive forces. This pattern, with minor variations, holds for the other western pueblos also.

Since the household, determined by kinship and marriage, is an economic unit and group welfare is dependent upon co-operative effort, living in close geographic proximity had its practical advantages. In basic plan, contiguous rooms could be added to accommodate new families as needed. So the requirements of the social structure to maintain cohesion along lineages or segments of them and for expansion are met architecturally by the agglutinated dwellings. We may rightfully ask that, if this is a widespread and firmly fixed pattern today, was it not also true for the large pueblos of Pueblo III times? And if we are entitled to assume this, as I think we must, some inkling of the beginning, at least of the formalization, of the extended-family type of housing may be found in the architectural record of Pueblo II or, in round terms, about A.D. 1000.

Many, though not all (Brew, 1946, p. 224), of the Pueblo II settlements were small, architecturally representing a metamorphosis from the earlier pit houses to the predominantly large pueblos of later times. They undoubtedly were extended-family dwelling units situated in the midst of or near the fields; or, to put this in another way, during Pueblo II it would appear that more extended-family groups were living as independent units than was the case both in Basketmaker III and in Pueblo III. Later the agglutination of numbers of these units, together with normal population increase, resulted in the large towns of Pueblo III and IV. Eggan (1950, p. 130) believes that the "matrilineal lineage principle was utilized in organizing the large pueblos on the Hopi mesas." Once again it would be my contention that this was also true on earlier time levels. It remains for the archeologist to adduce supporting evidence. This move must also have been accompanied by the development of new political controls. What it was that brought people together in towns has been expressed in the pueblo formula of a community stronghold near water. The concept of banding together for mutual defense has much to recommend it, but there may also be other factors, one being the requirements of the religious system in promoting rain-producing ceremonies.

Still another effect on the settlement plan arising from the concentration of people concerned the maintenance of the agricultural activities. Previously, it would appear that household groups, living as small independent communities, were close to their fields. Nucleation meant that some fields were far away. This demanded more time in transit to and from field work and greater risk of loss of crops to marauders. The distant farmhouse, strategically located with respect to the fields, was the solution. This served jointly as a temporary home, as an observation post, and for crop storage at harvest time. On the whole, archeologists have not paid much attention to these units, but, generalizing on my own experience, it would appear that the farmhouse was a function of urbanization and that few, if any, will be found dating from before about 1000. The inference may be drawn that the distant deployment of farmhouses was associated with times of peace, which, if correct, considerably reduces the force of the argument that towns arose in response to a need for mutual protection.

Numerous aspects, such as the clan and ceremonial systems, the effects of population influxes and diffusion, regional and temporal differences, the influence of natural events like volcanic eruptions (Colton, 1933, 1936) and droughts, and other problems, would need to be considered for a thoroughgoing interpretation of the pre-Spanish pueblo settlements in terms of sociopolitical factors. It is a task well worth the effort.

The Hohokam settlements of the Gila Basin present a strikingly different picture from that of the Pueblos, and the data are far more difficult to assess, first, because the connection between the Hohokam and existing groups has not been clearly demonstrated and, second, because there is far less archeological information than exists for the Pueblos. Except for the fourteenth-century intrusion of pueblo architectural principles into the Hohokam territory, the village types remained almost unchanged from the beginning of Hohokam history at about the time of Christ to 1300. The same compelling conditions of water and soil determined the location of their abodes, but villages were even more localized to main valleys than among the Pueblos and Basketmakers because of the larger unwatered and inhospitable areas of the desert. Even so, this did not result in the compact, concentrated house clusters seen to the north. Village size appears to have been the product more of the magnitude of the population and local ecological factors than of social or political forces or the necessity of defense, which may have merged earlier independent units in some places. The organization of Snaketown, judged on the basis of rubbish mounds (only about 5 per cent of the site has been excavated), would appear to indicate random house clusters, dispersed over a large area. To a greater or lesser degree this applies to other Hohokam villages, too. What this means in terms of societal arrangement can only be surmised— possibly some segregation by kin. But other than DiPeso's recent work in the Santa Cruz Valley on a late (post-1000) time level, Hohokam archeology has revealed little to suggest the existence of sharply defined social units or a rule of residence.

The presence of ball courts does, however, reflect an overriding binding force, undoubtedly primarily religious, though the competitive aspect of the games (inferred) was probably determined by the social organization of the group. Among the Anasazi and Mogollon, the Great Kiva was firmly in-trenched. The location of this structure was generally central, or nearly so, with respect to the domestic structures. The ball courts among the Hohokam, on the contrary, were frequently marginal, at the edges of the living areas. What conclusions may be drawn from this I do not know, but it could be a hint of intervillage competition of the kind still existing in the kick-ball races of the Papago.

We know that the ball courts do not occur in all Hohokam villages, from which we may gather that differences of importance between them did exist. Those villages with courts may have had a moiety or phratry division from which competing "teams" could be drawn and also the necessary leadership, whether religious or secular, to determine the time and the conduct of the games.

The outstanding achievement of the Hohokam with political consequences and implications was the development of their irrigation system. It was only by intervillage co-operation that individual ditches, 20 or more miles in length, up to 60 feet in width, and 10 feet in depth, could have been constructed. Aggregate canal mileage in the Salt River Valley alone has been calculated to be in excess of 200 miles (Turney, 1929), which, even in our present mecha-nized society, would be regarded as a large-scale operation. In some instances several villages drew benefits from the same canal. The planning, construction, and maintenance of these ditches reflect some degree of centralized authority, possibly in the nature of an intervillage council. At the same time, the infer-ence can be drawn that villages were under strong political leadership, for labor recruitment would have been at this level.

Other important effects on the society deriving from public waterworks programs would have been new concepts regarding water rights and possibly landownership. The nature of these is not recoverable. Elongated river cob-bles have been found by present-day farmers in the Salt River Valley, set verti-cally in the ground, sometimes in alignment, suggesting field or "property" boundaries, but modern reclamation blotted out the field systems before this was called to archeologists' attention.

Wittfogel and Goldfrank (1943) have noted the influence of waterworks and irrigation in shaping agrarian societies, with special reference to the eastern Pueblos. They point out: "If the Pueblos represent a waterwork society in miniature, then we should look for certain authoritative forms of civil and magic leadership, for institutionalized discipline, and a specific social and ceremonial organization." If this is true for the Pueblos, it may have been infinitely more so among the Hohokam, who had superior technological mastery of irrigation.

Another consequence of Hohokam canal-building which materially affected their dispersal has, I think, been overlooked. For all arid-country dwellers, water determines the site of residence. Given the proper topography, ditches could be built to lead water for miles away from the river which supplied it. This permitted settlements to spring up far from natural water sources in the midst of the preferred fertile plains. A notable example of this was Los Muertos in the Salt River Valley, which flourished in the fourteenth century as one of the Southwest's larger population centers, 6 miles from Salt River. At least three small ditches directed water from the main canal to reservoirs conveniently placed in a cluster of two-score domestic compounds (Haury, 1945, pp. 30–42).

This emancipation from naturally occurring water was one of the unique advances of prehistoric community life in the Southwest. Under this system, village well-being was in delicate balance, for the water flow had to be kept up. Once again from this we infer the existence of a central authority and organized activities connected with the repair, cleaning, head-gate tending, and protection of the canal systems. It passed out of existence as a pattern, however, with the decline of the desert people after 1400 and was not revived until the last century, with the digging of wells.

Before leaving the Hohokam area, mention should be made of several characteristics which have never been adequately explained. The basal platforms for houses, or platform mounds, of the Salt, Gila, and Santa Cruz River valleys surely mean something in settlement terms. Historically late and dating from a time of considerable cultural mixture, they exist as architectural anomalies in the Southwest. Also the fortified hills and strongholds of Papagueria (Hoover, 1941) with their related villages have not been fully assessed as to the implication of warfare affecting the desert Hohokam in late prehistory. The defense villages of the Papago should shed light on this.

By way of recapitulation, Pueblo and Hohokam development can be briefly summarized as follows: Both have similar beginnings in so far as village plan is concerned, the groups having been given permanence by ecological factors and economic pursuits. In time (Pueblo II), among the Anasazi, pueblo architecture grew out of an increasingly sharpened feeling of kinship bonds and a rule of residence. After 1000, lineages were drawn together in towns. This was accompanied by new ideas pertaining to farming, to civil and religious conduct, and to the achievement of political autonomy. The Hohokam villages, on the other hand, show a weakness in all the elements which characterize the Pueblos throughout their history. House organization suggests no strong lines of descent or the dictates of a residence rule. We may infer that their strength lay along political lines, geared to an agricultural economy by irrigation. Diffusion tinged this culture with Meso-American elements, far more so than among the Pueblos. But, in spite of this evident contact, social classes, cities, emphasis on warfare, the religious architecture and ceremonial centers of the South did not take hold, which argues against their migration out of the South as a full-blown group. I mention this seemingly unrelated fact to emphasize that both Anasazi and Hohokam were in the Southwest at the time of Christ, that their proximity to each other, yet divergent development observable over many centuries, provides us with cultural phenomena of exceptional interest.

As noted before, most of the efforts to project social structures backward into the archeological past based on the settlement patterns have come from the pens of the ethnologists, not from the archeologists. I do not intend this to be a rebuff to my colleagues—we have had our own time getting our archeological house in order through intensive historic and taxonomic studies. But it does appear now, with the trend toward broadened horizons, that inference as to the non-material aspects of archeological groups must be as much a part of our reports as is the description of architecture and pottery.

The crux of the matter is, of course, how far we can go in making such inferences and interpretations. The ball courts, irrigation canals, and symbolic art of the Hohokam tell us that their society must have been structured; but how do we arrive at its precise nature? Obviously, this accomplishment is an impossibility. The limits to which we can go are set in part by the nature of archeological data; beyond this the frontiers will be established only by our own ability or inability to evaluate the information available to us.

TYPES OF VILLAGE-PLAN LAYOUTS IN THE SOUTHWEST

By ERIK K. REED

AN IMPORTANT distinction and a really basic trait of the Anasazi proper in the northern Southwest, up to about A.D. 1300, is the unidirectional or front-oriented town plan. In the period between about A.D. 450 and 750, "Modified Basketmaker" or "Basketmaker III" (settlements of pre-ceramic horizons are not well enough known to permit any determination of village plans), the typical site consisted of (1) storage cists, (2) pit houses, and (3) refuse area—generally arranged, in that order, usually on an approximately northwest-southeast axis, though irregular and scattered.

Most of the men who were kind enough to review the first draft of this paper in the summer of 1954—including E. W. Haury, J. O. Brew, W. W. Wasley, W. R. Bullard, and others—argue that I have created, and am creating, a false impression of regularity in Basketmaker III as against lack of organization in early Mogollon sites. Bullard states the case thus: "Much of early Anasazi information is based on excavation of single units within a community; Mogollon information is based more on whole community plans. Whereas the typical Basketmaker unit consisted of a pit house with associated storage rooms, the typical Mogollon unit lacked the storage rooms. The unidirectional plan is based largely on association of pit house with its storage rooms. Compare site plans of Shabikeschee and the SU site. Contrasts are not so great when large segments of communities are compared at BM III level." Admitting the justice of these comments, I still think that the difference, conspicuous in later periods, is foreshadowed in early Anasazi sites.

In the period known as Pueblo I, from about A.D. 750 to between 900 and 950, the storage cists have become light surface structures, typically a crescentic row of contiguous rooms, and the features of the pit house have changed, but the ordering is the same and is much more regular: (1) surface rooms, (2) pit houses, (3) refuse area. The same basic arrangement carries through, with few exceptions and with increased rigidity, in later phases in the San Juan area: pueblo-kivas-refuse (and burial) areas, even when the pueblo has become quite large, with kivas incorporated. There is always a definite front and back, with a general axis of orientation.

This principle of village layout is observed throughout the San Juan area and the northern Little Colorado drainage (at least as far south as the Zuni-Puerco district); on the lower Little Colorado as far southwestward as the

Wupatki district and also west and north of the Colorado River; and weakly developed in the Paria River area and the Virgin River drainage in southwestern Utah and southern Nevada. Not enough is known about early sites in the upper Rio Grande to make a definite general statement for that area, which is also of Anasazi character in other diagnostic cultural features up to the 1300's; but available data clearly suggest the prevalence in early periods of the basic Anasazi plan, or modifications thereof, with definite organization and orientation along a single direction.

This distribution corresponds, approximately and generally, to that of several traits—circular kivas; rough, gray culinary pottery; wrapped-haft stone axes; lambdoid artificial cranial deformation; and perhaps also the keeping and eating of turkeys—which distinguish the Anasazi proper from other prehistoric southwestern groups (Reed, 1946, 1948, 1949a, 1950, 1951b). The major apparent exceptions are (1) the upper Rio Grande in the 1200's, discussed later, and (2) the Kaibab plateau, north of the Grand Canyon in western Arizona, and parts of southeastern Utah, where definite patterning on these lines is not clearly observable (but might be determined by further work).

South of the Little Colorado Valley in Arizona and south of a transitional zone in western New Mexico running from the Zuni country and Quemado south of Acoma to between Isleta and Belen, between U.S. Highways 60 and 66, the Mogollon traits corresponding to those just listed for Anasazi are rectangular ceremonial chambers or none identifiable; polished brown ware; ¾-grooved (for a J-haft) polished stone axes; vertical occipital cranial deformation; and wild turkeys hunted, evidently, rather than domesticated, in general or in much of the area.

There are definite instances of turkey-keeping in late pueblos of Mogollon tradition in eastern Arizona, and my statement on this project (1951a) will have to be modified. Otherwise, so far as I know, my interpretation of certain aspects of Mogollon-Anasazi relationships, as adumbrated in an earlier paper (1942) and worked out in an unpublished thesis, has held up fairly well, although there is a current view which I am compelled to accept to a degree, or in a sense, that the Sinagua should be grouped with Hohokam and Patayan instead of Mogollon. The rejection of my thesis recently voiced by Drs. Martin and Rinaldo (1954) is just an objection to "lumping" without any controversion of the facts, analysis of the reasoning, or invalidation of any part of the interpretation. The legitimate and logical refutation by Dr. Wendorf (1953, 1954) of an incidental corollary of my general theory, specifically attempting to correlate languages and archeological complexes in the Rio Grande, is well taken—whether or not correct—but does not affect the main idea.

In the Mogollon and (or including) Sinagua, as in Hohokam (see Haury, this volume), no such regularity of plan is observable in early sites, and quite different principles of organization are found in later ones. Mogollon pit-house villages seem to me to have no visible scheme of organization at all; the dwellings (i.e., the entrances) even face in different dirctions, although sometimes with a general east or southeast trend. Small pueblos in much of southwestern New Mexico often are just groups of rooms pulled together into an unplanned unit. At least some of the Tularosa Phase sites are, however, essentially Anasazi in plan, Fred Wendorf has pointed out, which is all right, as it consorts with other Anasazi influences observable as far south as the Tularosa Valley.

Larger pueblos may also be agglomerations, more or less linear, at least among the Sinagua (e.g., Tuzigoot and Wupatki), or else are organized in squares (or circles or ovals) around a central plaza or around several courts, in the region above the Mogollon Rim (e.g., the Puerco Ruin at the Petrified Forest, sites in the Zuni country) and in the Mimbres. Out of this or else from the grouping-together of several agglomerations, there seems to have developed the alignment pattern—a series of uneven rows or house-blocks with streets and courts between.

Most of the compounds in southern Arizona seem to be unorganized, the dwellings either scattered, with no particular alignment and orientation, or else forming agglomerations, held together only by the inclosing wall and not by any inherent design. In certain of these sites, such as the Casa Grande and Soho Phase house-mound inclosures, there is a single central focus of interest, and presumably these should be classed with plaza-type pueblos. Some post-1300 compounds, e.g., the Clear Creek site, have the houses regularly facing inward.

In absolutely none of these plans, in (so far as I know or can find out readily) not a single site south of the approximate boundary indicated here and in previous papers, except apparently in the Tularosa Valley, is there a unidirectional orientation along a single axis, with a marked distinction between front and back. There is no "front" in many of these ruins; they face out equally in all directions or face in to a plaza from all sides. Among the mesa-top Sinagua sites the approach to the site, dictated by topography, may be considered as the front, A. H. Schroeder points out; but I feel that this does not invalidate the general statement.

Now this site orientation is a really significant difference, fully as important as the circular kiva and far more meaningful culturally than methods of hafting axes or of firing and finishing pottery. It surely must reflect something basic in personality structure, outlook, national character—something comparable to the difference between the Spanish inward-facing patio-type house on the edge of the street and our front-facing dwellings with the lawn on the outside. Exactly what it means I do not know; a psychologist and an architect—or Lewis Mumford—might be able to tell us. But it must have some definite significance, very possibly reflecting differing kinds of social organization.

Strangely, the Anasazi type of town plan disappeared, apparently upon abandonment of the San Juan and adjacent districts about or soon after A.D. 1300. Other characteristic Anasazi traits continued in the upper Rio Grande generally (but not among the western Pueblos), after the early 1300's: circular kivas, black-on-white painted ware and rough, dark, unpolished utility pottery, and full-(spirally)grooved stone axes.[1]

The modern western Pueblos (the Hopi towns, including Tewa or "Hano," the village of the Tanos from the Rio Grande on First Mesa above Walpi; Zuni, and other prehistoric Zuni villages; Acoma) all seem to fit or approach the alignment type or a combination of alignment and plaza type, with no single central focus. The crowded mesa-top Hopi villages are irregular linear agglomerations, but with inside, if not necessarily central, courts, and may be considered an adaptation of the alignment pattern, uneven rows or blocks arranged along courts rather than surrounding them. Oraibi, the only Hopi pueblo still on its pre-1680 site, is definitely patterned in rows and streets like Acoma, the best example, where, incidentally, the "streets" are "one-sided," that is, the houses all face in the same direction.

The old part of the modern pueblo of Zuni consists of rather extensive house-blocks inclosing small courts, disposed irregularly about a main, more or less central, plaza, in which the eighteenth-century Franciscan mission church is located. I suspect that this effect of what seems to be a single center may be ascribed to Spanish influence and that it was not a true occurrence of the plaza type but a linear-alignment plan into which the Spanish plaza with the Catholic church was absorbed.[2] In the late pre-Spanish and proto-historic period, however, apparently through the seventeenth century, both Hopi and Zuni towns were generally hollow-square (or -oval), plaza-type layouts.

In the upper Rio Grande, the hollow-square or plaza type (often multiple-plaza) seems to have become predominant by the 1200's, possibly even earlier, and to have continued through Pueblo IV, the glaze-paint and biscuit-ware period, 1350–1680—for example, Pecos, the large Galisteo Basin ruins, Kuaua,

---

1. Reed (1949*b*) and Wendorf (1954). Lambdoid cranial deformation vanished entirely, so far as is known, and turkeys were being kept in the sixteenth century at Zuni (not at Hopi) as well as at many Rio Grande pueblos (not Pecos or Taos).

2. In the same way that in the Mariana Islands, near the western extreme of the domain of that same viceroy of New Spain who from a distance ruled New Mexico, the plaza has been incorporated into the linear single-direction Micronesian village plan without actually changing it seriously. In the small, comparatively undisturbed, farming villages on the southeast and south coasts of Guam, the parallel rows of Micronesian-type, pile-supported, rectangular houses, built of modern materials, still all face toward the sea; the plaza is merely a vacant space, with houses facing on only one side—actually, facing *across* the plaza rather than into it —instead of the whole settlement centering toward it, as in a Spanish town.

Unshagi, Pindi, Cuyamunge, the major Pajarito Plateau ruins,[3] the biscuit-ware sites of the Chama Valley,[4] and others. Among the modern Rio Grande pueblos, only the Tewa have retained the hollow-square or multiple-plaza layout.[5] All five Rio Grande Keresan villages[6] are essentially of the parallel-alignment type, like the western pueblos, with no single central area; so is Jemez; so are the Tiwa pueblos of Sandia and Isleta near Albuquerque, although both of these also have central plazas.

Of the two more northerly Tiwa-speaking towns, there is too little left of Picuris to present a definite picture (but it gives a plaza effect), and Taos is a peculiar, even unique, layout—two large agglomerations, each a pyramidal four- or five-story pile without a specific directional orientation, and scattered additional small buildings, all tied together by an inclosing wall. The large open space lying between the two main structures is not a true plaza, though forming a definite center of the settlement (and of activities). Here it is possible to speak of a "front" and a "back"; yet the several buildings are not aimed toward the front.

The underlying philosophy, so to speak, of Taos pueblo actually resembles at first glance the basic principles of organization, or lack of organization, of southern Arizona compounds or of the irregularly scattered agglomerations of certain ruins in central New Mexico.[7] In any case, Taos is neither a hollow-square (plaza) type nor a parallel-alignment (rows and streets) type, and I have difficulty in trying to interpret it as a survival of the Anasazi front-oriented, unidirectional type, *unless* it is viewed as facing east, uphill, away from the normal approach, in which case the whole thing falls into place, with kivas at the "front," and looks like a partly disintegrated Pueblo Bonito.

Interpretation of the changes during the last few centuries in the upper Rio Grande, from the front-directed Anasazi plan to the hollow-square layout

3. Puye, Tsankawi, Potsuwi ("Otowi"), Tshirege, and Tyuonyi. The last is a hollow circle instead of a square and retains a definite hint of Anasazi directional orientation: the original building was evidently a typical Anasazi pueblo, with kivas in front, and complete inclosure came later. Rainbow House, a small contemporary ruin just down the canyon, is of Anasazi plan.

4. Te-ewi and Leafwater, Tzama itself, and others; Riana in a slightly earlier (Wiyo black-on-white) period.

5. Tesuque, San Ildefonso, Nambe; confused but basic and original at Santa Clara; disrupted at San Juan, presumably by closer contact with the Spanish than elsewhere from the summer of 1598 on, and San Juan is now more on the parallel-streets plan than of the central-plaza type.

6. Zia and and Santa Ana on the lower Jemez River and Cochiti, Santo Domingo, and San Felipe on the Rio Grande shortly above the confluence of the Jemez. San Felipe does have a definite central plaza, however, and Cochiti actually is rather scattered.

7. The large brown-ware (with Chupadero black-on-white and glaze-paint polychrome) sites of the Salinas district, historically Piro (including "Jumanas"). The late Dr. H. P. Mera considered these as "discrete or rancheria arrangements" as against the compact "confluent" pueblo form (Scholes and Mera, 1940, p. 292), and they are indeed rather irregularly laid out and disorganized in plan, though resembling generally the multiple-plaza type.

(ubiquitous, apparently, during Pueblo IV) to predominance of parallel alignment, except among the Tewa, is beyond me.

The continuance of the plaza type in the surviving Tewa pueblos fits nicely and confirms the clear indications from pottery and other lines of evidence (including documentary sources from 1540 on) that the northern Tewa were the biscuit-ware-making people of the entire district about the confluence of the Chama and the Rio Grande and had been in this same area since well before 1300. The linear alignment in parallel rows with streets is all right for Keresans, with their many other connections with the western Pueblos, and also for Jemez, which shows important western and/or Keresan influences (cf. Eggan, 1950). It could be explained for Sandia as possibly due to the Tiwa sojourn in the first half of the eighteenth century. The site of their pueblo there, Payupki, is a plaza layout (Mindeleff, 1891, Pl. 13). Why the linear parallel alignment superseded the unified hollow square in the west I have no idea. The latter seems to have been widespread, characteristic of most groups except Sinagua, throughout Pueblo IV.

J. D. Jennings has wondered whether the shift from front-facing arrangement to inward-looking plaza type might reflect the "freezing" of Pueblo society into ultra-conservatism; I like this kind of explanation and hope it can be made to fit the timing.

But the distribution in space does appear susceptible of historical, if not cultural, interpretation, at least during the thousand-year period before the abandonment of the San Juan and the general era, between 1250 and 1450 or so, of instability and shifting, resettlement and readjustment, and consolidation into the historic Pueblo cultures. A general correlation, undoubtedly not without exceptions, can be outlined as follows:

1. Front-oriented or unidirectional plan (definite orientation of the entire site and its major component parts in a single direction): Anasazi to 1300.

2. No particular organization, scattered separate houses or unsystematic agglomerations of rooms (facing more or less equally in several or all directions): Yuman-Patayan, Hohokam, Sinagua (including large late pueblos), early Mogollon pit-house villages and small pueblos, many southern Arizona compounds.

3. Plaza or multiple-court layout (facing systematically inward to one or more centers): most of the larger later Mogollon pueblos (Mimbres, Cibola–Little Colorado), possibly the Hohokam house-mound sites, all known large Pueblo IV sites of the upper Rio Grande, the modern Tewa pueblos.

4. Parallel alignments (systematic but not single-directional orientation, not organized around a center or centers): no known pre-Spanish examples but the great majority of modern towns (all western pueblos and Keresan pueblos, also Jemez and Isleta).

My colleague, A. H. Schroeder, with whom I have discussed this and who has been of considerable help on it, has further suggested the following correlation with the foregoing points, which I am not quite ready to indorse, although it also is the *kind* of explanation I want:

1. Extended-family (clan) architectural plan of Pueblo II, dominant also in Pueblo III arrangement on a larger scale: clan control, formalized town.

2. Non-clan society architecture, based on immediate family: no group control—individual selection based on economy; rancheria type.

3. Result of Anasazi diffusion into non-clan areas, creating formalized town with political (?) control—or result of Mexican influence on the Hohokam, which diffused north and east through the mountains across to the upper Rio Grande, introducing formalized central control.

4. Clan blocks of Anasazi dominate architecture of west, and moiety society that of east.

Possibly, with further consideration, a general hypothesis can be worked out along this line (and following up the penetrating suggestions which have been offered in the last twenty-five or thirty years by Strong, Steward, Florence Hawley, Eggan, and others), which will fit with the historical facts indicated by material culture. Town plans will surely prove as important as potsherds for this kind of synthesis.

SOME DISTRIBUTIONS OF SETTLEMENT PATTERNS IN THE PUEBLO SOUTHWEST

By FRED WENDORF

IN THIS paper we shall discuss varieties of southwestern pueblo village arrangements and probe the possible significance of these groupings in terms of indicated function, social and political structure, and religious organization. Two cultural traditions, each occupying a distinctive geographical environment, will be examined: the San Juan Anasazi, as seen from the desert plateau of the upper Chaco–San Juan drainages; and the Mogollon, as exemplified in the mountain valleys of the upper Gila and its tributaries.

THE CHACO ANASAZI

The Chaco Anasazi resided in what is now northwestern New Mexico, in the broad, grass-covered, and almost flat Chuska Valley. The valley has the appearance of a vast basin, over 75 miles long and 60 miles wide, surrounded on all sides by high and timber-covered mountains. The monotony of the valley floor is occasionally broken by deep canyons and vertical-sided mesas. The average elevation is approximately 6,000 feet, but rainfall is scant, ranging from less than 9 to slightly more than 13 inches per year. The mountains which surround the Chuska Valley receive somewhat greater moisture, and runoff from these higher land masses provided an important supplement to the water supplies of the aboriginal inhabitants. The Chaco drainage area apparently never supported a living stream, and permanent flowing water was, and is, virtually absent, occurring only in the San Juan and its northern tributaries.

The Chaco Anasazi were agriculturalists, but the absence of permanent flowing water and the scant rainfall required that only the areas which met the specialized requirements of sand-dune or flood-water farming could be utilized (Hack, 1942). Such areas are numerous, but few are extensive, and for the most part they are widely separated. Thus the area is ideally suited for exploitation by widely scattered small groups, and only a few areas can support sizable permanent populations. At the same time, the openness of the terrain and the comparative ease of communication and contact between the scattered communities retarded the development of regional subcultures. Throughout the Chuska Valley and in all time periods there was a surprising uniformity of cultural pattern.

Settlements of the Chaco Anasazi, from the earliest known horizon (*ca.* A.D. 500; Basketmaker III) until approximately A.D. 1050 or 1100 (beginning of Pueblo III), consist of a few fairly large communities located in particularly favorable areas and numerous, widely scattered small villages situated closely adjacent to similarly favorable but smaller arable plots. Each of the small villages, regardless of size, contained living and storage areas, and one or more subterranean ceremonial structures (kiva). From all outward appearance they were ceremonially, and presumably politically, independent. Steward (1937, p. 95) has suggested that each of these small villages was inhabited by a unilateral kin group living on its inherited land.

Farmhouses, that is, structures occupied only temporarily during the growing or harvest season and lacking the ceremonial structure consistently associated with the small villages, are not known for this period, although they possibly exist.

The larger communities appear as clusters of several discrete units with no apparent consistent arrangement of the various units with respect to one another. Each unit was closely similar to the isolated smaller villages and contained living and storage areas and its own kiva. In addition, many of these larger villages have a large ceremonial structure (Great Kiva) which lacks any visible physical relationship with any particular living unit (cf. Shabik'-eshchee, Roberts, 1929). It appears likely that these Great Kivas were the scene of ceremonies performed for the benefit of the entire community, and, if so, then they must have been an important integrating factor. We have no means of determining whether the small isolated villages also participated in these community ceremonies and thus were, at least partially, affiliated with one or another large village, but the persistent retention of the distinct socioceremonial units within the large communities suggests that these large villages were themselves imperfectly integrated and, perhaps, that landownership remained with the individual kin groups occupying the village units.

Between A.D. 1050 and 1100 or a few years later, there was a marked change in the Chaco Anasazi settlement pattern. The smaller villages remained as before, each with its own living, storage, and ceremonial units; but the large communities increased considerably in size, and, of more importance, they appear firmly integrated. The lines between the socioceremonial units of the previous period are now blurred. The living rooms are consolidated into one or more large blocks, and the small kivas, although still remaining, can no longer be clearly associated with a particular group of rooms. It seems likely also that, with the increase in community integration and consequent loss of lineage autonomy, landownership was gradually transferred from the kin group to the community. The kin group, no longer localized but still retaining group solidarity through ceremonies, was now a clan (Steward, 1937, p. 99).

At about the same time we note the first clear evidence of dual divisions within the large (and even some of the not so large) villages. This generally takes the form of two Great Kivas, both of which were apparently in simultaneous use, and sometimes, as at Pueblo Bonito (Judd, 1954, p. 17), of a physical division of the village into approximately equal parts. It seems likely, on the basis of modern Pueblo parallels, that these dual divisions functioned primarily in the ceremonial realm. By controlling or channeling rivalry and opposition, they served to retard the development of factions and thus were an important factor in retaining community solidarity.

Farmhouses without associated ceremonial chambers now appear, probably, as Haury suggests elsewhere in this volume, as by-products of urbanization. The techniques of flood-water farming were highly developed, including the use of check dams, reservoirs, and distribution canals (Hewett, 1936; Judd, 1954); but even the most favorable areas could not support the very large populations which had concentrated in the Chaco Canyon and a few other sections of the Chuska Valley. Exploitation of some of the more distant areas on a part-time basis became the compromise solution.

Structures of probable ceremonial function, but not conclusively affiliated with any one community, also appear at this time. These structures are very similar to the Great Kivas associated with the large villages. These specialized ceremonial structures not only closely resembled the Great Kivas in architectural detail but also apparently had the same functional relationship to the adjacent large communities that the Great Kivas had in integrating the lineage units of earlier communities. They suggest that community consciousness was expanded beyond the consolidated villages and that this was accomplished through a development of the ceremonial structure which paralleled that taking place in the social realm. This expanded community consciousness foreshadowed and facilitated the concentration into still larger communities at a later date.

Whether a specialized priesthood had developed by this time is difficult to determine with any degree of satisfaction. It is clear that the Chaco Anasazi were expending major efforts in the building of religious structures, and it seems plausible that these efforts were guided by priests, some of whom may have had multicommunity affiliations.

Specialization in crafts and trading also may have been developing, but this may have continued on a part-time basis, with the individual's major efforts expended in subsistence activities. Hence this concentration of population is not true "urbanization" as this term is generally understood.

The precise nature of the influences which led to this almost sudden village integration is not clearly understood. It is altogether possible that these changes were the result of internal factors alone; the necessary foundations were certainly present. However, at the time this concentration was taking place, there appeared in this area several new features which caution us not to reject completely the possible role of strong outside influence. E. N. Ferdon

(1955) has called attention to a possible platform mound, colonnades, and other "Mexican" architectural features which now appear in the Chaco. Apparently, there was a strong surge of southern influence which coincided in time with the concentration of population in the Chaco. It remains to be determined whether this influence appeared as the result of the development of large population centers or actually played a causative role.

Around A.D. 1300 or perhaps a few years before, the Chuska Valley was abandoned by the Chaco Anasazi. This was not an isolated event, for the years between 1300 and 1540 saw a general reduction in the area occupied by Puebloan peoples and important population changes throughout the Southwest. During this interval many large communities were built along the Rio Puerco, the Little Colorado, and the White Mountain areas, which were abandoned within a few years. By 1540 the Pueblo population, including the Chaco Anasazi, had concentrated into a few large communities—at Hopi, Zuni, Acoma, and along the Rio Grande. There is no general agreement as to the cause of these movements, although they have been the subject of considerable discussion (see O'Bryan, 1952). Arroyo-cutting, soil exhaustion, drought, and attacks by enemy peoples are among the many suggested solutions. This consistent and ever increasing concentration of population offers us a significant clue toward an understanding of the factors which led to the San Juan abandonment. There is abundant evidence for an intensive drought in the Chaco–San Juan area between 1275 and 1300. Similarly, Bryan and others have recorded a major period of arroyo-cutting between 1200 and 1400. There can be little doubt that these perhaps related events had a disastrous effect on the native agricultural economy. The question might be raised, however, whether a population faced with only problems of adverse climate would concentrate into still larger communities; the reverse might be expected—a scattering into small groups to small, undesiccated areas or a general movement to the still favorable and nearby San Juan Valley. Internecine warfare between the pueblos, perhaps triggered by the loss through arroyo-cutting of important agricultural lands and consequent increased competition between the neighboring groups, might account for the concentration into large communities but would not explain the abandonment of the entire area. Some group would have emerged victorious and continued to occupy the valley. Attacks by an outside group, coupled with a deteriorating natural environment, is one explanation which satisfactorily fits the known facts.

Elsewhere (Wendorf and Reed, 1955) it has been suggested that the San Juan Anasazi were Keresan speakers, and it seems likely that they moved to the vicinity of Acoma and the Keres district along the Rio Grande. These Keresan villages were closely integrated. Landownership lay with the community, and clans, while present, had only limited ceremonial or political status. The villages (except Acoma) have dual ceremonial organizations, each with its own Great Kiva. Areas some distance from the pueblos were farmed, often with the aid of canal irrigation, but only temporary "farmhouses" were erected. Permanent residence was maintained at the village.

This pattern of closely integrated large villages persisted until around 1860, when the Navajo and Apache were subdued and it became possible for small groups to reside permanently near the more distant fields. Within a few years many families began to live more and more of each year near the fields which they cultivated, until finally they returned to the parent village only on ceremonial occasions. For the most part this remained the typical settlement pattern—scattered farming villages, often with a greater total population than the main community but still ceremonially and politically dependent on that community. A possible trend of further fragmentation is discernible in a few instances, notably Laguna, where ceremonies are occasionally performed in farming communities.

THE TULAROSA MOGOLLON

The Mogollon, who lived in the high mountainous region of the upper Gila drainage, and in particular those in the Tularosa Valley, present many interesting similarities to and differences from the Chaco Anasazi in the sequence of settlement patterns. The Tularosa, for most of its length, flows through narrow and rock-lined canyons, but from Aragon to a few miles above Reserve, a distance of approximately 12 miles, the Tularosa Valley averages nearly ½ mile in width. In this section the bottom lands of the valley were ideally suited to agricultural purposes. Rainfall averages around 15 inches per year, perhaps 5 inches more than falls in much of the Chuska Valley, and the Tularosa was a dependable flowing stream, ideally adapted to irrigation. It is not surprising, therefore, that this small area supported a dense population.

High mountains, for the most part unsuitable for farming, separate the Tularosa from adjacent drainages. These mountains served to isolate the Tularosa Mogollon from their neighbors, and consequently the widespread cultural uniformity noted for the Chaco Anasazi is not found among the Mogollon. Although there are numeorus general similarities characteristic of the Mogollon area as a whole, there are also minor variations which are peculiar to small subareas. The population tended to concentrate in the geographically isolated valleys.

Our knowledge of settlement types in the Tularosa Valley during the early ceramic horizons is extremely limited. Only two dwelling sites occupied within the considerable interval from before A.D. 300 to 1100 have been excavated; however, in general, these and the surface survey suggest that the Tularosa villages were not markedly unlike those in adjacent areas: a few fairly large pit-house villages, each generally containing one structure which is larger than the remaining houses, and an unknown number of small villages of from one to three houses, all the houses in which are of about the same size. There is no consistent village plan; house locations apparently were determined by terrain. During the early part of this period there was a tendency for villages to be located in defensive positions, on the tops of high, almost inaccessible, mesas. Later the communities were situated on low benches closely adjacent to arable fields.

These villages provide us with few clues as to landownership, ceremonial structure, or kinship. However, it seems likely that ceremonies for the benefit of the community were performed in the larger pit structures and that these served a function similar to that of the Great Kivas of the Chaco Anasazi.

The small villages lacking community ceremonial structures may have been occupied by unilateral kin groups or extended families living on their own land, with each village ceremonially and politically independent of the large communities. However, the absence of identifiable ceremonial chambers makes this less certain than among the Anasazi. The individual pit houses are small, and probably each sheltered a nuclear family.[1]

That the larger villages were not unstructured bands is suggested by the village plan which develops in this area between A.D. 1100 and 1200. An excellent example of this development may be seen at a large village near the junction of Apache Creek and the Tularosa. Around A.D. 1100 this village consisted of eighteen or more rectangular, masonry-lined pit houses scattered along the crests of two closely adjacent ridges. A single large depression near the edge of one of the ridges was probably a Great Kiva. An inspection of the village plan discloses no significant groupings not determined by topography.

But around A.D. 1150 the pit houses were abandoned in favor of above-ground dwellings. Our excavations strongly suggest that the people who had been living in the pit houses also built the pueblos. The pueblos, however, were not built as a single integrated structure or even as two such structures with one of them on each ridge; instead, the inhabitants erected at least five separate units, each unit containing from ten to twenty rooms. This architectural change was not accompanied by a marked increase in population, for many of the rooms served for storage. These groups of discrete units forming one community integrated by a ceremonial chamber are strongly reminiscent of the Chaco Anasazi large-village plans, with the exception that they lack the small "clan kivas" of the latter. Also, since each house group probably sheltered several families, it seems probable that each house contained a unilateral kin group. At least this seems to be a logical explanation for the families to join together into separate groups within the community. Certainly, there would be no motive for unrelated families to erect such structures. We further suggest that landownership remained with the kin group occupying the unit pueblos. Lineage ceremonies, if any, may have been performed in one of the rooms within the house-block or in the plaza or patio adjacent.

1. Some of the houses in the Pine Lawn Phase are large, and Martin and Rinaldo (1950, p. 560) have suggested that each was occupied by an extended family; however, the one site of this period thus far excavated in the Tularosa Valley had small houses.

The possibility exists that this lineage system was borrowed from the Anasazi at the same time that pueblo architecture was introduced. Direct evidence for the lineage does appear simultaneously with the pueblo; however, the previous architectural style (pit houses) effectively concealed any social structure, and, since the unit pueblos were erected without any apparent period of social adjustment, we feel that the lineage was a well-established feature of the Tularosa Mogollon.

The architectural changes in the large communities were duplicated at the smaller villages; the isolated pit houses were replaced by small one-, two-, or more-room pueblos, similarly isolated. Temporary structures, or farmhouses as the term is used in this paper, may appear at this time. Certainly, many of the one- and two-room structures of this period give little indication of prolonged occupation, but their presence in this small, yet densely occupied, valley raises a perplexing problem regarding landownership. There are few areas in the valley which could not be farmed from almost any of the permanent villages. That they would erect a temporary structure within walking distance of their permanent habitations seems unlikely; and so we must conclude either that some of the land in the valley was owned by families living outside the valley, who returned to this area during the growing season, or that the "farmhouses" were actually intended to be permanent dwellings which were abandoned shortly as the population began to concentrate into large villages. We favor the latter possibility.

Around A.D. 1200 the many small villages which were scattered around the valley began to concentrate into a few large communities, at first by joining existing villages but later by shifting to new and more easily defended locations.[2] During the initial phases of this consolidation the villages comprised a single block, often of more than a hundred rooms, each with one or sometimes two kivas. There was a tendency for several of the large pueblos to be grouped within a few hundred yards of one another, and in several instances isolated and very large Great Kivas were found in the areas between the pueblos and some distance removed from the nearest domiciliary structure. Again we see a parallel with the Chaco Anasazi, in that the Mogollon isolated Great Kivas were structurally similar to the Great Kivas incorporated within the pueblos, and they undoubtedly served a similar function—the ceremonial integration of otherwise discrete units and the enlarging of the community consciousness through an already established ceremonial structure.

Around A.D. 1250 there was further consolidation of the Tularosa pueblos into less than a half-dozen very large communities. None of these pueblos has been excavated, but, to judge from surface indications, each village contained

2. The chronological seriation of these villages as later than those described in the foregoing paragraph is dependent upon their containing greater amounts of such relatively late intrusive types as St. John's polychrome. We have assumed, perhaps incorrectly, that these percentage differences have chronological significance.

several Great Kivas. We have no evidence for isolated Great Kivas at this time in the Tularosa. Indeed, the big pueblos are not clustered in a small area, as in the Chaco, but are scattered throughout the valley.

There is no evidence as to whether the lineages evident in the earlier unit pueblos survived the consolidation into large communities and hence became clans, as among the Chaco Anasazi, unless the multiple Great Kivas can be inferred to represent such a social organization. Perhaps the time interval between the building of the large villages and the abandonment of the area was too brief for a clear-cut development in either direction.

Around A.D. 1300 or shortly before, the Tularosa was abandoned. As in the case of the San Juan, there is a general lack of agreement as to the cause of this abandonment. Furthermore, we are unable to determine precisely which, if any, of the historic-period Pueblo groups the Tularosa people may have joined, although present data favor Acoma or Zuni. It is clear that the social and religious structure of the Tularosa Mogollon was closely similar in gross features, though not in detail, to that of the Chaco Anasazi. The lineages, if they survived as incipient clans, would have been readily assimilated into the already functioning clan system at either Acoma or Zuni.

In other districts of the Pueblo region, comparable sequences of archeological types and trends can be observed and, wherever sufficient data are available, interpreted in terms probably quite similar to the foregoing attempts to outline demographic and socioceremonial history.

DEMOGRAPHIC CHANGES IN THE EARLY PERIODS OF COHONINA PREHISTORY[1]

By DOUGLAS W. SCHWARTZ

INTRODUCTION

IN THE southwestern corner of the Colorado plateau in northwestern Arizona, immediately south of the Grand Canyon, lies an area which prehistorically was occupied by the Cohonina Branch (Fig. 1). Archeological work on this branch has lagged far behind that in the Anasazi country to the east or in the Hohokam area to the south. Although the Museum of Northern Arizona has conducted work on the Sinagua Branch on the southeast fringe of the area (Colton, 1946) and has undertaken a few excavations within the area itself (Hargrave, 1938; McGregor, 1951), the amount of work is relatively meager.

The archeological remains in this area may not be so spectacular as those of the Anasazi and Hohokam, but, nevertheless, the area is important for a number of reasons: (1) for its intermediate position between the Anasazi and the Patayan (or Yuman) of the lower Colorado River; (2) for its possible relationship with the historic upland Yumans who lived in the same area; and (3) for the completion of the prehistory of the entire Southwest.

An attempt is made in this paper to order previously unstudied material, to add this to the work which has been published on the area, and to propose from this certain hypotheses on the early history of the Cohonina.

Specifically, the Cohonina Branch is located west of the Little Colorado River, south of the Grand Canyon, delimited by the San Francisco Peaks on the southeast, on the south approximately by U.S. Highway 66, and on the west by the edge of the Colorado plateau. This is generally the drainage of Cataract Creek, which empties into the Colorado River in the recesses of the Grand Canyon. The limits of the branch, which cover some 3,600 square miles, were set by Colton (1939, p. 25) on the basis of ceramics. This country is semiarid, with a dominant piñon-juniper growth.

Historically, this area was inhabited by the Havasupai, a Yuman-speaking, part-agricultural, part-hunting and gathering people, who had cultural affiliations both to the east with the Pueblos and to the west with the other Yuman-speaking people.

1. This work was principally financed through the Yale Department of Anthropology and the research program of Yale Peabody Museum supported by the Wenner-Gren Foundation for Anthropological Research.

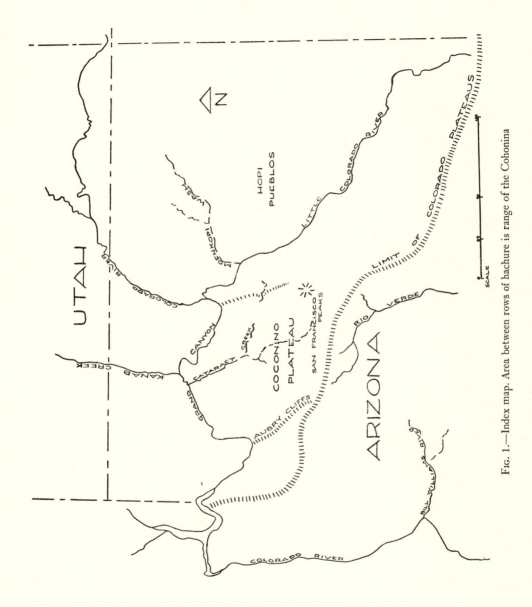

Fig. 1.—Index map. Area between rows of hachure is range of the Cohonina

METHOD

The material in this analysis comes basically from surface sherd collections made at 104 sites. Most of these sites were in the Gila Pueblo survey collection, which were studied for the first time through the co-operation of Dr. E. W. Haury at the Arizona State Museum, where the collections are now housed; the rest of the sites are from work of the Museum of Northern Arizona (Wilder, 1941).

The method employed is essentially that developed by Spier and used on the Zuni material but later changed and refined to meet the needs of individual areas by Colton, Ford, and others. The core of the analysis is the determination of population change. The steps briefly are as follows:

1. The plain pottery from each site was used as an index to determine the branch affiliations of the sites. In this case the utility pottery is all San Francisco Mountain gray ware, and hence the sites are identified as Cohonina.

2. The painted pottery, mostly traded in from the Kayenta area, was used to determine the time range of the individual sites, since these types had previously been dated with the help of dendrochronology.

3. The range in time of each site was plotted as a bar on a graph.

4. The bar graphs were divided into 25-year periods, called "habitation units."

5. The number of sites occupied during each of the 25-year periods throughout the total time span were then counted and plotted on a line graph.

6. The material was divided into six study units on the basis of location, in order to determine whether there were any geographical differences throughout the total area.

7. The assumption was made that the relative increase or decrease in habitation units bears a direct relationship to the rise and fall of population, without the necessity for taking into consideration the exact numbers of people. The similarity in size of the sites throughout the time span makes this type of comparison possible. The analysis, then, is based on settlement density and its fluctuations.

RESULTS

The results of the analysis showed a high degree of consistency in the frequency of occurence and change of habitation units over the total area studied. The pattern of fluctuation is regular enough to justify formulation of certain hypotheses.

Occupation of the area lasted from the early 600's to approximately A.D. 1200. The possibility of an earlier prepottery stage exists, although there is little or no evidence for it either in the literature or in the material studied. A chart of the over-all population change is given in Figure 2.

The population increased more or less steadily between A.D. 600 and 900.

Between 900 and 1100 it leveled off, for 100 years after 1100 there was a tremendous decline, and in the post-1200 period no sites were located in the area. This indicates the general trend of the changes, but, for the purposes of this study, the material may be separated into periods.

In the earliest period, between A.D. 600 and 700, there was an extremely low habitation density. This might be termed the period of exploration, when the water sources were being located, when favorable agricultural areas were being sought, and, in general, when a few pioneering families were learning the all-important lessons of survival.

By the second period, 700–900, which might be termed that of growth, all the area studied had been occupied, and the habitation units were increasing

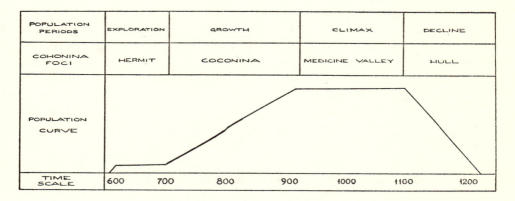

FIG. 2.—Period, foci, and population chart

at a rapid rate, tripling by 800 and doubling again by 900. No doubt the improvement in techniques for dealing with the new environment had much to do with the increase in population, although new people may also have been migrating in from the outside.

The period from 900 to 1100 is a climax of occupation for the region, at which time the population leveled off. Most of the published and excavated sites have come from this period, probably because they outnumber the early and later ones and are thus most likely to be found and excavated.

For the century following this 200-year population peak there is a period of rapid habitation decline. Then, after approximately 1200, the culture of the Cohonina Branch is lost to the prehistorian.

In summary, Cohonina population changes might be expressed in terms of four major periods: exploration, growth, climax, and decline. The last three of these correspond in time to foci set up by the Museum of Northern Arizona for the area: Cohonina, Medicine Valley, both fairly well described, and Hull, which has been suggested. Although material from the early period, 600–700, has been mentioned in the literature, no focus designation has been assigned; therefore, the term "Hermit" is suggested, the name originating from a geographical area in which early sites were found.

INTERPRETATION

From a theoretical standpoint, the most interesting of these periods is the one of decline, since it corresponds to population disturbances in other parts of the Southwest. At least two possible explanations have been advanced to account for the apparent drop in population in the Southwest during this general time—movement out of an area or various kinds of depopulation or extinction.

If there was a momement out of this area at the close of the twelfth century, the archeology of the surrounding regions does not show it. A habitation drop resembling that in the Cohonina country also took place to the north across the great span of the Grand Canyon (Hall, 1942) and to the east in the Kayenta country (Colton, 1939, p. 59). The material to the west is only slightly known, but there is no significant indication of a migration in that direction. In the Verde Valley, to the south, there does appear to have been an influx of people, but these were the Sinagua moving from the southeastern corner of the Cohonina periphery (Fig. 1) and creating a void, which, in turn, was not filled by the Cohonina. Therefore, it seems reasonable to assume, on the basis of the present evidence at least, that the Cohonina did not leave their homeland after A.D. 1100.

Disease, climatic change, and nomadic pressures have been postulated as possible causes for depopulation or extinction in other parts of the Southwest (O'Bryan, 1952). Colton (1936) suggested that the aggregation of people into the great villages of Pueblo III times brought to epidemic proportions disease encouraged by lack of sanitation. This increased the infant mortality, thus depopulating whole areas. Although this seems to be a very logical hypothesis for the Kayenta country, the coincidental habitation decline in the Cohonina area, where there was no development of apartment-like structures, does not substantiate it.

Changes in climate, postulated in other areas of the Southwest, whether the Great Drought or an epicycle of erosion, are a little later than the period of decline in the Cohonina area. However, the second of these alternatives cannot be completely ruled out and needs more investigation.

The chance that nomadic groups exerted pressure on the Cohonina exists as a perfectly good alternative hypothesis for the explanation of the drop in population. Although this theory has been tossed about in archeological literature for a number of years, it still persists and even seems to be growing again in popularity (O'Bryan, 1952). One of the best arguments in its favor is that a population drop appears at relatively the same time over a wide area, in cultures which are not only in different environments but at various levels of intensity or achievement. Shoshonians have been suggested as the possible early invaders, but the Athapaskans are still in the running.

One new alternative hypothesis which might be suggested to explain the population drop in the Cohonina area and possibly in other areas in the Southwest is that of a change in the culture. This could have been either a shift to a type of life which left no material remains or a change in location within the area to a place that has not yet been investigated archeologically. The Grand Canyon and its side canyons, which are within the Cohonina range, could have served this purpose.

SUMMARY

In summary, the population of the Cohonina Branch grew and vanished during a 600-year period. An understanding of these demographic changes can add much to the interpretation and understanding of the culture change of this prehistoric group. The reasons for the disappearance of these people are still a question here, as in many parts of the Southwest; but recent work in the Grand Canyon, focusing on the later periods of Cohonina prehistory, suggests that a change in culture and internal location may have been the cause of the population drop, thus making it more apparent than real. The significance of this change in culture for the understanding of the historic groups in the area is a problem to which only the archeologist holds the prehistoric key.

CALIFORNIA SETTLEMENT PATTERNS

By ROBERT F. HEIZER AND MARTIN A. BAUMHOFF

ALTHOUGH there is now available for reference a respectably large amount of published data on prehistoric occupation sites in California, our understanding of regional patterns and sequences is regrettably deficient. We are barely at the point where an initial attempt at synthesis can be tried, and efforts in this direction are now being made by the staff of the University of California Archaeological Survey. On file now, in several repositories in the state, are records of the location and surface features of about ten thousand sites out of an estimated total of fifty thousand.

A valuable tool of interpretation of California archeology is available in the form of the extremely full and detailed ethnographic record compiled principally under the aegis of A. L. Kroeber. For example, a method has been devised for calculating the probable population of archeological sites. The data required for development of the formula (log population = constant $\times$ log area) were secured from ethnographic accounts of central and northern California native groups containing plans of villages, number of houses, and population. Since the formula checked in a variety of cultural and ecological situations, it has been assumed to have reasonable validity. Details of the method and its application may be found in Cook and Treganza (1950, pp. 231 ff.) and Heizer (1953, p. 321).

The probable validity of this method of calculating former population numbers may, in future, be further checked by analysis of vital statistics data derived from complete excavation of cemeteries and further sifting of the abundant ethnographic data. Pertinent to this matter is the observation first made nearly a half-century ago by Kroeber (1909, p. 4) that the archeological patterns throughout California are variable but that in the major areas the distinctive regional patterns became established early and the basic material types and economic techniques persisted through time. The idea of early establishment and subsequent maintenance of regional culture types finds some support in the reiterated expression that California is an area where early populations became isolated and persisted (summary in Heizer, 1951b).

From data presently available, it appears that central and southern California were occupied early—perhaps in the Anathermal Temperature Age of the Postglacial (Antevs, 1948, 1951)—with the rain-forest region of northern California occupied somewhat later by more specialized fishing-based riverine and coastal populations. Further, for a long time the native population density of California must have been rather light, but it expanded as time went on as a result of increased ability by the occupants to exploit the environment as they perfected techniques of gathering, preparation, and storage; about fifteen hundred years ago began the population explosion which achieved, by the opening of the historic period (A.D. 1770), one of the densest Indian population areas of North America (Kroeber, 1925, chap. 57; 1939).

With the exception of the bottom lands of the Colorado River in the southeastern border of the state, where the several tribes (Yuma, Halchidhoma, Mohave) practiced agriculture, the remainder of California was occupied by hunting-fishing-gathering groups. Further, aside from the desertic areas of southern California, where water and food were thinly distributed, and the mountain regions over 4,000–5,000 feet above sea level, where winter snows blanketed the ground, California was sufficiently endowed with an abundant variety of food resources to enable permanent occupation. By this statement it is not meant that each village was occupied each month of every year of its life, since seasonal population shifting due to weather (from the hot valleys to the mountains in summer), drainage problems (spring overflow in the plains), seasonal endemic disease peaks, and the like obtained widely. However, it is clear that movement was confined to restricted areas which were felt as owned by tribelet groups and defended from trespass. Such conditions of territorial stability were generally true throughout California by the opening of the historic period, and the archeological data can be interpreted, without straining them, to read that a similar situation had existed for some centuries, if not millennia, earlier.

For working purposes a division of the state into nine archeological areas has been made (see Fig. 1). These several areas, while they essentially reflect ecological zones, also have cultural distinctiveness. Whereas Kroeber (1925, chap. 59) first recognized three major culture areas (northwestern, central, and southern), he later (1936) subdivided these into six distinctive subculture areas, pointing out the tribe, in each instance, which exhibited the climax development of that particular configuration of native California culture. His 1936 map accords fairly well with that shown here, and from this concordance one may infer that the local subtypes of ethnographic culture are capable of projection backward in time. This can be affirmed by actual data, as stated earlier, though the farther back in time we go, the more divergent becomes the culture strain until affinities are either so vague or so generalized as to become meaningless.

A number of regional culture sequences are known. These are sound so far as they go, since they are based upon stratigraphic successions, but they are usually either known or suspected to be incomplete and are often floating in time because they have not been correlated with sequences which are anchored by older carbon 14 or terminal (historic period) dates. These regional sequences, in so far as they may be related to changing settlement patterns in California, will be cited later.

Throughout California the most common type of occupation site consists of an elliptical refuse mound, variable in depth and size, and consisting of carbon-blackened earth, fire-broken cooking stones, food refuse (mollusk shells, animal bone, etc.), lost or discarded implements, and usually graves concentrated into cemetery plots. Along the ocean coast the shell component

Fig. 1.—Archeological areas of California. *I*, northwestern California; *II*, north coast ranges; *III*, San Francisco Bay; *IV*, the Great Valley; *V*, Sierra Nevada; *VI*, northeastern California; *VII*, south coast ranges; *VIII*, south coast; *IX*, southern California desert.

may be very large because of intensive use of molluscan foods. In favored spots such shell mounds may be very large and are often stratified because their advantageous situation has been repeatedly recognized. In valley regions of alluvial soils or in the rocky foothills, the internal composition of occupation sites will vary according to the local availability of firewood, stone, food resources, and the like. Recognition of this fact of variability in the composition of occupation sites led S. F. Cook and others to follow up the pioneer work of E. W. Gifford, in which he investigated the constituents of a series of California coastal shell mounds (Gifford, 1916). The more recent work along this line was based upon the assumption that a fairly specific reconstruction of certain aspects of prehistoric life and times, not normally obtainable by a study of artifacts, house floors, or skeletal remains, could be made, provided that we had precise data on the nature and amount of the durable residue secured by screening and sorting a large midden sample. The development and successful application in California of this method, hitherto untried and since ignored by archeologists, may be found in several published accounts (Cook, 1946, 1950; Cook and Treganza, 1947, 1950; Cook and Heizer, 1951; Greengo, 1951; Heizer, 1953; Meighan, 1955b).

NORTHWESTERN CALIFORNIA

Northwestern California, dominated by the Klamath Range, is rugged and mountainous. Steep-walled and narrow canyons carry drainage waters to the ocean. The area is very heavily forested and is deficient in game except in savanna areas formed by Indian fires. Site locations are at stream mouths along the ocean front and along large streams and rivers and their main tributaries. The economy here was water-oriented. Salmon, shellfish, and sea mammals furnished the main subsistence; hence settlements were located in favorable spots for securing them. The interior forested sections lack such sites. Coastal sites are usually on fairly steep slopes overlooking the beach, and houses were arranged roughly in rows. Village locations were selected partly as vantage points to watch for sea mammals. Interior sites are at the mouths of small streams where they empty into the rivers. They sit on old stream terraces and command a view of the river. Most favored spots were those which received the sun's warmth (Waterman, 1920, p. 204).

Archeologically, this area is little known, since only 3 sites have been excavated (Loud, 1918; Mills, 1950; Heizer and Mills, 1952). Only minor changes in the material culture over the last thousand or fifteen hundred years can be detected in the data now available, and it appears that the archeological remains are those left by the ancestors of the recent tribes of the area. Most, but not all, archeological artifacts can be readily identified as to function because of their close similarity to, or identity with, ethnographic forms.

Sites tend to be subrectangular in outline, their mass consisting of food and living refuse. In size they range from 100 by 250 feet to 400 by 750 feet, and in depth from 1 to 8 or 10 feet. The outline of sites is determined by the linear arrangement rather than by bunching of houses (cf. Waterman, 1920).

Cemeteries lie either within the settlement area, a custom which persisted into the ethnographic period, or in special spots near the village, where they could be kept in view by the occupants of the settlement.

One coastal shell mound has been analyzed for constituents (Cook and Heizer, 1951, pp. 303 ff.) and was found to have a higher charcoal and bone content than central California coast shell mounds.

NORTH COAST RANGES

The north coast range archeological area comprises the mountainous region lying north of San Francisco Bay as far as Cape Mendocino, where it borders on the northwestern region. Ethnographic information indicates that the people in this area were organized into groups called "tribelets" (Kroeber, 1932, p. 257). These groups were semipolitical units which centered around one large village of perhaps twenty-five houses and included one or more auxiliary villages which contained fewer houses. The chief lived in the large village, which was also the site of the ceremonial house. Archeologically, the main villages can sometimes be located by the presence of the pit of one of these large, semisubterranean dance houses. Round Valley, in the Yuki area, has been surveyed intensively, and all the archeological sites have been located there (Treganza, Smith, and Weymouth, 1950). The map shows ten dance-pit sites grouped into three clusters. It is likely that each of these clusters represents a prehistoric tribelet, with the main villages changing place from time to time because of fire, war, disease, or the like.

In the rugged mountains of the north the villages were along stream courses or on the peripheries of the small valleys, according to ethnographic accounts (Goddard, 1923). A southern exposure was always sought (Foster, 1944, p. 157). According to Treganza, Smith, and Weymouth (1950), the archeology of this northern district shows a similar situation.

In Napa Valley the sites all occur along the banks of streams in the large, well-watered valleys. This is true ethnographically (see Barrett, 1908; Kniffen, 1939; Stewart, 1943) and archeologically (Heizer, 1953; Meighan, 1955b). Around Clear Lake the villages clustered on the margins of the lake and on islands in the lake (Gifford, 1923).

Population was relatively dense in this area, especially in the south. Kroeber (1925) has estimated the number of people at 12,250, and Cook (1943), after reconsidering the data, has raised this to 13,550. This is about 60 persons per 100 sq. km., or slightly higher than for the northwestern area. This large population was evidently achieved by an optimum adjustment to the local food resources (acorns, fish, and deer, with a sizable increment of water fowl in the lake area). This adjustment was evidently attained in late times, because most sites show substantially the same late culture.

The earlier cultures of this area are recognized by Meighan (1955b), who defines a Borax Lake complex from the material described by Harrington (1948). Meighan believes this to be the basement culture in the area, which persisted with some changes into the Mendocino complex and was finally replaced by the late cultures sometime between A.D. 1 and 1000. Sites of the Borax Lake and Mendocino complexes are located on small knolls or fans on the margins of alluvium-filled basins. There are no cemeteries known from the earlier sites of the Borax Lake complex, but one cemetery has been found in the later Mendocino site. In the later prehistoric and ethnographic periods it was customary to cremate the dead and bury the ashes within the village.

SAN FRANCISCO BAY

The archeology of the San Francisco Bay area is relatively well known, having been begun early by Nelson (1909, 1910), Uhle (1907), and Loud (1924), and has lately been submitted to an intensive reanalysis by Beardsley (1948, 1954).

Nelson's survey of the bay gives the best data as to geographical location of villages. This information may be taken as extending back in time as far as the sequence goes, perhaps twenty-five hundred years (a radiocarbon date of 2339 ± 150 B.P. has been determined for one site [Davis, n.d., p. 107]). This is shown by the fact that many sites have two or more components, including representatives of both the Middle and the Late Horizon cultures of central California (Beardsley, 1954, pp. 100–101).

Most large shell mounds are located in sheltered coves, although some lie on the exposed bay margin. Most sites are found near streams, without regard to whether the land is timbered or barren. On a stream there may be several sites, with the largest one nearest the shore. Usually they are near the water except in the northwest, where they also occur inland 4 or 5 miles.

A very careful analysis of the avifauna of one of the bay shell mounds has been performed by Howard (1929). This, together with a knowledge of the growth and seasonal patterns of the birds, leads her to conclude that the site was occupied both summer and winter, which thus makes any seasonal migration of the people unlikely.

The composition of many of the bay mounds has been scrutinized carefully by several investigators (Gifford, 1916; Cook, 1950; Greengo, 1951). A rough average, calculated from five sites (Cook and Heizer, 1951, Table 7; Greengo, 1951, Table 2), yields a composition as follows: 65 per cent residue, 25 per cent mollusk shell, 10 per cent rough stone, and trace amounts of bone, charcoal, and obsidian.

Greengo (1951) and Gifford (1916) have also analyzed several bay mounds by percentages of the various species of shellfish. Greengo has demonstrated that the mussel (*Mytilus* sp.) maintained the highest percentage throughout the sequence. The principal secondary species was the oyster (*Ostrea lurida*), which is most abundant in older sites and the lower portions of stratified sites and was replaced by the soft-shelled clam (*Macoma nasuta*) in the later middens. This change may have been contemporaneous with the introduction of Late Horizon material and thus have been culturally determined; but Greengo thinks the succession came about because a changing environment (silting-up of the bay) encouraged the population of clams to increase and that of oysters to decrease in late times.

Sites on the coast show that mussel was important there also. The principal secondary shellfish were clams (*Saxidomus nuttali, Schizothaerus nutallii*) and crabs. The frequency of *Saxidomus* is higher in the later middens. Greengo attributes this change to an increased interest in this species which culminated in the Late Horizon, when disk beads made from the shells of these animals were used for money all over central California (Kroeber, 1925, p. 248).

The mounds of the area all have more or less the same shape. "The typical shell heap . . . is oval or oblong in outline, with smooth slopes, steepest of course on the short transverse diameter; and the longer side is generally parallel to the shore line or stream to which the pile may be contiguous" (Nelson, 1909, p. 325). In size the mounds vary greatly—from 30 to 200 yards in longest diameter and from 3 to 20 feet in depth.

The population of the area in historic times is known only from mission baptismal records. From these Kroeber (1925, p. 464) calculates that the total was 4,900, or about 50 persons per 100 sq. km., a much lower density than in the neighboring north coast ranges. This lower population is evidently due to the fact that here the primary economic dependence was on shellfish rather than on acorns, as was the case in the rest of central California.

The population seems to have been stable over a period of two thousand to twenty-five hundred years, since there are as many Middle Horizon sites as there are Late ones (Beardsley, 1938, Table 1). The relatively heavy population elsewhere in central California is attributable to an optimum adaptation to an acorn economy in Late Horizon times, whereas the bay people had apparently attained an optimum adaptation to the less advantaged littoral economy in Middle Horizon times which they never relinquished. Perhaps this is part of the reason they were by-passed by the "florescence" of culture which took place among the Pomo and neighboring groups in late times.

THE GREAT VALLEY

The great valley of California is a gently sloping plain 500 miles long and from 20 to 50 miles wide, comprising a total area of some 16,000 square miles. The archeological sequence (Early, Middle, Late Horizons) has been worked out for this area, with many sites assigned to specific time periods. The summary of settlements given later has been derived from the following sources: Schenck and Dawson (1929); Heizer and Fenenga (1939?); Lillard, Heizer, and Fenenga (1939); Heizer (1941); Hewes (1941); Beardsley (1948); Heizer (1949); Smith and Weymouth (1952).

There are five sites known from the Early Horizon. They all occur on sub-surface clay knolls barely protruding from the valley floor. The deposit mass is extremely compact and contains a heavy increment of clay. The latest of these sites has a radiocarbon date of 4052 ± 160 years (Heizer, 1951a, p. 25). Three of the sites are cemeteries, with little sign of having been occupied as villages. The other two contain both occupation debris and burials. This would indicate that the dead were buried on high ground, where they were above the river flood waters. The bulk of the occupation sites were doubtless on the lower ground and have since been flooded out or, more likely, buried under sediments which have accumulated since that time.

Nineteen sites have been excavated which are attributable wholly or in part to Middle Horizon. These all occur either on existing or former waterways—usually sloughs of the Sacramento or San Joaquin. The sites on sloughs indicate that the river courses have changed since the time of occupation. Cemeteries are found within the sites, a fact that implies that the dead were buried in the villages.

Twenty-two sites of the Late Horizon have been excavated, although many more are known to exist. These sites all occur on waterways which still exist or were known to have existed in the historic period. The middens are black, with none of the solidification noted in Early Horizon sites. Since the Late settlements occurred in the same localities as the Middle ones and, in fact, overlay them in many places, it is clear that the settlement pattern here has remained essentially the same over many centuries.

Nine of the Late Horizon sites in this area have been subjected to physical analysis by Cook and Heizer (1951). The variations found within the area are almost all ascribable to differing environments. One site containing a high quantity of fish bone was situated on the main Sacramento River and near a small fresh-water lake, so it is evident that this site was used as a fishing station. Similarly, the rock content increases as the foothills are approached and native stone becomes more available; shell is more frequent downstream, where river mussel is concentrated in the more sluggish waters; there is a higher percentage of animal bone content in the sites of the lowland marshy areas, where the elk was present, than in the deer country in and near the foothills.

The population of the great valley at the opening of the historic period (1770) has been calculated by Kroeber (1925) at about 33,000 and by Cook (1943) at 35,000. This is between 40 and 50 persons per 100 sq. km., or an intermediate figure for California. In the central part of the valley, at least, this same population must be susceptible of projection back at least as far as Middle Horizon times, because Middle Horizon sites are about as plentiful as Late Horizon ones and the time spanned was of the same order of magnitude. There is no way to ascertain the population of Early Horizon times because most of the sites have been destroyed. However, if the size of the Late Horizon population is accounted for by its adjustment to an acorn economy, then the Early Horizon population must have been smaller, since their relative paucity of grinding tools attests their small reliance on this food product (Heizer, 1949, p. 38).

Figures for the population of individual sites have been calculated by Cook and Treganza (1950, p. 234) on the basis of site area, as noted previously (p. 32). For four Late Horizon sites the populations are 10, 25, 52, and 228.

NORTHEASTERN CALIFORNIA

In northeastern California Heizer (1942) has described sites near Tule Lake, and recently Squier and Grosscup (n.d.) have issued a preliminary report on their work in that area. They have established a sequence of four phases but have not indicated which sites belong to which phases, so that no sequence of settlement patterns can be established. In general, it would appear that archeological sites are almost ubiquitous on the shores of past and present lakes. For the most part, these sites consist of scattered camp-site areas without midden deposit. There are also many caves in the area, all of which seem to have been utilized aboriginally.

SIERRA NEVADA

The population of the Sierra Nevada was concentrated on the gentler western slopes, which are characterized by several kinds of environment closely associated with elevation. Bordering the valley in the low foothills is the Lower Sonoran Life Zone. This consists of a belt of oak and grass, above which is a chaparral zone. The latter, lying at an average elevation of 1,000 feet, is characterized by plant species of extreme arid-land types. This xerophytic chaparral is thought to have been formed because of long-continued burning by the Indians and by natural incendiaries (lightning, etc.) (Jepson, 1923, p. 6). Next come the Transition Life Zone (2,000–5,000 feet) and the Canadian and Hudsonian Life Zone (5,000 and 9,000 feet), which are of importance because the deer go there in the summer and because there is good fishing. Vegetal food is minimal at higher altitudes.

According to ethnographic information, only the land up to the Transition Zone was occupied the year around. Above that the snow was so deep that it was hard or impossible to live (Barrett and Gifford, 1933, p. 135). The higher lands, however, were much used for hunting and fishing in the summer, and caves there sometimes served as burial places (Wallace, 1951; Heizer, 1952).

For the sites at higher elevations there are two studies. In the Yosemite Park region Bennyhoff (1953, 1956) has carried out extensive surveys and some excavation. The altitude of the park ranges from 4,000 to 10,700 feet, the sites occurring principally in the Transition and Canadian Life Zones. In the Transition Zone, 82 per cent of the sites had bedrock mortars associated with them. This indicated that the people were dependent upon acorns, to some degree at least, when they were living in this zone. Higher up in the Canadian Zone fewer sites were above the oak and yellow-pine belt, so acorns and pine nuts had to be carried up to them. Most Canadian Zone sites are small camps with only sporadic occupation.

In the Yosemite area in general, "locations were selected on the basis of available water, good drainage, sunny exposure, limited vegetation, and an accessible hinterland. Boulders suitable for mortar rocks were needed in the oak belt" (Bennyhoff, 1953, p. 31).

The other study of sites in the high sierra is that of Heizer and Elsasser (1953), which covers the area around Lake Tahoe. Two culture complexes were isolated in the region—the Kings Beach and Martis complexes. Kings Beach sites can be identified as the camping spots used by the historic Washo as summer fishing stations. Kings Beach artifacts are rarely found at the same site as those of the Martis complex; apparently, the Washo had a superstitious fear of the pre-Washo sites (Heizer and Elsasser, 1953, p. 22). Both Martis and Kings Beach sites are located near water, but there is some evidence to suggest a difference in settlement pattern. "Martis Complex sites may have been located with reference to good hunting and seed-gathering localities, while Kings Beach Complex sites appear to have been located primarily with reference to fishing sites. This generalization might not be wholly true, however, since some excellent fishing stations are occupied by Martis Complex sites" (Heizer and Elsasser, 1953, p. 19).

The population of this area was estimated by Kroeber (1925) at about 16,750. This is about 25 persons per 100 sq. km., a relatively low figure for California. This is accounted for by the fact that much of the land at high altitudes was not inhabited at all.

SOUTH COAST RANGES

On the coast, archeological sites occur on the beaches and on the bluffs above the beaches. There are smaller sites along the streams in coastal valleys, but these, like the shore sites, are characterized by an abundance of shell in the midden. In the interior, sites occur in valleys along streams or in caves in the mountains (Meighan, 1955c).

There was some contact between better-off interior groups and the coast peoples, but the environments were so different that probably there were two types of culture with relative separation of coastal and interior groups. This is indicated by Spanish mission-period observations and dialect differences.

SOUTH COAST

The south coast is a zone on the Pacific Coast perhaps 50 miles in depth and extending 500 miles from Point Sal in the north to Baja California in the south. D. B. Rogers (1929) first proposed a threefold sequence in this region (Canalino, Hunting, Oak Grove), and he has been supported in this by Olson (1930) and Carter (1941). To the south another rather early culture was discovered by Heizer and Lemert (1947) and subsequently excavated by Treganza (Treganza and Malamud, 1950; Treganza, n.d.). This culture, named "Topanga," is similar to Oak Grove in some respects but has a number of distinctive artifact types which link it with M. J. Rogers' (1929a) San Dieguito culture, still farther south.

These generically similar early cultures of the south coast region have a common settlement pattern. The site deposits consist of soils which are hard and indurated, showing a long period of leaching and weathering. They occur on well-drained knolls in country with an abundance of oaks and are often a considerable distance from a year-round supply of water. Seed-grinding implements (basin metate and mano) are abundant in the midden deposits.

The late, or Canalino, culture is similar to others farther south on the coast (M. J. Rogers, 1929a; McCown, 1945; Meighan, 1954). These late sites usually show a high degree of adaptation to marine life; they are very large, some being as much as a mile long, and all are directly on the sea shore.

Samples from D. B. Rogers' sites have been subjected to physical analysis (Cook and Treganza, 1950, Table 3). The Oak Grove site shows little bone and shell, bearing out Rogers' contention that these people relied primarily on vegetal food for sustenance. The Hunting culture sites contained great quantities of shell, indicating main reliance on shellfish by this population, despite the name assigned to them. The Canalino site contains more bone but less shell than the Hunting site, thus indicating that the shellfish economy was amplified with fish and sea mammals. The plank canoe, a late prehistoric feature, led to more efficient economic use of the sea.

A word should be said about the Channel Islands off the coast of southern California. Archeological work has been carried on there by D. B. Rogers (1929), Olson (1930), Orr (1951), and Meighan and Eberhardt (1953). The work of Meighan and Eberhardt on San Nicholas Island has led them to believe that only a late culture period is represented there. About half the sites are found on the beach, the others being on the plateau which forms the center of the island. The factors determining location of sites are (1) accessibility of the beach, (2) proximity of fresh water, and (3) elevation (choice of a high spot with an unimpaired view). The heaviest occupation was on the northwestern third of the island—evidently because there was a better water supply there than elsewhere.

The population of the south coast area was calculated at about 22,000 persons by Kroeber, or about 60 per 100 sq. km. Whatever the true population was at the time of contact, it must have been larger in the late periods than it had been previously because the late sites are both more numerous and much larger than the earlier ones.

SOUTHERN CALIFORNIA DESERT

With the southern California desert region, we enter the Great Basin physiographic province. The greatest part of this region is taken up by the Mohave Desert, which has a typical basin-and-range topography with very little water and scanty plant cover consisting of Joshua trees, cactus, and greasewood at the lower elevations, together with some piñon and juniper higher in the mountains. Two of the more favored parts of the region are the Colorado River Basin and the comparatively well-watered basin formed by Mono and

Owens valleys. In the Colorado Basin, access to water provided by the river of that name made primitive agriculture possible. Because the Mono Basin–Owens Valley lay under the eastern escarpment of the Sierra Nevada, it received all the eastern runoff from these mountains. This provided food of great variety and sufficient quantity to support a population as dense as any in the Great Basin.

Julian Steward's (1938) important ecological study of the Great Basin indicated that the desert peoples placed primary economic reliance on vegetal products, notably nuts of the piñon pine (*Pinus edulis* of *P. monophylla*). Because of the difficulty in gathering sufficient food in this harsh environment, the people were unable to gather into groups larger than family size for the greater part of the year. This means that most village sites in the desert area would be very small. Steward's data given for the people near Death Valley show that living sites were located with reference to springs and other watering places but usually a slight distance away, perhaps to keep from frightening game which might be attracted by the water. Winter villages, which might contain several families, were similarly located.

In the southern Paiute area, where a small amount of agriculture was practiced, the villages evidently contained only a single family and perhaps a few others (Kelly, 1938). This ethnographic situation is mirrored in the archeological pattern of small, scattered sites.

In the more favored areas the pattern differed. Among the Owens Valley Paiute there were large villages on each of the creeks tributary to the Owens River (Steward, 1933, Map 2). These villages evidently attained a population of 200 or more in favorable circumstances (Steward, 1938, p. 51) and were occupied the year around because the variation and quantity of food produced in a small area made continual migration in search of food unnecessary.

On the Colorado River the people appear to have lived in considerable concentration on the flood plain of the river. Forde (1931, p. 101) quotes several early accounts to the effect that "during the floods of April and May the Yuma move away from the banks of the river in order to escape its inundation, camping on the nearby uplands until the river returns to its channels." The population of one of the villages was estimated by Diaz in 1774 at 800 (Forde, 1931, p. 101). Even allowing for exaggeration, this would indicate that the villages were very large. No doubt their size was a function of the relatively intensive agriculture of this region. In Owens Valley, late sites are found along streams that empty into the Owens River (Riddell, 1951) and also along the river itself. In the Mono Basin, Meighan (1955a) has made an intensive survey of sample areas, and he finds numerous large sites high up in the mountains near stands of piñon, with fewer and smaller sites on the plateaus where piñons are absent. Caves were occupied in this area, probably as winter retreats.

The general pattern of late settlements in this part of the Great Basin, then, is that of small camps on the desert wherever water occurs and larger camps in the mountains near piñon groves. Caves and rock shelters were occupied at least sporadically. Almost all the open sites in the desert are lacking in deposits of any depth; presumably they are subject to constant wind erosion. In the mountains a small deposit sometimes accumulates but seldom more than 2 feet. Caves may have any amount of deposit up to several feet. The extent of an open site may be as small as 50 or 100 feet, or it may be as large as a mile in length.

Occupation of the flood plain of the Colorado River by Yuman villages is not attested archeologically. M. J. Rogers (1939, p. 8) says: "There is little archaeological evidence to suggest this practise. What there is would indicate that flood camps were located on the sandy benches of dry washes, and almost never on the gravel terraces above the river bottom." In the Mohave Desert the late (pottery) sites are found near "recent or present day water holes" (Campbell, 1936, p. 296) or in caves and rock shelters in the hills (Campbell, 1931, pp. 30–32). In the Panamint Mountains near Death Valley late sites were found near springs, on mountain tops among piñon and juniper stands, and in caves and rock shelters (Meighan, 1953).

The earlier cultures in the Mohave Desert have been defined by M. J. Rogers (1939). The settlement patterns of these earlier cultures seem to have been similar to one another. The sites are usually found near extinct lakes or channels, and some occur near present-day watering places (Campbell et al., 1937). Absence of grinding tools leads Rogers to believe that this culture was economically based on hunting rather than on seed-gathering.

SETTLEMENT PATTERNS IN EASTERN
UNITED STATES

By WILLIAM H. SEARS

A SETTLEMENT, for the purposes of this paper, may be defined as an archeologically discernible site, a unit of space which was characterized during some culturally definable period of time by the presence of one or more dwellings or other structures. The arrangement of structures on a site with respect to one another forms unit patterns. The arrangement of these, in turn, through a wider segment of space, might be termed a complex pattern. To rephrase, we must consider both individual community plans and the arrangement of these communities with respect to one another.

Our problem, then, is to discover the sorts of patterns in these two classes which have existed in eastern United States, to outline the changes in patterning through time, and, as far as possible, to sketch the sociopolitical implications of the space-time distributions observed. Partly because of my own limitations and partly because of the character of the available evidence, the discussion must lean rather heavily on the Southeast.

A major problem, clearly, is classification of the various sorts of settlements which have been observed, so that we may be consistent at least within this paper. A great many terms drawn from archeology, ethnology, and common usage have appeared at various times. Some systematization or classification has been attempted too, usually as a by-product of other discussions. It seems best here to use more or less accepted terminology and to define the terms with reasonable precision. Since examples are a necessary part of definition in this case, much of the space-time distributional data can best be included in the definitions.

Under unit patterns, perhaps the simplest that is archeologically observable is the *camp*. This term would cover sites with areas between a few hundred square feet and perhaps an acre. Refuse or midden deposits are thin, which, taken into account with such items as distribution of fireplaces, scarcity of post molds, and lack of post-mold alignments, indicates communities of several impermanent, lightly built shelters erected without any definite community plan. The same evidence is also indicative of short-term and/or seasonal occupation. Our best examples are the Paleo-Indian and Archaic sites, with the southeastern shell mounds forming exceptions in some cases to the rules of scanty refuse and short-term occupation.

The space-time distribution of camps covers the entire eastern United

States from the first advent of man to the historic period, at which time our concern ends. In the Southeast, their importance diminishes at an ever increasing rate from the beginning of the Christian Era. To the north and east their importance in later years increases with, and is a factor of, distance from the Southeast. In northeastern New England, camps and small villages persist as the sole settlement patterns until the historic period.

A *village* occupies an area of several acres. Estimates of the number of dwellings run as high as thirty or forty. Post-mold alignments, other evidences for type of shelter, and depth of refuse on these larger sites correlate to document the existence of reasonably sturdy dwellings which remained in place and occupied for extended periods of time. It seems probable that some definite, if not overly controlled, village plan existed in most cases. Examples might include the Hopewellian sites in the Midwest, as well as the Adena villages, and sites in the Northeast ranging in time from the Owasco Aspect level to historic Algonkin villages. In the Southeast and Midwest, villages often enter into complex patterns, with ceremonial units on single sites.

The spatial and temporal distribution of villages is then about the same as that of camps, which villages begin to replace or at least to supplement, at the Early Woodland or Burial Mound I time level in the Southeast and Midwest. Dates for this replacement or supplementation in the Northeast would be somewhat later. In terms of total population housed, the village is probably the most important unit, excepting the far northern and eastern areas, from the Middle Woodland or perhaps even Early Woodland period to the time of white contact.

Our third class, *towns*, includes the largest prehistoric communities. Areas run up into the hundreds of acres, and dwellings must have numbered up into the hundreds. Great depths of refuse and permanent structures of heavy construction, often rebuilt and strengthened several times in one spot, demonstrate very long-term occupation of single sites. Dwelling units were arranged in definite patterns, often in relationship to one or more ceremonial units, and the entire complex was often fortified. Examples range from the huge prehistoric Mississippian sites of the Southeast and those described by the chroniclers of the De Soto expedition to Iroquoian towns of the Northeast. In space and time the town, with or without ceremonial adjuncts and fortifications, definitely appears earliest in the Southeast, in the Mississippi drainage, and in the drainages of other southeastern rivers of the Coastal Plain. It appears there as one of the diagnostics of the Early Mississippi or Temple Mound I period and remains important throughout the prehistoric period. There seems little doubt that the spread of densely populated settlements to the north is a later phenomenon, again with lateness a factor of distance north. Before we reach the northern and eastern limits of villages, towns disappear in all periods.

The fourth and last class of unit settlement patterns is that of *ceremonial units*. This class includes as members burial mounds, temple mounds, earthworks generally, plazas, and such others as earth lodges and special-purpose mounds.

It is well known that all possible combinations of these unit patterns and ceremonial units occur. At the early time level, where camps are the sole settlement type, complex patterns are lacking. Camps do not, at this early time, seem to cluster with respect to one another. Their location seems to have been determined by purely economic factors, not at all by social or ceremonial considerations. Later, camps are a part of patterns whose total plan is determined by larger social and ceremonial centers.

Ceremonial centers, an often used term, is here restricted to sites which contain only structures of presumed ceremonial usage, such as the well-known midwestern burial mound and earthwork complexes, or to such structures, singly or in groups, as parts of larger towns. The Hopewell site and various of the Hopewell and Adena earthworks appear to be examples of ceremonial centers without directly associated settlements composed of dwelling units. The ceremonial-center designation is also best applied to the often isolated, single burial mounds, with comparatively minor occupational associations, if any. These may have served a number of villages and camps. Willey (1949, p. 369) has indicated that this seems to have been the case with numbers of the Santa Rosa–Swift Creek and Weeden Island mounds of the Florida northwest coast. Webb (Webb and Snow, 1945, p. 35) has suggested a similar patterning for the Adena culture.

Village clusters are particularly common. Many of the foci of archeology represent, in classificatory terms, a number of neighboring villages so closely related culturally that constant contact between them and probable participation in a common sociopolitical organization are definitely indicated. Very often these clusters seem to share a single ceremonial center, either an isolated one or a unit in one of the villages. In the later periods, villages and the smaller towns often form a complex pattern with respect to a town with a single ceremonial center included in it. Such patterns with town–ceremonial center as an apparent focus for spatial organization of large regions are restricted rather definitely to the Mississippi drainage and the lower Southeast. Complex village patterns run as far east as do villages themselves.

Town clusters—patterns with a number of towns, a greater number of villages, and a great many camps as part of the total complex pattern—are very important in the Southeast, particularly in the last few centuries before white contact. An integral part of such complex patterns is a large town which includes a ceremonial center of one or more temple mounds, often one or more burial mounds, a plaza or plazas, and other special-purpose mounds and structures. The major centers of the Southern Cult, such as Moundville and Etowah, are examples, as are the Monks Mound–Cahokia complexes, Kincaid, the Angel site, and so on. In the case of Etowah and almost certainly in the case of most, if not all, such large complexes, subsidiary towns will also possess ceremonial structures of one or more types, although these will not be found in the villages. A number of lesser towns of the Etowah culture have earth lodges, for example, and at least one had a temple mound. It is quite possible that other towns and perhaps larger villages had ceremonial centers in the form of larger buildings, a matter which can be determined by full and careful excavation, with allocation of the excavated structures to short-span subdivisions of the culture.

A final complex-pattern type, mentioned previously, is the town–ceremonial-center combination. These are, of course, the larger Mississippian sites with dense populations concentrated in restricted areas, often within palisade walls. The ceremonial centers, with their temple mounds, burial mounds, plazas, etc., determine by their esoterically prescribed patterning the arrangement in space of the individual dwelling units and consequently the total community plan. Great variation within this basic type is known to occur, ranging from the St. Francis variant with great thickness of debris and continued rebuilding in a restricted area (Phillips, Ford, and Griffin, 1951) to greater spreads around a larger plaza, such as the Ocmulgee, Etowah, and Kincaid sites. The appearance of these complexes is a diagnostic feature of the full, mature, or late Mississippian Horizon, the Temple Mound II period, in the Southeast. Larger fortified towns reach the Northeast in the protohistoric period, such as the Castle Creek site (Ritchie, 1944, pp. 61–68). The ceremonial units do not spread out of the Southeast, however.

The over-all development through time in the Southeast is clearly a matter of continual increase in settlement-pattern size and complexity. While we can be reasonably certain of many details concerning the unit patterns in only a few cases, and of the complex patterns in even fewer, certain facts do emerge.

First, the earliest and simplest settlements, the camps, reflect in their small size, impermanence, and lack of organization into complex patterns the hunting-gathering economic basis otherwise demonstrated in the thin, scattered midden deposits. The type of site then affords direct evidence for a type of social system somewhere near the ultimate in simplicity.

Second, when villages do appear, they initiate a trend of continual and ever more rapid increase in unit pattern, size, number, and complex-pattern development. This trend continues unabated through to the contact period. From this, the factors of increased numbers of dwellings, dwellings of larger size and greater permanence, and more definite unit patterning reflect or demonstrate changes of some importance in the social system. This is verified by the appearance of the complex patterns, both those involving multiple villages and those of villages compounded with ceremonial centers. We may suspect that the state–tribe, if you wish—as against the band or single kin-group organization of the camps is definitely present when units appear that are large enough to be classified as villages. The rather clearly sacred nature of such features as burial mounds and the various types of earthworks give us some clue as to the nature of these incipient states, united by bonds of kinship and strengthened by the sacred ties of a religion developing definite form and ritual. Quite possibly, a totemic system, interrelated with the religion, reinforced the basic kinship bonds both within and between villages.

This, like all classifications, is an arbitrary division of a space-time continuum. Arguments as to whether a particular site is a large village or a small town are quite clearly fruitless. Nevertheless, it is most obvious in southeastern United States that when certain limits of settlement-pattern size, complexity, and permanence have been reached, certain other elements make their appearance concurrently. Some of them are as follows:

1. Formal, precisely laid-out community plans. At this late time level, Mississippian or Temple Mound as you wish, the formality and complexity are extended down from the towns to the villages. The villages are, of course, a necessary and important part of the scene.

2. Increasing importance of unit patterns compounded with ceremonial units, particularly the temple mounds, plazas, and earth lodges. Burial mounds remain on the scene, with internal changes.

3. Fortification of towns becomes important and prominent.

4. Definite patterns of community interrelationship over wide areas appear, the development of complex settlement patterns. Generally, as in the Etowah Valley, the pattern has as its major determinants a single large town with ceremonial center and the drainage system of a single large river.

These features and others are quite recognizable determinants of the Mississippian periods and the Mississippian cultural type, the Temple Mound II horizon. Southeastern archeologists have suspected for some years that major and rather abrupt and drastic changes in the economy were prerequisites of these Mississippian developments. Generally, it seems to have been believed that there was a marked increase in agricultural productivity as against that of the Hopewellian period, due to the introduction of improved crops and agricultural techniques. The temple mounds, with the ritualism which they reflect, as well as the Southern Cult, are then considered to have been related to—perhaps a necessary relationship to the aboriginal mind—the new agriculture. At times there seems to have been at least an unvoiced suspicion that the gentlemen who administered religious and civic affairs from the temple mounds were really prehistoric county agents sent from a capital somewhere around Mexico City.

Certainly, there is no doubt of increases at this time in population density, social complexity, dwelling size, and permanence, as well as in religious formality. Nor can we doubt the increase in social importance of organized, heavily ritualistic, and probably dogmatic religion.

Yet I wonder, as have others, if we need postulate the introduction of anything new from outside North America as a causative factor in these developments. Looking at the problem from the settlement point of view, from the top down, as it were, rather than from the 5-foot square and 6-inch level up, what we see is—to restate the problem very simply—increasing community size, permanence, and complexity of organization plus large-area organization complexity. Ignoring other factors for the moment, these are, practically, necessary by-products of increased population density which can only reflect more available food. The food could have come from new crops and techniques or, more simply, from utilization of existing crops and techniques on more and more of the available land. As long as the land held out, population increase continued at an ever accelerating pace.

We may suggest, then, that when maize agriculture was perfected during the Hopewellian period, it produced populations too large for the then extant social systems. The social systems of the Hopewell communities and the intimately interrelated religions, both reflected in community plans, would tend to falter under pressure. This hypothetical conception of conditions at this time level—cultural level, really—may be reflected in the continued difficulty met in attempting to characterize the inter-Hopewellian-Mississippian cultures, such as Troyville and Jersey Bluff. Cultures in this period tend as a group to be somewhat formless, to lack the clearly defined flavor of the preceding and succeeding periods. As periods they are usually characterized by evidence for rather rapid internal change through their short duration, confirmation of our hypothesis of rapid social adjustment. The cultures which follow them, such as Coles Creek and the various Early Mississippi units, clearly grow from these formless levels, although they retain for some time distinctive traces of the various regional Hopewellian manifestations in which their roots lie, a cultural generation back. As development proceeds, we find increasing evidence for intercommuncation, evidence ranging from widespread ceramic types and ceremonial regalia to greatly increased uniformity of settlement patterns. With the continued population pressure on land suitable for the extant agricultural techniques—pressure reflected in the rather sudden appearance and great popularity of fortifications—we may expect greater interpersonal and intercultural contact. When the expanding populations were forced into contact, as well as into conflict, religious and other ideas must also have been interchanged. The situation must have been quite similar to that on the Plains in the eighteenth and nineteenth centuries, where the cultures of groups with very diverse backgrounds became increasingly more uniform, in spite of nearly continuous conflict.

I would suggest, then, that the great achievements of the southeastern cultures, from perhaps A.D. 1000 on, from the first appearance of the Mississippian culture type, were not due to new crops, a new religion, or a great rush of new ideas. They resulted rather, as a natural consequence, from the continued application of a productive complex of food plants and agricultural techniques to more and more of the fertile bottom lands of the Mississippi and other major river drainages. The more obvious by-products, such as temple mounds and the Southern Cult, may have had—probably in some part did have—some sources in areas outside the United States. The point is that these elements may not be causative but may simply have been taken over and integrated into the indigenous developments noted. That is, major social changes, including changes in religious form and in the intimately interrelated settlement patterns, were inevitable from the beginning of the Middle Woodland period. Their precise forms in the later periods may be due, in some part, to outside influences.

That the ceremonialism is not a necessary part of the process, is not a causative factor in the expansions and developments which can be observed, is, I think, somewhat clearer when we look at areas farther north and east.

The soils and climates of the southeastern and middle western bottom lands, perhaps accompanied by a historical accident of earlier introduction to maize agriculture, certainly produced a faster-moving series of developments there than anything which took place in the Northeast. Nevertheless, assuming that the harsher climate slowed down the process, the development of settlement patterns in the New York–Pennsylvania area parallels that of the Southeast. By the early historic period, A.D. 1600 rather than the southeastern 1000, we reach the level of carefully laid-out villages with fortifications and, judging in part from this, of population pressure on the land resources available to the then extant agricultural technology. This parallel development, if southeastern-influenced, makes its way quite successfully without the ceremonial units, at least without those archeologically observable. With minor exceptions, the burial mounds at the Middle Woodland level are omitted, and certainly culture seems to have advanced quite successfully without either temple mounds or the Southern Cult. To belabor a point, the northern climate may have inhibited the advance of agriculture somewhat, but I cannot see that it was unfavorable to temple mounds, copper plates, and engraved conch shell.

The inhibiting effect of the climate on agriculture does, of course, increase with distance north and east and is reflected in the diminishing size of settlements and in the greater distances between them. The New England Algonkins did not, culturally, pass the Middle Woodland level of cultural development. But they at least got that far, with a social system which must have been much like that of the classic Hopewell communities but without resorting to elaborate burial mounds.

SETTLEMENT PATTERNS IN THE LOWER MISSISSIPPI VALLEY

By STEPHEN WILLIAMS

THIS paper will consider the problem of the relationships between the archeological remains and the physiographic features in this area, with emphasis on certain cultural changes which have taken place through time. I will begin with a brief but detailed consideration of the physiography and some of the attendant problems, for "the student of prehistory in the Lower Mississippi Valley must . . . attempt to reconstruct cultures that no longer exist in an environment that exists only in a profoundly modified state" (Phillips *et al.*, 1951, p. 36). Then I shall present an outline of the archeology of the area, period by period, and trace the developments in the settlement patterns which can be discerned.

For the purposes of this study the Lower Mississippi Valley may be divided into north and south physiographic divisions. The northern division includes all the valley above a line drawn from Memphis, Tennessee, to Helena, Arkansas, and thence northwest across the valley, as shown on the map (Fig. 1). Within the northern division the main regions are the Eastern and Western Lowlands, which are separated by Crowley's Ridge. The Eastern Lowland includes the St. Francis Basin and the Cairo Lowland, which are divided by the low Sikeston Ridge. The major tributaries of this division are the St. Francis and Little rivers in the east and the White and Black rivers in the west. The southern division, combining what Fisk (1944, p. 22) called the "central" and "southern" divisions, includes all the alluvial valley south of the line delineated above. This division contains a number of important basins, beginning at the northern end with the Yazoo Basin, known locally as the "delta," and with the Tensas Basin to the south and west. Grand Prairie Ridge on the west side of the valley, north of the Arkansas River, is the largest prairie area within the valley proper. Macon Ridge, a dissected alluvial plain, separates the Boeuf Basin from the Tensas. The most southern part of the valley is known as the Deltaic Plain and is made up primarily of the Atchafalaya and Lake Pontchartrain basins. The major rivers of this division are the Yazoo and the Sunflower in the east and the Arkansas, Ouachita, and Red in the west.

The major land forms of the valley are the flood plain, the prairies, and the high ridges and bluffs. The flood plain is a very complex form and may be further divided into four basic parts: low ridges, glades, back swamps, and

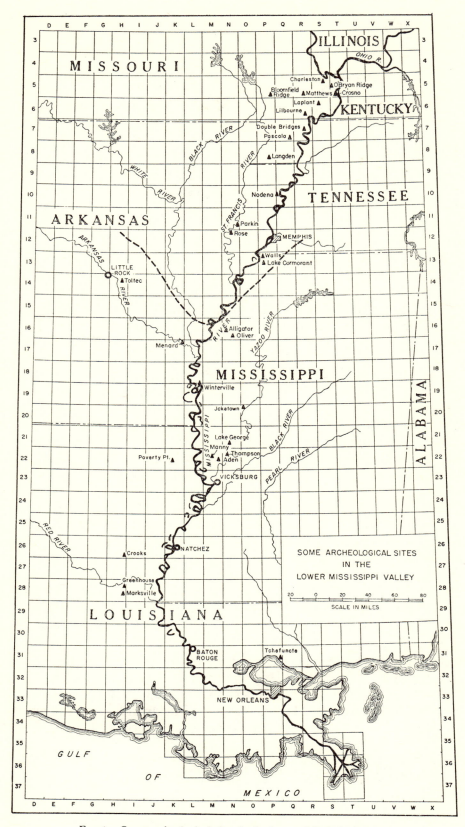

Fig. 1.—Some archeological sites in the Lower Mississippi Valley

sandbars. The low ridges are the most important part of the flood plain and were formed as natural levees in the main meander belts of the major rivers. The soils of these ridges are light and fertile, and, since they were often covered with canebrakes, they could be easily cleared. The ridges are separated by the glades, which are often wet for months at a time and support a dense forest growth. The back swamps are large, low areas back of the recent meander belt which are true swamps and were heavily forested with cypress, tupelo, and the like. The fourth part of the flood plain is the flats or sandbars along the recent river channels. The prairies, of which a few of the more prominent have been mentioned, are remnants of older and slightly higher alluvial surfaces which in earlier times had a long grass cover with groves of oaks and similar hardwoods. The soils of this land form vary considerably, with some, such as that on Sikeston Ridge, being light and sandy, while Grand Prairie Ridge is made up of tough, clayey soils. Crowley's Ridge in the northern division is the only major high ridge in the valley. It is an erosional remnant topped with clay and loess. Several other similar upland remnants of much smaller dimensions occur within the valley, such as the Commerce Hills at the north end and the Bastrop Hills in the south. The valley is bordered on the east and west by uplands, which meet the valley trough in many places as rather well-defined bluffs. Especially on the east, these bluffs are capped with loess deposits.

Although an exhaustive discussion of the effects of the physiography on the aboriginal cultures of the Lower Valley is beyond the scope of this paper (see Phillips et al., 1951, pp. 5–36, for a detailed treatment of this subject), some preliminary findings may be presented at this time. First, one can expect a lack of early remains within the flood plain proper as a result of the destruction of all such sites by later alluvial action. None of the prairies—the older alluvial surfaces—is of sufficient geological age to be a likely location for sites of this period, and, in fact, none has been found in these areas. Only the upland remnants like Crowley's Ridge are old enough, and the few sites assignable to the early traditions have been found on this ridge. So far, only scattered finds have been made, and no well-defined sites with a majority of eastern fluted-point types have been located. However, this area is certain to be the only place to look, and some sites of later preceramic periods have also been found on the ridge.[1]

Second, one fact stands out above all others when looking at the valley as a whole: only a very small part of the land was habitable. Of the four areas of the flood plain itself, only the ridges and possibly the sandbars were available for use for any length of time during the year. The prairies and upland remnants were also habitable, but the aboriginal peoples seem to have been

1. These statements are correct only if Fisk's geological dates are accepted; some recent geological opinion would place the prairies as Late Wisconsin in age, and there are now some archeological finds in these areas which tend to support this earlier dating.

rather selective and made only partial use of these areas. Less than 20 per cent of the land area of some present-day counties in the valley shows soils which reflect formerly habitable land. An appreciation of this problem is daily being made more difficult by the modern drainage projects and land-improvement programs which have wrought vast physiographic changes in the last fifty years.

Of course, the soils, as mentioned previously, do tend to reflect the former ecological conditions, but the over-all impression of much of the Lower Valley today is one of a vast expanse of fertile land with easily tilled soil. The further conclusion that these present-day conditions have considerable significance in viewing the history of the past is too easily made. This is not to say that the whole valley was not in its way quite favorable for the support of a substantial population both on a hunting and gathering stage as well as during the agricultural periods, but the special problems of this physiography must always be kept in mind.

This relative scarcity of land which remained dry under foot the year round and which could be used as a place of more or less permanent habitation caused the favorable sections of the area to be used over and over again as village sites. Because of this pattern of site reoccupation or long intermittent habitation, most sites, no matter whether their refuse deposits are 5 feet deep or only 1 foot thick, contain more than one cultural component. Surface collections from such sites, which are the vast majority found so far, are difficult to handle, and the seriation of sherd samples must be treated with the greatest care if justice is to be done to the resulting picture of cultural development.

In selecting a suitable site location within the limits already set, the question of whether the soil was tillable in terms of the aboriginal techniques was of major importance, too, during a considerable part of the time span covered by our present knowledge. The ridges formed by the natural levees were the most favorable lands and were almost always used by the agricultural peoples. The prairies were also occupied for a considerable period, but sites very definitely tend to cluster along the prairie edges. This settlement pattern may have been an attempt by the inhabitants to exploit more than one ecological zone, because these prairies were often ringed by swamps. The upland remnants and bluffs were, of course, very difficult to utilize for agriculture, but I would make the suggestion that the inhabitants of the sites which do occur along the eastern bluff of the Mississippi made use of the bottom lands below. Crowley's Ridge, in contrast, lacks any major sites assignable to the later periods, and, significantly enough, there are no good farm lands close by.

Limitations of raw materials available for manufactures in such phases of cultural activity as the lithic industry also played a fairly important role in all the cultural periods recognized. One obvious reaction to the scarcity of stone in the alluvial materials is the baked clay or Poverty Point objects which may have persisted longer than was formerly supposed. The association of some types of these objects with pottery-using complexes is certainly suggested (Ford *et al.*, 1955, pp. 46–52).

To turn to a more detailed consideration of settlement patterns through time, a tentative sequence for the Lower Mississippi Valley is presented in Figure 2. Precise correlation of all the regional sequences within the valley does not seem possible or warranted by the data available at this time. The nine periods have been named in such a way as to maintain as much continuity with past classificatory practices as possible, despite some obvious differences in emphasis which this chart reflects. The phases themselves in each period are listed in a north-to-south sequence, as are the period names. Perhaps looking at the archeology of the valley in this north-to-south direction is the major reason for some of the views which follow, but there seem to be real cultural differences at the two ends of the valley, and for that reason I will try to point up some of the important differences between the northern and southern divisions described here.

In the first period, here termed the "Early Lithic," evidence of any kind is scanty indeed, as has been noted before. The few finds are of a kind to provide little direct evidence concerning settlement patterns, except to suggest the very general conclusion of the use of small camps. Most of our evidence comes from Crowley's Ridge in the northern division, but this distribution may actually reflect only differences in the interests of the collectors.

Despite the well-documented and now even fairly well-dated (by carbon 14) remains to the east of the valley, few sites of the Archaic period are known. Some projectile points of the Dalton type (Scully, 1951) have been found in the northern division, and these sites have been grouped into the Bloomfield Ridge phase (Williams, 1954). Here, too, the scanty evidence points to small camp sites. Some sites of this period may exist within the valley proper, but the very age of most of the alluvial deposits militates against this possibility. It is interesting to note the use of shellfish as an important part of the diet in the southern division in some of the succeeding periods. It has been suggested (Phillips *et al.*, 1951, p. 429) that some of these shell mounds may contain material of this Archaic period, but none has been found so far.

In the third period, here called "O'Bryan Ridge–Poverty Point," one finds considerably more data available. In the north the sites are small villages not more than a few acres in extent (Griffin and Spaulding, 1952, p. 1). Those in Missouri have been grouped in what I have called the "O'Bryan Ridge phase." There are scattered traces of this culture toward the south until one reaches the impressive site of Poverty Point and its cultural affiliate, Jaketown (Ford *et al.*, 1955). The large mounds and embankments at Poverty Point (Ford, 1954) are without precedent, but both seem to indicate quite a sizable assemblage of people or a great length of occupation or both. This first appearance of circular embankments and mounds in the Lower Valley is something of a cultural and temporal anomaly, which the present excavations at this site may explain. At Jaketown there are also low mounds which seem to have been constructed at this time, but no good evidence as to their exact use was discovered. The first example of a house is also known from Jaketown; it was circular, with the small posts set singly in a slightly staggered pattern (Ford *et al.*, 1955, p. 34).

In the Tchula-Tchefuncte period the first ceramics seem to appear, and in the northern division mound-building on a small scale also seems to begin. In the south well-defined burial mounds are present, but no good evidence of

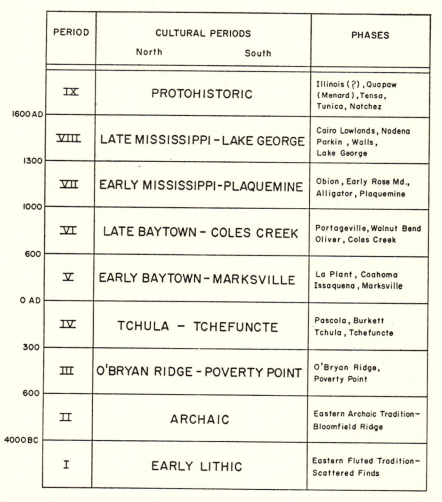

	PERIOD	CULTURAL PERIODS		PHASES
		North	South	
1600 AD	IX	PROTOHISTORIC		Illinois (?), Quapaw (Menard), Tensa, Tunica, Natchez
1300	VIII	LATE MISSISSIPPI – LAKE GEORGE		Cairo Lowlands, Nodena Parkin, Walls, Lake George
1000	VII	EARLY MISSISSIPPI – PLAQUEMINE		Obion, Early Rose Md., Alligator, Plaquemine
600	VI	LATE BAYTOWN – COLES CREEK		Portageville, Walnut Bend Oliver, Coles Creek
0 AD	V	EARLY BAYTOWN – MARKSVILLE		La Plant, Coahoma Issaquena, Marksville
300	IV	TCHULA – TCHEFUNCTE		Pascola, Burkett Tchula, Tchefuncte
600	III	O'BRYAN RIDGE – POVERTY POINT		O'Bryan Ridge, Poverty Point
4000 BC	II	ARCHAIC		Eastern Archaic Tradition – Bloomfield Ridge
	I	EARLY LITHIC		Eastern Fluted Tradition – Scattered Finds

Fig. 2.—Tentative sequence in the northern and southern divisions of the Lower Mississippi Valley.

house type is available except one indication of a possible circular structure (Ford and Quimby, 1945, p. 88). Sites may be characterized as relatively small, with adjacent burial mounds within the flood plain. I have called the phases in the north "Burkett" and "Pascola" (Griffin and Spaulding, 1952, p. 1); those to the south, "Tchula" (Phillips *et al.*, 1951, pp. 431–36) and "Tchefuncte" (Ford and Quimby, 1945), are better known. There seems to be a definite southern distribution of sites during this period, but this may be related to a lack of complete analysis of the data from the northern division.

During the fifth period, Early Baytown–Marksville, there is good evidence of the split between the northern and southern divisions, which may well be an indication of the growing strength in the south of what Sears (1954) and others have called the "Gulf tradition." A single site, La Plant (Griffin and Spaulding, 1952, pp. 1–2), with the very distinctive dentate rocker-stamped pottery is known in the north. Other sites in this area continue the use of burial mounds with the non-Hopewellian ceramic tradition that characterized the period (Phillips *et al.*, 1951, pp. 436–40). In the south there is a major center around the Marksville and Crooks sites (Ford and Willey, 1940), which shades off into the later Issaquena phase (Phillips, n.d.) in the lower Yazoo Basin and the Coahoma phase farther north. Sites are characterized by a number of conical burial mounds near the village area. A few sites, primarily in the Yazoo Basin, have circular embankments, as seen at the Thompson site (Fig. 3), but there is little indication that the entire inclosed area was utilized as a village, as evidenced by a lack of cultural material over a great part of the site.

The sixth period, Late Baytown–Coles Creek, is marked in the south by the introduction of the platform mound and a definite population increase. This increase has been carefully charted in the southern division around the Yazoo Basin (Phillips *et al.*, 1951, p. 340) and on the Gulf Coast (McIntire, 1954, p. 40). In the south the period is characterized by a typical Coles Creek phase site such as Aden (Fig. 4); the mounds are not large, generally less than 15 feet high, and are usually rather precisely arranged around a plaza. In the north the period is marked ceramically by the appearance of Wheeler Check Stamped pottery, as in the Portageville and Walnut Bend phases, but the probable occurrence of pyramidal mounds in this northern area is a vexing problem still unsolved. The cultural complexes are much better defined in the south, as in the Oliver phase (Peabody, 1904) and the Coles Creek phase (Ford, 1951). The typical houses at the Greenhouse site were fairly large and circular. They were built both with and without wall trenches for the supporting posts.

The seventh period, Early Mississippi–Plaquemine, is characterized in the north by the beginning of the fortified villages with platform mounds in the Cairo Lowland (Williams, 1954), as well as the start of the great St. Francis type villages (Phillips *et al.*, 1951, p. 329) to the south. Large mound groups are strikingly absent from this northern division, despite the obvious example of Cahokia much farther north. In the south this is definitely the period of great mound construction, as characterized by the great sites of Emerald and Anna (Jennings, 1952, p. 266), to mention only a few of these large ceremonial centers. Something of the careful precision of mound placement seems to have been lost, and sheer size seems to become of more importance. The typical structures were square to rectangular wall-trench houses, although there seems to be some evidence of a shift to single wall-post construction in the latter part of the period (Quimby, 1951). The correlation of some of the

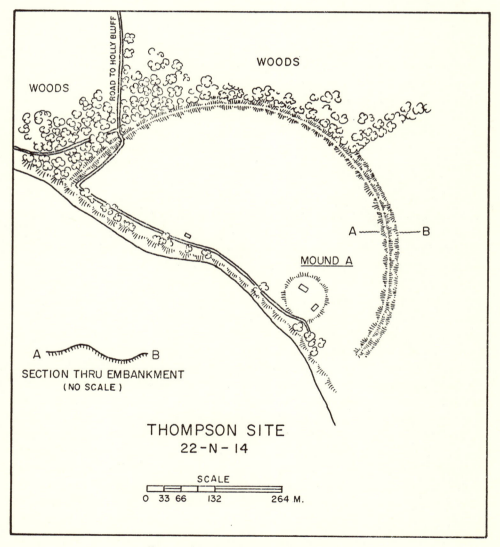

Fig. 3.—Sketch map of the Thompson site

northern phases, particularly Obion (Kneberg, 1952) and Alligator (Griffin, 1946), with this period is difficult, and they may have been placed too late. The Early Rose Mound material (Phillips *et al.*, 1951, pp. 287–89) fits in here by definition, as does the Plaquemine phase (Quimby, 1951) far to the south.

The Late Mississippi–Lake George period (the eighth) has more regional phases than any other period. Of course, the data are more plentiful here, but certainly a general pattern of increasing cultural diversification through time

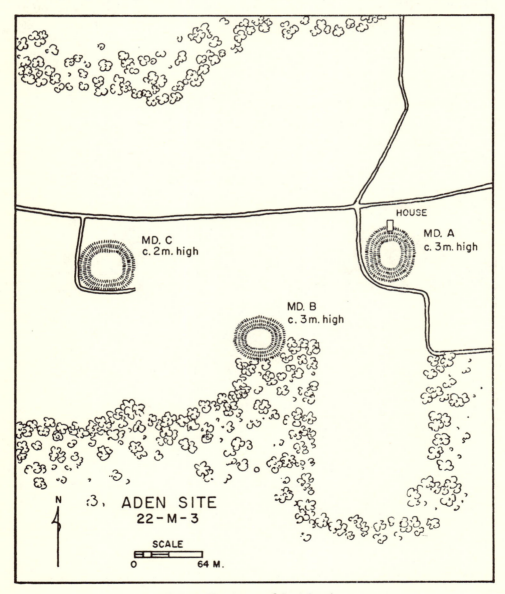

MD. C
c. 2 m. high

HOUSE

MD. A
c. 3 m. high

MD. B
c. 3 m. high

N

ADEN SITE
22 – M – 3

SCALE

0   64 M.

FIG. 4.—Sketch map of the Aden site

seems to be indicated. The Crosno site (Fig. 5) is typical of the Cairo Lowlands phase (Williams, 1954), with its rectangular embankment and single
platform mound about 18 feet high. The structures were mainly rectangular
with wall trenches, but here, too, there was some evidence for a shift to single
wall-pole construction, despite the contrary evidence of one circular wall-
trench structure at Crosno (Williams, 1954), which was the most recent
found. Circular structures seem to have continued on as a special kind of
ceremonial building in this area, as the only round building at Nodena (Williams, n.d.) was a temple on a low mound, while the rest of the fifty-odd
structures at the site were all rectangular to square with single-post construc-

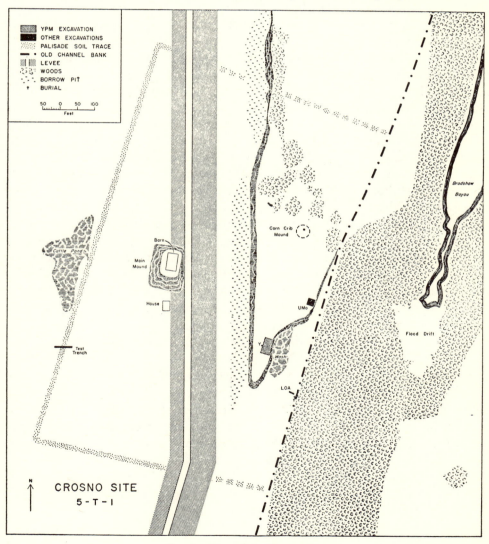

Fig. 5.—Map of the Crosno site

tion. The Nodena, Walls (Griffin, 1952, pp. 233–36), and Parkin (Griffin, 1952, pp. 231–33) phases represent the amount of cultural diversity recognized within a rather small area in the northern division. In the southern division this definitely seems to be a period of decline in mound-building, not exactly correlated with a decline in other cultural features, for in the Lake George phase the strongest influences from the Mississippian tradition appear.

The final, or Protohistoric, period is imperfectly known archeologically in most of the valley except with regard to the Natchez, who continued to build rectangular wall-trench houses grouped in fortified villages (Quimby, 1942). A number of intrusive burials into the older mounds are known from this period, as at the Oliver site (Peabody, 1904); and the Menard phase (Griffin, 1952, pp. 237–38) around the mouth of the Arkansas River may represent the historic Quapaw (Phillips et al., 1951, pp. 392–419). The rest of the tribes indicated for this period are known only slightly through ethnographic and archeological sources. However, this was a time of general cultural decline and population decimation, with vast parts of the valley practically uninhabited at the period of white contact.

A few conclusions of a more general nature may be brought together at this time. Remains of the first two periods, Early Lithic and Archaic, are absent from the flood plain, and the evidence that does exist shows a small population living on what are now upland remnants. Despite the enigmatic data from Poverty Point and Jaketown, the burial mound seems to have entered the Lower Valley in the Tchula-Tchefuncte period and had its popularity peak in the following Early Baytown–Marksville period. The pyramidal platform mound and carefully laid-out villages appear first in Late Baytown–Coles Creek times and are developed into the large ceremonial centers of the Early Mississippi–Plaquemine period in the south. Fortified towns, concentrating a fairly large population into a limited space, begin in this seventh period, as seen in the Cairo Lowland and St. Francis Basin. In the last prehistoric period there is a further development of these towns and increased populations. The Protohistoric period spans the decline of these towns and their populations.

In general terms, one sees a continuity of culture through time in the southern division of the valley until the impingement of the Mississippian tradition makes itself evident on the Gulf tradition. In the north such cultural continuity is not present; rather, one sees a number of breaks in the regional traditions both before and after the Late Baytown–Coles Creek period.

PREHISTORIC SETTLEMENT PATTERNS IN THE NORTHERN MISSISSIPPI VALLEY AND THE UPPER GREAT LAKES

By JAMES B. GRIFFIN

INTRODUCTION

IN ATTEMPTING to apply the concept of settlement patterns to the prehistoric occupation of the northern Mississippi Valley and the upper Great Lakes, one finds this area woefully weak in data which can be successfully employed to present a sound picture. There are many reasons for this. One is that relatively few village sites have been excavated by professional archeologists. Even when such excavations have been made, the archeologists have rarely been able, because of lack of funds, to excavate an entire village area of the larger and more advanced prehistoric groups. Another difficulty has been that, with few exceptions, individuals conducting such excavations were interested primarily in the materials to be gathered from the excavation and in the historical problems connected with the materials. There has been neither an excavation nor a survey in this area which has been oriented to the specific approach of obtaining adequate information on settlement patterns, such as Willey (1953) assiduously conducted in Peru. It should be recognized, of course, that the area covered by Willey in the Virú Valley is not much greater than that of a good-sized county in the north-central states. Another difficulty is that there are also very few sites from the early periods that have been at all adequately excavated. Although we have some rather excellent maps of the ceremonial earthwork patterns of Hopewell and Adena in Ohio, there is very little information which could translate this into the cultural complex of village and ceremonial area in existence at the time. This is also true, of course, but to a somewhat lesser degree, of the large Mississippi sites of a later time and of a somewhat different area.

The settlement-pattern material available will be presented according to the accepted major time periods and the normally associated cultural groups at present recognized in the area. The first of these periods is the Paleo-Indian, which is an assumption based upon the occurrence of fluted blades in some numbers in this region and the fact that these fluted blades are not now known to be a part of any of the Archaic complexes. It is probably only a question of time until villages or camps are located which will definitely link the fluted blades with an associated artifact complex similar to that from eastern and southeastern sites.

The sites of the Archaic period are somewhat better known and represent a number of varied archeological complexes which are linked together because of the absence of ceramics and other traits of later cultures; because of the common possession of certain large projectile points, grooved axes, and other polished-stone forms; and on the basis of a general way of life. Following the Archaic is the temporal division known as Early Woodland, which comprises such units as the Adena of the Ohio Valley, the Black Sand and Red Ochre cultures in Illinois, and the Baumer and Sugar Hill complexes in southern Illinois. Perhaps segments of the Glacial Kame culture and Old Copper in Wisconsin can also be included in this general Early Woodland category. The Middle Woodland and Hopewellian period is, of course, characterized in the upper Mississippi area and the Ohio Valley by Ohio Hopewell; by the related Hopewellian occupation in Illinois, eastern Iowa, Wisconsin, and Michigan; and by certain segments in Indiana. In the same and immediately surrounding areas contemporary with the Hopewellian culture bearers, there are other Woodland groups. While a number of minor stages can be recognized in the succeeding Mississippi period, in most instances in the north these are not too well defined, and it will perhaps be best to concentrate our attention on some of the major Middle Mississippi and Late Woodland sites in the area.

It can be agreed that the initial consideration is to agree on a definition of "settlement"; for this purpose I may follow Sears, who recognizes a settlement as "an archaeologically discernible site, a unit of space characterized during some one culturally definable period of time by the presence of two or more dwellings or structures." I may point out at this time that this is essentially the concept included in the term "community" or "component" of the Mid-Western Taxonomic Classification. It is somewhat narrow, however, in that it requires recognition of "two or more dwellings or structures." For many components or communities we do not have these data. One of our great difficulties is, in fact, the question of what is an archeologically discernible site which represents a cultural unit during a definable period of time and also represents a functioning cultural group.

PALEO-INDIAN AND ARCHAIC SETTLEMENTS

For the usual convenient purposes I will also follow the division of dwelling areas into a threefold grouping of camp, village, and town. A camp site is one with an area forming only a few hundred square feet to perhaps an acre in size, with little refuse in a pit or midden, a scarcity or absence of post molds indicating permanent structures, and no formal community plans. Such remains are obviously of short-term and possibly seasonal occupation. This is the type of settlement pattern which we associate with the Paleo-Indian and Archaic levels. It should be remembered that we have little or no evidence for dwellings or structures during this long time span and must assume their presence.

The famous Indian Knoll site (Webb, 1946), while a little over 2 acres in size, almost certainly does not represent a relatively short occupation by a fairly large group of people but rather a seasonal, or at least recurring, occupation by relatively small bands of people over a fairly long period of time. Few, if any, of the Kentucky shell heaps are larger than this, and most of them are smaller. Even in the West Virginia and Pennsylvania area of the upper Ohio this small size of 1 acre or less is common (Mayer-Oakes, 1955). No data are given on the size of the Faulkner site in southern Illinois, but the McCain site in southern Indiana has some deep refuse deposits and also some side-slope dumps. In the latter area there are refuse deposits some $4\frac{1}{2}$ feet deep, while in the heaviest normal areas of occupation depths of $2\frac{1}{2}$ to $3\frac{1}{2}$ feet were reached. These depths are somewhat unusual for non-shell-heap sites of the Archaic stages. The evidence on this site is not too clear as to the area covered by the aboriginal occupation, but the area mentioned in the text would come out to about $\frac{1}{2}$ acre. In the lower Illinois Valley, in the so-called "Titterington Focus," there is evidence that the people of the late Archaic period made burials in mounds located on the bluffs and also buried in the valley floor in village sites or cemetery areas. The recently reported Old Copper sites are burial areas and, as such, hardly give an idea as to the size of Old Copper settlements, although there are no indications of large size or deep deposits. Reference is occasionally made in articles on Archaic sites to small clay areas which may represent house floors; but, so far, little or no excavated evidence has been provided for specific dwelling types or their placement in this period. It is also evident that in this area during the Archaic period some settlements were placed in caves, cave mouths, and rock shelters. Explorations of these have been carried out in southern Ohio and in the adjacent areas of Iowa, Minnesota, and Wisconsin and also southern Illinois. Here, of course, the occupation pattern conforms to the shape of the shelter available. The glacial cover over much of the region included in this survey effectively limited the number of such sites favorable to man's occupancy in prehistoric times.

EARLY WOODLAND SETTLEMENTS

Leaving the Archaic in this unsatisfactory state, we can move on to the Early Woodland period, which is usually characterized in the upper Mississippi and Great Lakes area by references to the Adena culture. The evidence we have from Adena is, of course, based almost entirely on the excavations of burial mounds. In quite a number of cases, Adena burial mounds are located in areas along bluffs or in areas overlooking streams which were not a part of the village occupation area. The size and complexity of some of these mounds reflect, perhaps, both the stability of population in a particularly localized area and also an increasing development of burial ceremonies. No one has yet attempted a study which would correlate the size and number of burials and associated features in a mound with the types of artifacts found with the burials. This would, perhaps, provide a rough seriation of burials and artifacts which could be utilized to determine, for example, whether the Adena burial mounds were introduced to the Ohio Valley in a complex form from a higher-culture area (which to me seems most unlikely) or whether the development of the Adena burial complex is a function of its location in the Ohio Valley and that its complexity increases through time as it approaches the Hopewellian horizon.

We are told (Webb, 1942) that the C. and O. mounds in eastern Kentucky afforded an excellent opportunity for the study of an Adena village; yet there is actually very little attempt made in that paper to produce such a study. It is fairly evident, as the report states, that the village was old and well established when subfloor burial pits were dug and that these pits contain the group of burials over which a mound was later erected. In this case, several structures crossed one another on the village floor and had occupied the area successively before the burial pit had been dug. It is stated of one of the villages at the C. and O. site that it was relatively rich in artifacts compared to the mound, but this does not give us too much idea as to the intensity of the occupation. It is probable that the village site here is about 1 acre in extent. In the Mount Horeb area, Unit B, which is the Peters village, was located within an inclosure having an area of some 25 acres or so. It is stated that this has been a favorite collecting ground for amateurs and that they have recovered considerable Adena material (Webb, 1943). Whether all 25 acres were occupied at one time by an Adena village or by villages over a fairly long period is a question which has not yet been satisfactorily answered. The nearby Grimes village site, of some 8–9 acres, is also a place where a considerable amount of Adena village-site material has been recovered. These are, of course, the largest areas to be regarded as village sites. The question is whether the entire area was occupied at a particular time, so that one could assert that Adena villages occupied up to 8 or 9 acres. Apparently, this is not the conclusion reached by Professor Webb, who indicates in his summary on the Adena people that they rarely, if ever, lived in large, compact villages but were located in scattered house groups with probably a few houses closely associated (Webb and Snow, 1947, p. 314). These groups, he thinks, were separated by several hundred feet from their nearest neighbors. This is perhaps based on the evidence from the C. and O. site. He also states that the Adena village debris is thin and that this was often placed in mounds built on village-site areas. In order to provide a requisite number of people who might have been responsible for some of the large mound sites and complicated and extensive burials, it was suggested that several such habitation groups, scattered widely over a few square miles of area, might have combined to constitute a community and be responsible for such large burial structures.

The evidence for the Red Ochre culture in the Illinois Valley is again almost entirely of burial mounds located on heights overlooking the valley and its tributary streams. Here, too, there is little evidence of village occupation. Available data, some unpublished, would indicate that the Early Woodland sites in the area are small camp areas of roughly less than 1 acre in extent, with scattered projectile points, Early Woodland pottery, and a few other items indicating the occupation area. The Sugar Hill camp in southern Illinois of the Early Woodland period occupied only about $\frac{1}{3}$ acre, with village refuse some 16–24 inches deep. The Baumer site was located along a ridge parallel to the Ohio River. This ridge covered an area 1,500 feet long by 350–450 feet wide. Various exploratory trenches were placed in the site, and the implication is that the village area covered most of the ridge. If so, this would be a considerably larger village area than is normally associated with an Early Woodland occupation.

In spite of the association of Adena mounds with circular earthworks and the apparent size of some of these circles and houses, there is no indication that, in Sears's terminology, the Adena people had a settlement pattern of a size which would equate with his concept of a village, that is, an area of several acres with thirty to forty dwelling units and a considerable depth of refuse. On the other hand, the Adena settlements are obviously not camps. Once again, a classificatory device is found to be too narrow and restrictive.

MIDDLE WOODLAND SETTLEMENTS

There is considerable difficulty in recognizing the "settlement" pattern of Ohio Hopewell because little or no attention was ever paid to village sites. This led to an idea that there were no Hopewell villages and that Fort Ancient sites were the dwelling areas of the Hopewell people. Ceremonial earthwork and burial-mound construction, however, reached elaborations not even approached by later Indian groups. At the Hopewell site, Ross County, Ohio, the great inclosure contained 111 acres and the adjoining rectangle some 16 acres. Fort Hill in Highland County, Ohio, has a wall 1½ miles long inclosing some 48 acres. Fort Ancient, which was built by Hopewell people, has 4 miles of embankment. These and other large earthwork centers provide evidence of increasing stability of population, of increasing social cohesion and control, and of greater population density.

The excavation over a period of years of the Turner site near Cincinnati indicated extensive village occupation and resultant debris within the 30-acre inclosure and many non-mound burials. The late Clifford Anderson, who dug with Moorehead at Hopewell, told me that they found rather extensive evidence of a village site. Surface collecting, however, is not very productive at the present time. Robert Goslin, of the Ohio State Museum, has assured me that village-site material was incorporated into the main Seip Mound and that it was found on the floor of the mound, outside the mound, and in the wall of the earthwork. There is village-site material inside Fort Ancient, and an extensive village east of the "fort" walls was excavated in the middle 1930's to provide fill for park building construction. In his report on the Ginther group, Shetrone (1926, p. 65) clearly indicates the Hopewell village debris on the surface and under the mound. This mound was portrayed by Squier and Davis as pyramidal, but excavation did not produce "evidence to indicate that the mound ever had been geometrically rectangular in form." In the same report Shetrone comments:

> In the same field and adjoining the Shilder mound on the north-east, are a number of tipi-sites and fireplaces. The presence of these is readily noted when the ground is freshly plowed, or in the greater luxuriance of the grain under cultivation. They are characterized by an abundance of burned stone, flint-chips, broken pottery-ware and fragments of mica. In two of these, beneath the plow-lines, were found flake knives of the drab flint, exactly similar to those taken from the Shilder and the Ginther mounds. It is everywhere evident, from the remains of tipi-sites and other indications, that the entire face of the terrace, from the Cedar Bank group southward past the Ginther works to the Hopeton group, was the place of habitation of the peoples who constructed and utilized these several works.
>
> That the Ginther mound, the Shilder mound and the accompanying tipi-sites pertain to the great Hopewell culture group of prehistoric peoples will be evident to the student of Ohio archaeology, if not, indeed, to the casual reader. Whether future explorations will continue to bear out Squier and Davis' seemingly unwarranted surmise that the flat-topped mounds contain no remains, remains to be seen [pp. 69–70].

In the Illinois and adjacent Mississippi Valley there are Hopewell village sites by the hundreds, but none of them has the associated ceremonial earthwork patterns of Ohio or such large burial tumuli. While most of these village sites are relatively small, 1–3 acres, some may be as large as 5 acres. There is little evidence of house structures, but the two published examples are oval in ground plan. One house at the Havana site is 19 feet wide by 38 feet long and with a main central rectangular fireplace (McGregor, 1952, pp. 50–51). The other structure is reported from the Sister Creeks site and was not regarded as a house but as an inclosure, 60 by 28 feet, with a double row of post molds. The outer row of post molds very clearly forms a paired pattern, resembling, in that aspect, the well-known Adena arrangement. No central roof supports were recognized (Cole and Deuel, 1937, p. 155). The majority of the Hopewellian village sites are located in the main valley floor or adjacent tributary valleys and have extensive mound groups—from a few to thirty-five mounds—in association with them. Where stream flood plains were narrow, the burial mounds were sometimes located on adjoining bluffs.

It can be seen from the foregoing data on the specifically Hopewellian sites in the northern Mississippi Valley that there is little justification for far-reaching generalizations in regard to the settlement pattern of these peoples. That there was a population increase is plain; that there were different types of settlement and association of living areas with ceremonial centers in different regions, such as Ohio and Illinois, is also clear. In fact, the only region east of the Rocky Mountains to have extensive elaboration of ceremonial activities in connection with the village sites during the Middle Woodland period is in southern Ohio. It is not reasonable to regard this order of social integration as characteristic of the Middle Woodland period as a whole and equate it in an "evolutionary" scheme with, say, the early Formative sites in Meso-America or the Cultist period in Peru. This is in marked contrast to the succeeding Mississippi period, where the mound and plaza arrangement diffused widely throughout the east. Most Hopewellian sites are villages, but no one site has yet produced two house patterns, let alone thirty to forty.

MISSISSIPPI PERIOD SETTLEMENTS

With the advent of the Mississippi period, the amount of evidence increases considerably, and we can in some instances be fairly precise about village size and arrangement. At this stage, however, as with earlier groups, we also have some difficulty in determining the size of the living village. There is evidence indicating that the earliest pyramidal mounds were relatively small and associated with occupational debris of the transition between Hopewell and Mississippi. There are but four mounds in the Pulcher group, south of St. Louis, and they are located along a Mississippi bank line. The village size is about 15 acres, and a central plaza is not apparent.

The more developed Middle Mississippi settlements are, at the least, villages in Sears's classification, and some appear to be towns. At some sites, such as the Linn site of southwestern Illinois or Aztalan in Wisconsin, the settlement area is inclosed within a fortification. The pyramidal mounds are also within the wall, and the resultant picture is of a fairly orderly, planned settlement. None of these sites has been sufficiently excavated and reported upon to allow us to speak about the house arrangements and their relationship to other features of the site. The Linn earthworks inclosed some 30 acres, Aztalan roughly 20 acres, while the Angel site is said to have over 100 acres of archeological significance. More diffused sites would include Kincaid, of some 125 acres in southern Illinois; Cahokia, of about 3,000 acres in the American Bottoms opposite St. Louis; the Kingston Lake site in Peoria County, Illinois, of about 15 acres; and small sites, such as the F^v 664 village in Fulton County, Illinois, of some 2–3 acres. Monks Mound at Cahokia covers 16 acres, 2 roods, and 3 perches of ground. A better example of the contrast between the way of life of the Mississippi and that of the earlier periods could hardly be provided.

There are a great many sites with Middle Mississippi material which do not have large mound groups and cover no more than a few acres. These are located on somewhat smaller streams tributary to major rivers. These larger streams usually have the outstanding ceremonial centers in their valleys or on immediately adjacent upland. Dr. J. C. McGregor has survey evidence which indicates that a great many of the Spoon River Focus sites of the central Illinois Valley are located on upland areas in defensible positions.

The known and implied settlement pattern of large Middle Mississippi sites has not been stressed in this paper because it will be presented in some detail by Sears and Williams (this volume). The most extensive development of the mound-plaza–dwelling area did not take place in the region with which this paper deals, even though some of the outstanding sites of this type are located in the north.

In the upper Illinois Valley, the Fisher site near Joliet occupied about 5 acres and included some twelve burial mounds and fifty house sites. It was, however, occupied intermittently, and it is difficult to say what was the size of the specific living Indian group. The Fisher houses, which were thought to be circular, turned out to be rectangular to square when excavated, with a double wall and about 16 by 20 feet in size for the normal dwelling. A large structure was 25 by 35 feet. The houses were grouped about a roughly rectangular area 400 by 250 feet in size, corresponding to the Mississippi plaza pattern (J. W. Griffin, 1945). Plum Island, near Starved Rock, has a village of about 2–3 acres which is predominantly of this prehistoric period. The Oneota sites are apparently of the same order of magnitude. Others which still show strong Woodland characteristics are the Young site, of 4 acres; the Riviere au Vase, of ½ acre in eastern Michigan; and the Raymond village site in Jackson County, Illinois, of ⅓ acre. On the whole, sites of the Late Woodland culture type would range from about ½ acre to 3–4 acres at the most.

These data on size of the settlements contrast rather markedly with early French statements. In 1695 the Miami were said to have two villages with a total population of 4,400–4,800. In 1718 they were said to have six villages with a population of 5,600–6,400 (Kinietz, 1940). The village average in the first case is about 2,300 people and in the second about 1,000. It is also stated that the Miami and the Mascouten made use of forts and had at least one long house to a village for councils and ceremonies. Their permanent villages were near the agricultural fields, and during the winter communal hunt the old people remained in the village. La Salle claimed to have gathered at the French post at Starved Rock near Utica, Illinois, some 20,000 Indians, including 4,000 warriors. One village was said to have three to four hundred cabins, with four fires to a cabin and two families to each fire. Probably such a concentration did not take place until the establishment of European trading posts.

Sites of the Fort Ancient culture reach 4 acres or somewhat more in size. They are located on the first or second terrace or in some cases on bluffs overlooking streams. There is relatively little published evidence on house structure. The Baum pyramidal mound was built on top of the remains of a 36-foot circular house, and a similar structure was built on the second structural stage of the mound. The house in the Baum village, and presumably the Gartner site as well, was circular and about 12 feet in diameter. Mills excavated almost fifty of them but recorded that there was evidence of rebuilding, so that one cannot be certain as to the number of dwellings occupied during a single season. In the Fort Ancient sites along the Ohio and especially in those which come close to the historic period, the rectangular house is more normal. Excavations of Fort Ancient sites in Kentucky during federal relief days (the 1930's) definitely indicate the rectangular house as the most common form.

The Monongahela sites in southwestern Pennsylvania had small oval to circular houses from 10 to 25 feet in diameter inside an oval stockade (Mayer-Oakes, 1955). The houses were arranged in a circle within the palisade, with an open area in the center. Many of the villages are located in defensive positions. In excavated sites the average number of houses was twenty-five, and in at least some cases there had been two successive stockades, with thirty-three houses within the first palisade and twenty-seven houses within the later and outer wall. There is considerable evidence for occupation of such sites over a fair period of time to allow for the construction not only of the palisades and houses but also for refuse pits, burials, and other features. The general occupation pattern is thus similar to Late Woodland sites east of the Appalachians and to northern Fort Ancient sites.

Along the south shore of Lake Erie the late prehistoric villages of the Erie and related peoples are an acre or so in extent. They are located along old beach lines or on bluffs overlooking streams. Village debris is fairly heavy, indicating extensive occupation, but house patterns have not been worked out. Some of these sites are protected by walls and ditches or by palisades and, because of the relative absence of occupational debris, may have served primarily as defensive rather than year-round living areas.

SUMMARY

The general shift in type and size of prehistoric settlements is evident from the foregoing discussion. It is apparent why no formal classification has been attempted for settlement patterns. The early preceramic periods have relatively small sites without much evidence of dwelling structures or of specialization in the ceremonial, economic, or military activities of the people. During the Early and Middle Woodland periods there is a gradual increase in the size of the areas covered by habitations. The most striking change, however, is the construction of mounds for burial both on and near the dwelling site. In Ohio Hopewell there is a further and spectacular addition in the form of the extensive and complex earthworks, which are primarily of a little-understood ceremonial nature. The Mississippi period has a marked quantitative and qualitative advance in the normal dwelling-area size, in number and extent of the specialized ceremonial and military alignments, and in other features of a more advanced cultural stage. By the time of European exploration, the dominant settlement pattern in the upper Mississippi Valley and upper Great Lakes was more like that described for the Fisher Focus than for the Cahokia area. The reasons for the disappearance of the large ceremonial villages are not yet completely understood.

PREHISTORIC SETTLEMENT PATTERNS IN NORTHEASTERN NORTH AMERICA[1]

By WILLIAM A. RITCHIE

INTRODUCTION

THIS attempt at the definition of prehistoric settlement patterns in the Northeast is undertaken in the hope that here, as in the Virú Valley, (Willey, 1953), they may be shown to have economic, sociopolitical, and religious implications, useful in the reconstruction of areal history, and, further, that they may suggest functional correlations or causal interrelationships in culture (Steward, 1949, p. 6).

There are several reasons why the present task holds exceptional difficulties. In the first place, sites in the north were generally smaller and less permanent than those in the south, their organic contents have very largely disappeared through decay, and they are now much scarcer, owing to greater destruction by modern civilization and amateur activities. Yet, notwithstanding these serious limitations, it has been feasible through excavations, supplemented by ethnohistorical sources for the latest period, to assemble some pertinent data on community organization, burial ceremonialism, warfare, and, more inferentially, possible sociopolitical practices for certain of the principal cultural groups and temporal horizons in the Northeast. It must be frankly confessed, however, that the deductive use of analogy and extrapolation, employing, as ethnographic patterns within the area, the northern Algonkian tribes for the earlier cultures and the Iroquoian tribes primarily for the later, predisposes the writer to the delusions of circular reasoning and the foibles of syllogistic logic.

THE PALEO-INDIAN PERIOD

Warrant for the Paleo-Indian horizon in the Northeast is extremely scanty, comprising primarily a random scattering of fluted points of a general Clovis type. When the find-spots are plotted, however, various small local centers seem to emerge, usually within a stream valley. The distribution of fluted points sustains the inference of a wide range of movement by these earliest hunters, otherwise indicated by the exotic character of the stone employed in the particular locality where the point was found.

In recent years, discoveries of definite fluted-point assemblages in the Northeast create the likelihood of augmenting our meager knowledge of this

1. Published by permission of the director, New York State Museum and Science Service ("Journal Series," No. 7).

horizon by the addition of data bearing on faunal associations and geological and chronological relations (Witthoft, 1952; Ritchie, 1953; Byers, 1954, 1955). At present it would seem that the Pennsylvania and New England components depict favored camping spots, each repeatedly visited by the same small foraging groups, as suggested by individual site consistency in typologies and techniques. A shore camp on the waning Champlain Sea is possible on geological considerations at the Reagen site (Lougee, 1953, p. 275), which may be the youngest of the three components, thus providing depth perspective for even the earliest cultural horizon in the Northeast.

THE ARCHAIC PERIOD

The most ancient manifestations in the Northeast, so far dated by radio-carbon measurements, go back to 3500 and 3000 B.C., thus establishing contemporaneity with obviously related cultures in the Southeast. In all probability, the climatic conditions of the Altithermal (which may have been a primary factor for the presence of the Paleo-Indians in the eastern United States) still prevailed (Sears, 1942, p. 733; Lewis, 1954, p. 249). There are also reasons to envision significant geographical differences from the present which exerted as yet unassessed effects on the cultures of this period (Quimby, 1954, pp. 318–19). As yet, the regional and temporal variations in the developmental pattern of the Archaic cultures have been only partly defined. At least two distinctive traditions, each linked with a physical type, have been determined for New York State, viz., the Lamoka and the Laurentian, and the latter seems to have constituted the basic Archaic tradition over much of the Northeast.

Certain broad generalizations concerning the Archaic are deducible from the archeological data, but these afford us relatively little insight into the settlement patterns. The basic economy represented a long-established adjustment to a forest milieu, with possibly somewhat later modifications for littoral subsistence. The earliest coastal encampments may now be submerged, as suggested by the Boston fishweirs (Johnson, 1942), Grassy (Johnson and Raup, 1947), and Grannis (Sargent, 1952) islands. The tools for felling and working wood were well developed throughout the period, including, at various times and places, the celt, adze, gouge, grooved ax, chisel, and heavy scraper. Fundamental reliance on the hunting-fishing activity is attested by the wealth of projectile points of many varieties, presumably for the arming of darts and spears; bone fishhooks; barbed bone points, both fixed and detachable; net and line sinkers; and possibly bone trapsticks. Food-grinding equipment was even more standardized among the cultures of this period, embracing an assortment of mullers, flat mealing stones and mortars, and cylindrical pestles, the latter possibly denoting use of the shallow wooden mortar. The discovery of carbonized acorn hulls and nut shells in New York sites of this age and their associated faunal remains testify to an oak-deer-turkey biome.

The nature of the settlement sites supports the assumption of a simple acquisitive economy, since, with few exceptions, they are small in size, with little or no surviving organic residue, suggesting the temporary camping places of tiny nomadic bands who scattered themselves widely along the banks of the larger streams and ponds and the smaller lakes, and at advantageous spots along the coast. The preferred situation was a knoll, terrace, or ridge of well-drained, warmer, sandy or loamy soil, at or close to a hydrographic outlet point, preferably the mouth of a stream. Proximity to rifts, riverine pools, still-water rivers, large swamps and marshes, and shallow lake ends indicates that the capture of food animals, with the limited available techniques, formed the primary consideration in the selection of habitations. It is probable that the nomadism of these bands was imposed less through preference than through necessity; for, in some instances in the Northeast, sites covering more than an acre of deep midden accumulations (Ritchie, 1932) provide good parallels to the large, semipermanent, shell-midden settlements of the southeastern Archaic.[2] The evidence here points to generations of more or less continuous abode in a locality especially favored by nature with variety and abundance of animals and plants. In most cases, however, of accumulated aggregates of refuse, artifacts, and burials, repetition of periodic residence as part of a seasonal cycle of activities would seem the more likely explanation (Ritchie, 1940, 1945).

Most regrettably, only the meagerest vestiges can be drawn upon in the reconstruction of northeastern Archaic house structures. At Lamoka Lake thick, indurated patches of laminated refuse, occasionally associated with a short post-mold series, led to the postulation of pole-framed rectangular structures, some 12 by 18 feet in floor size (Ritchie, 1932, p. 87). At the Brewerton stations similar compacted areas of alternating refuse and sand, without accompanying post molds, suggested sanded dwelling floors (Ritchie, 1940, p. 8). Stout antler points and certain forms of flat, perforated bone tools at these and related sites hint at bark and woven-mat house covers (Ritchie, 1932, Pl. X, Figs. 2–4, 13, 14; 1940, Pl. XXIX, Figs. 31, 41–45, 62, 63; 1945, Pl. 10, Figs. 4, 26).

The general picture emerging from current understanding of the northeastern Archaic cultures as a whole envisions small mobile bands of foraging people, following a seasonal cycle of economic pursuits, resident in temporary settlements of flimsy, bark- or mat-covered wigwam dwellings, situated on higher ground along sizable waterways, which afforded access to food and the routes of travel by means of dugout canoes. Significant elements of this way of life persisted, especially in the eastern half of our area, well into later times, and, indeed, they continue into the present among certain of the north-

---

2. Webb (1946) describes a typical Kentucky example. Numerous others might be cited for the Southeast area. There may well be an additional climatic factor involved here, inasmuch as the indicated population size of the groups progressively increases from north to south.

eastern Algonkian hunting tribes (Speck, 1935; Cooper, 1946; Flannery, 1946).

Rather dubious analogies of a sociopolitical and religious character may be attempted between these recent and ancient hunters of the Northeast. In the light of the total evidence it seems reasonable to suppose that the basic sociopolitical units of Archaic times comprised small multifamily groups, the members of which were mutually interdependent through co-operative efforts for success in food procurement and that such autonomous groups existed within a loose and shifting band organization, founded upon kinship and friendship (Steward, 1936). We may further hypothesize, on archeological grounds, shamanistic attention to details of hunting magic and the religio-magical observances attending burial; else how explain the rattles, flutes, amulets, red ocher, skull burials, and other paraphernalia and mortuary practices discovered at the Frontenac Island site (Ritchie, 1945). Something of the same order, apparently, is recorded for the Red Paint culture of Maine (Willoughby, 1898; Moorehead, 1922, pp. 20–143; Smith, 1948). A general lack of social stratification in Archaic societies is indicated by the absence of especially prepared and accoutered graves, and this furnishes a further parallel with the simple hunting bands of the northeastern Algonkians.

The problem of landholdings and territorial ranges of Archaic bands is still more difficult of approach. It seems very doubtful that the family-hunting-territory system existed at this early date, if, indeed, it is prehistoric at all (Leacock, 1954). In terms of the wide distribution over large regions within the area of many highly specific tool and weapon types, particularly in projectile points, one might infer a vaguely defined, unstable, band-controlled territory, combined with free interchange of ideas, over a time span now known to have encompassed several millennia.

THE EARLY AND MIDDLE WOODLAND PERIODS

In the Northeast the cultures of the intermediate Early and Middle Woodland periods are, on the whole, more poorly defined than those of either the Archaic or the Late Woodland horizons. It appears that over much of the area Late Archaic period cultures, deeply rooted in the Laurentian tradition, were progressively fertilized by the introduction, through diffusion, stimulus diffusion, and to some extent the spread of new peoples, of complexes containing, among other traits, ceramics, new ornamental forms of stone and copper, and a growing emphasis on a cult of the dead. The changes are gradational eastward, the process being already under way in northern New York with the influx of a new assemblage of people (?) and culture about 2500 B.C. (Ritchie, 1955).

A second ceramic tradition, comprising the typical "Woodland wares" of the area, stratigraphically overlies the earliest ceramics (Vinette 1 ware and its derivatives) wherever a pottery sequence has been defined. The appearance of this second group of dentate and cord-impressed styles, with emphasis on rocker and other stamping techniques, seems to usher in the Middle Woodland horizon. Many of its distinctive types occur widely across the Great Lakes and northeastern areas (Ritchie and MacNeish, 1949).

No appreciable modification in the way of life of the northeastern groups is implied by the archeological data for the earlier part of the Woodland period. Early and Middle Woodland wares appear sequentially in many of the sites, along with quantitative and certain qualitative changes in stone artifacts, particularly projectile points, suggesting the introduction of the bow and arrow in the latter part of the period (Ritchie, 1946, pp. 15–17; Rouse, 1947, pp. 18–22; Bullen, 1949, pp. 78–86; Smith, 1950, pp. 144–55). In so far as can be judged, the basic economy and camp type of settlement persisted well into Middle Woodland times, which may have seen the introduction of maize horticulture.

With the appearance of an Early Woodland burial cult, however, there occur the first tangible inklings of social differentiation, and before the close of Middle Woodland times a variety of modifications on this basic theme had taken place over much of the area. Broadly conceived, ceremonial centers made their appearance, at first as small cemeteries on sacred burial precincts, set apart from the habitation quarters, in marked contradistinction from the prevailing Archaic custom of simple interment in the camp refuse. Because these cemeteries contain a variable proportion of more carefully prepared graves with richer offerings, it seems logical to assume some sort of social hierarchy. The use of symbolic ritualistic objects and substances, like red ocher, suggests a religio-ceremonialism under shamanistic or priestly control, a primitive church operating as an integrative social force (Ritchie, 1955).

Later on, burial-mound construction, embodying diagnostic Hopewellian features, was practiced over a limited western portion of the area, but at no time or place are there the larger expressions of a ceremonial center, such as the earthen inclosures of southern Ohio (Ritchie, 1938). There is some indirect evidence of the use of charnel houses in the presence of unburned and cremated bone bundles in mounds and cemeteries.

THE LATE WOODLAND PERIOD

The apparent religio-ceremonial orientation of Early and Middle Woodland times declined in the tabescent stages of the latter period, and, by contrast, Late Woodland cultures in the Northeast are broadly characterized by a reversion to the secular emphasis of the Archaic occupations. The concurrent decline and final disappearance of certain aesthetic tendencies, expressed in various media and categories, and the attendant trade connections may well be interpreted as an intrinsic reflex of this change. An opposite development seems synchronously to have been taking place in the Southeast, with the emergence of Early Mississippi ceremonial centers (Ford and Willey, 1941, pp. 344–51; Sears, this volume).

For the Northeast this period witnessed the rise of the first large villages, covering 1 to several acres of elevated ground, consisting of semipermanent houses, and frequently inclosed within a protective palisade. The marked increase in population, attested by the larger and more numerous sites and the successively enlarged stockade lines of individual villages, may reflect the addition of abundant, storable, vegetable protein in the dietary of this time, following a suggestion to account for a similar growth phenomenon in the Southwest during Basketmaker III times (A.D. 500–700) (Linton, 1940, pp. 35–36). Definite storage pits and carbonized beans are now actually present in certain New York Owasco stations (Ritchie, 1936, p. 23; 1953, p. 11), for which radiocarbon dates on submitted charcoal samples have not yet been received. Maize horticulture, assumed to have entered our area at some stage of the Middle Woodland period, is now amply verified.

A trend toward closer cultural uniformity asserts itself, paradoxically, in combination with indirect attestation to contending populations, seen in the fact of village fortification and more dubiously in the arrow wounds in skeletal remains.

Now, initially, in our area data on house types are directly inferable from archeological findings of post-mold patterns, signifying the use of circular lodges with central hearths, some 12–15 feet in diameter and presumably of wigwam type.[3] Reference to the earliest documentary descriptions for the area furnishes a probable index to the impermanent superstructure—a domed or arbor roof of arched saplings, tied together with bark rope, and provided with a cover of bark, grass, or reed mats (Ruttenber, 1872, pp. 9–10; Murphy, 1875, pp. 179–80; Howe, 1943, pp. 298–99). The slender, curved, perforated, bone mat-needle is a common device of this period (Ritchie, 1936, Pl. IX, Figs. 10–13).

In the littoral region of our area open villages may have prevailed until the additional hazards of historic times. On western Long Island and possibly elsewhere among the Algonkian tribes of this region, a long-house type of dwelling is known to have been in use by at least the latter part of the seventeenth century. Said to have ranged in length from about 20 to 100 feet, it was, of course, a communal dwelling with a number of fires, and its obvious similarities to the long house of the Iroquois appear in the description by a Dutch traveler (Murphy, 1867, pp. 124–27).

The Iroquoian economy and settlement pattern of prehistoric and early historic times seems to have been anticipated in essential features—except, perhaps, use of the long house—on the underlying Owasco level of the same

3. Ritchie (1936, pp. 39–43), Rogers (1943, p. 31). Harrington (1924, p. 246) describes, without mention of post molds, oval, partly subterranean house floors on an eastern Long Island site of this period.

region. In the seventeenth century the main Iroquoian towns, which were shifted for short distances about every ten years to allow for soil and firewood exhaustion, were ranged across central New York State from the mouth of Schoharie Creek to the Genesee River. Larger villages comprised a hundred or more long houses, containing upward of 1,000 people, and lay on stockaded hilltops, usually remote from the water routes of travel.[4] Unlike most of their predecessors, the Iroquois were a forest-dwelling people with an extensive system of overland trails. Such Iroquoian towns would probably equate rather closely in size and general arrangement with the Late Mississippi towns of the Southeast, except that the former lacked the temple mounds, chiefs' houses, charnel houses, and other elements of the southeastern ceremonial complex. The council house of the Iroquois—the focus of political and religious activities—affords the closest parallel. Even at the present day, Iroquoian houses on the reservations tend to cluster around the council house (Fenton, 1951, pp. 40–41).

In the Iroquoian village community pattern, local autonomy prevailed, the facts of kinship and co-residence establishing social cohesion and underlying the creation of the confederacy (*ibid.*, pp. 39, 51).

Following the period of the Iroquoian wars (1648–75), village fortification was abandoned in Iroquoia. By 1800 the communal bark long house had been replaced by small individual family cabins constructed of logs on the Scandinavian model, probably introduced into Delaware by the Swedes and Finns in 1638.[5] Relinquishing of the co-residence system was attended by major modifications in settlement patterns. Thus each individual family cabin in a sprawling community was surrounded by its own piece of land, now tilled by the men, whereas, under the old compact communal-village system, work parties of clan women raised crops on land held in common (Fenton, 1951, p. 41).

The Indians' attitude toward the land was, however, probably not fundamentally altered by these enforced changes. Generally throughout the area the aboriginal philosophy in this matter was at the farthest remove from European concepts, which fact underlay the numerous difficulties of land transference during the Colonial period. Indian ideology conceived of the land, together with the life-sustaining animals, vegetables, and minerals it supported, as supernaturally given for the common use, hence beyond personal alienation. Privileges of land use rested with tribe or village, and apparently more than one tribe might synchronously utilize the same large tract in peaceful coexist-

4. The complete excavation of one of the smaller Mohawk villages (Caughnawaga, 1666–93) has been attempted (see Grassmann, 1952).

5. Kimball (1922, p. 8). To some extent, according to Fenton (by conversation), the long-house type of structure, with log walls and bark roof, continued to serve in a few places either as a communal dwelling or a council house even after 1800, as at Caneadea on the Genesee and Cold Spring on the Allegheny.

ence, while the removal of a band for a number of years seems to have eliminated even their temporary claim to these holdings (Snyderman, 1951, pp. 15–16, 18–20, 27).

CONCLUSIONS

In summary perspective, the development of settlement patterns in the Northeast reveals a more or less continuous process of amplification in size and complexity, in which it seems possible to discern certain interlinked general stages. In the first stage, encompassing the Archaic period, with a duration of at least two thousand years over various parts of the area, the sundry cultures were based upon a hunting-fishing-gathering economy, necessitating mobility or limited nomadism, associated with a seasonal cycle of food-producing activities, probably on the part of small, semi-isolated, individualistic, and relatively unstable bands composed of kinsmen and congenial outsiders, under temporary chieftainship.

Almost no vestige has been discovered of the probable flimsy shelters of this period, clustered at certain times and places in unorganized camps near available sources of food. Within such an economically oriented unit, simple social patterns founded on kinship, age, and sex probably prevailed. Religious notions related to magical beliefs and practices, perhaps under shamanistic guidance, while not susceptible to proof, are strongly attested by burial practices. Internecine hostilities among bands certainly existed, as demonstrated by wounds and mutilations of infrequent occurrence.

The changes that were to differentiate the Woodland period usher in the second major stage, which began in the western part of the area around 2500 B.C. The introduction of pottery and numerous other traits seems not significantly to have altered the economy or general mode of life, at least for quite a time; instead, the socio-religious structure of the cultures affected appears to have undergone revision under the growth of a persuasive cult idea. In due course, parts of the Northeast received the backwash of the most fully developed expression of this cult in Ohio Hopewellian, at which time our region attained its closest approach to a theocratic social order.

A shift in economy to include maize horticulture is probably a feature of this stage. Refuse accumulations are somewhat thicker, and there are other suggestions of more permanent and larger population groupings than characterize prior levels. The greatest elaboration of many aspects of culture, including religious ideology, were reached during Early and Middle Woodland times.

A marked regression in magico-religious activities and in some probably related aspects of the material culture characterizes the succeeding stage, dominated by the cultures of the Late Woodland period.[6] Economically, em-

---

6. Non-mortuary ritualism has been inferred from archeological evidences suggesting bear ceremonialism in the Owasco and early Iroquois cultures (see Ritchie, 1947, 1950).

phasis shifted from food-gathering to food production and storage. It is suggested that bean protein may have been added to the dietary at this time. Semisedentary village life is now definitely evinced, with a sharp rise (or concentration) in population, occupying single and communal dwellings of circular wigwam and long-house types. Demographic pressure is probable and may account for the indications of a sense of insecurity, if not actual contest, seen in the use of palisaded settlements. Smoking pipes and pottery attain their apogee in variety and artistic excellence within the area.

The final stage culminates the Late Woodland period, terminating in historic times in the intensification of the processes of intertribal conflict and conquest, presumably attendant upon growth pressures and a new economic motivation supplied by the European fur trade. This seems to have marked the high point of tribal confederacies among Algonkian and Iroquoian nations alike, organized primarily for defensive purposes but also employed offensively in the name of peace.

CHANGING SETTLEMENT PATTERNS IN THE GREAT PLAINS[1]

By WALDO R. WEDEL

HUMAN settlement of the Great Plains has been going on for probably ten thousand years or more. Much still remains to be learned about this long story, though its broad outlines seem to have emerged. It is already clear that the patterns of settlement have varied considerably, both through time and in space. These variations are not random or chance phenomena. They reflect in part the environmental factor, in part social and historical forces. While we cannot yet be certain of the degree of influence exerted in all cases by the several variables indicated, it is evident that any reconstruction or interpretation that ignores either is open to question.

Recent syntheses of Plains archeology have dealt increasingly with the matter of settlement patterns, though usually more or less incidentally and in connection with other objectives. Here I propose to assemble and briefly review these and other archeological and ethnohistorical data bearing directly on what Willey (1953, p. 101) has defined as "the way in which man disposed himself over the landscape on which he lived." Within the limits set for this paper it is obviously impossible to give comprehensive consideration to the entire Great Plains region as envisioned by the archeologist. The discussion is therefore restricted in the main to the central and northern portions, lying north of the thirty-seventh parallel of latitude between the Missouri River and the Rocky Mountains. Three subareas may be recognized (Wedel, 1949; Lehmer, 1954): the Central Plains in Nebraska, Kansas, and eastern Colorado; the Middle (formerly Upper) Missouri in North and South Dakota; and the Northwestern Plains in Wyoming and Montana, roughly west of the longitude of the Black Hills (Fig. 1).

Environmentally, the region under consideration offered native peoples a vast expanse of grasslands, generally flat to rolling, and cut through at infrequent intervals by a series of east-flowing streams. Locally, there are areas of greater relief, but nowhere are there serious topographic hindrances to travel on foot or horseback. The climate is continental in type, with dry, cold winters, hot, dry summers, strong winds, abundant sunshine, a high rate of evaporation, and wide daily and seasonal fluctuations of precipitation and temperature. Average annual precipitation diminishes from nearly 40 inches

---

1. Published by permission of the secretary of the Smithsonian Institution.

in the east to 12 inches or less in the west; and with this progressive decrease is associated a marked change in the native vegetation—from subhumid tall-grass prairies and heavily forested stream valleys in the east through mixed grasses to short-grass steppe and sagebrush, with little surface water and timber, in the west. A large part of the region, including most of the Northwestern Plains and adjacent sections of the Central Plains and Middle Missouri, lies beyond the 20-inch rainfall line and is climatically unsuited to de-

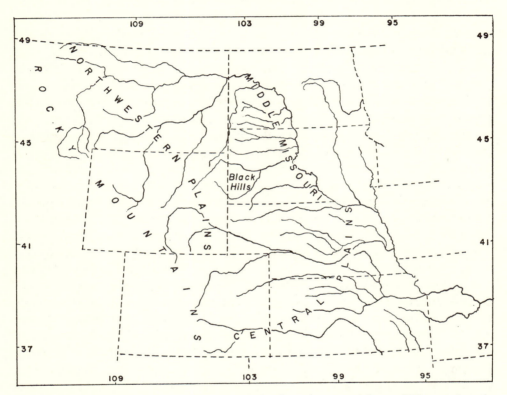

Fig. 1.—Archeological subareas of the Great Plains from the upper Arkansas Valley northward

pendable maize agriculture except by specialized methods. Everywhere the grassy uplands in prewhite days furnished an abundance of large game animals, with additional forms in great variety available in the timbered valleys.

In the ensuing survey of native settlement patterns, it is assumed that the prehistory of the Great Plains can be conveniently viewed in terms of the broad time horizons and culture complexes shown in Figure 2. Like all schematic representations of a dimly appreciated and complex phenomenon, where the basic data are often sketchy and incomplete and the chronology still in process of development, this one is not beyond question; and it will undoubtedly change as research and synthesis in the area move forward.

EARLY HUNTING COMPLEXES

The Early Hunting complexes are represented by archeological remains dating from approximately 5000 B.C. or earlier. Most of the evidence (Roberts, 1940, 1953; Sauer, 1944; Schultz and Frankforter, 1948; Holder and Wike, 1949; Wormington, 1949; Sellards, 1952) comes from scattered sites in the Northwestern Plains and at the western edge of the Central Plains in a region now characterized by low precipitation and sparse vegetation. Not uncom-

		Northwestern Plains	Central Plains	Middle Missouri
1800 A.D.	HISTORIC TRIBES	EQUESTRIAN BISON HUNTERS	DECADENT VILLAGE COMPLEXES	
1750 A.D.				
	COALESCENT VILLAGE COMPLEXES	DISMAL RIVER	ONEOTA	STANLEY LATE HEART LA ROCHE RIVER
			LOWER LOUP	etc.
			GREAT BEND	
1500 A.D.		PEDESTRIAN BISON HUNTERS		
	SMALL VILLAGE COMPLEXES	BUICK	UPPER NEBRASKA REPUBLICAN CULTURE	"MIDDLE MISSOURI TRADITION"
1200 A.D.				
	PLAINS WOODLAND COMPLEXES	FRANKTOWN GRANEROS PARKER	LOSEKE CREEK STERNS CREEK K.C. HOPEWELL KEITH VALLEY	SCALP CREEK ELLIS UNCLASSIFIED WOODLAND
500 A.D.				
1500 B.C.	HUNTING- GATHERING COMPLEXES	BIRDSHEAD CAVE II-IV SHOSHONI BASIN CAMPS McKEAN UPPER SIGNAL BUTTE II		
		McKEAN LOWER SIGNAL BUTTE I	NEBO HILL	
5000 B.C.				
8000 B.C.	EARLY HUNTING COMPLEXES	EDEN, CODY AGATE BASIN ANGOSTURA		
		PLAINVIEW, FRONTIER FOLSOM etc.		

FIG. 2.—Suggested chronology of certain cultures and complex horizons of the Great Plains from the upper Arkansas Valley northward.

monly, the sites are in localities that today seem inhospitable to human occupancy. They include bone beds, containing artifacts and suggesting kills or butchering grounds, and camp sites. They offer little or no information as to the size, composition, and organization of the human communities. Structural remains, posthole patterns, and food-storage devices, such as pits, usually associated in the Plains with fairly stable economies have not been found. Hearths sometimes occur, but they are usually few in number and seldom give evidence of prolonged use. The artifact inventory is almost entirely limited to stonework. It includes few or no grinding tools or other objects suited to the gathering and processing of vegetal foods. Instead, it features implements primarily adapted to the chase—knives, scrapers, choppers, and especially projectile points, the latter often relatively plentiful and of exceptional workmanship. There is no evidence of the dog. From the nature of the associated bone refuse, the chase involved predominantly the large game animals—at first, the elephant; later, species of bison now extinct; and, finally, modern bison.

From this evidence it is inferred that the early hunters were essentially nomadic, with the subsistence economy linked closely to the large gregarious herbivores. Local groups were probably of very limited size, perhaps consisting for much of the time of small bands or family groups. Bison-hunting, however, is most productive when pursued on a co-operative group basis; and such co-operative efforts may well be implied in some of the bone beds—that is, they may be the result of organized drives planned and executed on a larger scale than a single local group could successfully mount. Residence was probably in light dwellings covered with brush, grass thatch, or skins, with frequent movement from place to place as the availability of game, the exigencies of the seasons, and other circumstances dictated. The total population of the region must always have been small and sparse; but the widely scattered occurrence of typical artifacts suggests that, despite the lack of draft animals, the people may have traveled over considerable distances in pursuit of the herds.

The known sites of this period suggest temporary and often recurrent occupancy, reflecting the pattern of unstable settlement imposed by the migratory habits of the bison. It is by no means clear, however, that they necessarily or fully represent the yearly round of economic activities. It can probably be assumed that use was made of roots, seeds, and berries in season and of small game when the larger animals were, for one reason or another, not readily available. Since much of the region inhabited is characterized by severe winters, it is probable that residence during that time of year was in localities selected for dependable resources of shelter, fuel, water, and game.

HUNTING-GATHERING COMPLEXES

Following the Early Hunting complexes in and about the Northwestern Plains are several archeological assemblages (Mulloy, 1952, 1954a, b) that may be considered representative of Hunting-Gathering complexes. Carbon 14 dates indicate their presence before ca. 1500 B.C., subsequent to the period of heightened aridity termed the "Altithermal." Stratigraphically, there are indications of two horizons.

The assemblages occur in a variety of locations—at open camp sites, in dune areas, as occupation levels in and on stream terraces, in caves and rock shelters, and in association with mass kills of bison of recent species. Hearths of varied nature, some in the form of rock-filled basins suggesting roasting pits, are common at some sites. Clear-cut evidence of habitations is wanting. Groups of stone circles are thought to belong to this general time level, but it is not clear whether they represent habitations or specialized structures of other function. The deposits are sometimes of considerable depth and show

recurrent occupancy. That hunting was still an important part of the subsistence economy in some localities or at some periods is suggested by the high
proportion of projectile points, knives, scrapers, and other implement categories paralleling, in part, those of the Early Hunting complexes. Greater
emphasis on the grinding of foods, inferentially including some of vegetal
origin, is suggested by the presence of metates and *manos;* locally, there
seems also to have been greatly increased use of small game and occasionally
shellfish.

It has been suggested that this wider range of foods may reflect a diminished
supply of bison, perhaps for climatic reasons, and the consequent need for
adding whatever edible items could be obtained by foraging. Implied in this
view (Mulloy, 1954b, p. 59) are "small social groups—perhaps bands or even
independent family groups—moving about in a restricted and probably cycli-
cal nomadism exploiting the natural resources of an area to exhaustion and
then moving on to allow it to replenish. Perhaps each group had its own
collection of campsites and returned to each camp as a particular economic
resource, perhaps different from one camp to another, became available . . .
the evidence suggests small groups of miserable, perhaps chronically starving,
gathering nomads with a way of life more similar to that of such Great Basin
peoples as the Gosiute than to anything else in the region."

Ethnographic work in the Great Basin has given us a vivid picture
(Steward, 1938) of the way of life briefly outlined here from archeological
evidence in the Plains. That pursuit of large game was probably more important among some hunting-gathering peoples of the prehistoric Plains than
among the recent Great Basin tribes is suggested by the high proportion of
hunting implements at such manifestations as Signal Butte I and the McKean
site and by the bison kills of the Montana region, where organized co-operative drives can probably be inferred.

The sites at which remains of the Early Hunting and Hunting-Gathering
complexes have been found are generally along the mountain front at the
western edge of the Plains, along the breaks where the Plains are being dissected by stream action, and in the vicinity of detached mountain masses, such
as the Black Hills. These latter, offering in small geographic compass a variety
of environments, good wintering places for man and beast, and a succession of
ripening seasons for plants, would have been much more congenial to foot
hunters and gatherers than would the Plains proper (Hughes, 1949). Yet the
Plains seem also to have been drawn upon, as is indicated by the widespread
occurrence of typical projectile points and other artifact types at upland
localities now far removed from surface water or otherwise desirable camping sites. These finds suggest that there were perhaps seasonal or wet-weather
ponds, marshes, and waterholes, now dry, where game and perhaps edible
plants or plant products were once available and to which hunting and foraging groups were thereby attracted.

PLAINS WOODLAND COMPLEXES

The Plains Woodland complexes have been most fully investigated in the Central Plains, but they are also indicated on the Middle Missouri (Strong, 1935; Hill and Kivett, 1941; Champe, 1946; Hurt, 1952; Kivett, 1952). On present evidence, they appear to date within the Christian Era. Several variants have been recognized, all with pottery and some with indications of maize. Sites are usually small and inconspicuous, may be deeply buried in terraces, and have a wide distribution along the smaller rivers and creeks of Nebraska and Kansas. Habitation remains are scanty or absent; pottery and other artifacts are not plentiful by comparison with later complexes; and artifacts clearly recognizable as gardening tools are rare or absent. Shallow basins up to approximately 15 or 18 feet in diameter and sometimes containing fireplaces suggest dwellings—probably of light poles covered with grass thatch, bark, or skins and seldom numbering more than a half-dozen (single-family?) units per site. Burials include both primary and massed secondary interment, the latter perhaps suggesting prolonged, but not necessarily uninterrupted, localization of residence nearby.

The Hopewell village sites near Kansas City, with their traces of maize and beans, abundant cache pits, and sometimes comparatively deep and prolific refuse accumulations, look like fairly stable communities; and in some ways the culture manifested would seem to fit better into one of the later horizons of the region. Otherwise, what seems to be implied by most of the Woodland sites west of the Missouri is a simple, creek-valley, hunting and gathering economy, perhaps with incipient horticulture. Maize has been reported from Loseke Creek sites, squash and gourds for the Sterns Creek manifestation. The bones of elk, deer, small mammals, and birds seem to predominate over those of bison. This may reflect hunting and butchering methods rather than food preferences, for it is difficult to believe that any Plains Indian population, however small, scattered, and unstable, would have refrained long from pursuit of the bison if that animal were obtainable. There are other possibilities. If game was abundant in the brushy bottoms and adjacent prairies, small mobile population aggregates moving cyclically over a given territory might have been able to subsist for much of the time in a manner comparable to that of the western Algonkians, obtaining most of their meat from a relatively sedentary animal population within a day or two's travel from frequently changed camping sites instead of depending on the constantly roving herds. Or the known sites may represent chiefly winter locations, where, even when the herds were not readily available, it was possible to find shelter, fuel, and sedentary animal populations adequate to tide the human groups over this period. Roots, seeds, and berries were undoubtedly gathered as they became available, and grinding stones may indicate something of the manner of their processing.

Generally absent from Plains Woodland sites are recognizable traces of ceremonial or other specialized structures, defensive works, or other features implying large-scale community endeavors. The small burial mounds attributed to Woodland peoples in the eastern Plains and the ossuaries farther west may be exceptions.

SMALL VILLAGE COMPLEXES

Some centuries prior to the arrival of white men in the region, the Plains Woodland complexes were succeeded by a series of semihorticultural pottery-making cultures implying a much more stable pattern of settlement. Subsistence rested in part on a small-scale, hoe-linked, maize-bean-squash-sunflower horticulture and in part on hunting, fishing, and gathering. In the Central Plains the first of these complexes included several prehistoric manifestations featuring small, loosely arranged settlements—the Nebraska Culture in and near the Missouri Bluffs zone, the Upper Republican aspect of Nebraska and western Kansas, and a related complex, still unnamed, centering apparently in the Blue and lower Smoky Hill–Kansas River drainage.

Substantial earth-covered lodges, usually square or subrectangular in form, generally much larger than the habitations inferred for the Woodland peoples, and perhaps occupied by more than one family, were characteristic throughout. In the east these commonly stood in or over deep pits, whereas to the west the pits were usually shallower or wanting entirely. Villages show little or no sign of planning. In the Nebraska Culture they consisted of houses strung irregularly and at random intervals along the tops of narrow ridges and bluffs (Strong, 1935, Fig. 15; Cooper, 1940, Figs. 1, 4); others were probably scattered on lower terraces, where their arrangement is obscured. Upper Republican villages and many of those in the lower Kansas drainage were generally on terraces, where the topography exerted less restraint on the disposition of dwellings (Brower, 1898, p. 24; Wedel, 1935, p. 218 and Fig. 11; Kivett, 1949). Here they consisted of single houses randomly scattered at intervals of a few yards to several hundred feet or of clusters of two to four lodges, similarly separated from other small clusters or single units. Lodges usually included one or more small subfloor cache pits; and nearby there was often a small refuse dump. Such settlements, somewhat reminiscent of the larger clustering noted by the French among the seventeenth-century Caddo (Swanton, 1942, pp. 39, 42), did not lend themselves to fortification, and no indication of defensive works has come to light. The diffuse pattern of settlement, in fact, seems like good evidence that warfare was not an important consideration, for the rambling nature of the communities would have made them easy victims for raiding parties.

In the loess plains west of the Missouri there was a decided preference for residence along the smaller streams and creeks tributary to the Elkhorn, Loup, Platte, Republican, and Smoky Hill–Kansas rivers. Settlement was pushed to the edge of the Nebraska Sandhills and up the Platte and Republican drainages to or beyond the Colorado line—wherever, in other words, climate and soils permitted creek-bottom gardening, streams or springs could be depended upon for water, and timber for building purposes was available.[2] The apparent preference for residence on small streams may reflect in part the probability that timber was more abundant here than on the major streams, as was the case in the nineteenth century (see, e.g., Bryan, 1857, p. 475). The extreme westerly Upper Republican sites, in the Nebraska panhandle (Bell and Cape, 1936) and Colorado piedmont (Withers, 1954), may represent hunting stations, seasonally or otherwise intermittently occupied; or they may indicate people transitional from a semisedentary, partly horticultural to a purely big-game-hunting and gathering economy. Other sites in northeastern Nebraska suggest more compact and perhaps larger settlements (Cooper, 1936), possibly foreshadowing population shifts and regroupings that became much more pronounced in the next period to be considered.

The general picture here, then, is one of many small, widely scattered communities, probably seldom exceeding one or two hundred persons and usually considerably smaller. For aggregates of this sort the nearby creek bottoms furnished adequate garden space, and game could be readily obtained by foot hunters in the valleys and along the upland margins. The greater security afforded by successful horticulture and the more stable life thus permitted encouraged some enrichment of the material aspects of life, as compared with the Woodland peoples; this is reflected in the greater abundance of pottery and of artifacts in stone, bone, and other materials.

Commitment to fixed residence for considerable portions of each year implies that the social and political organization under which these hamlets and rural neighborhoods operated must have differed a good deal from those of earlier people. Different property concepts, more and tighter social controls, and generally closer integration of society for ceremonial and other purposes may be inferred. There is, however, no indication of social classes, of groups specializing extensively in particular arts and crafts, or of well-developed ceremonialism; such specialized structures as temples are lacking, as are burial mounds or other evidence of large community enterprises.

Outside the Central Plains recent investigations confirm the presence on the Middle Missouri of a small-village manifestation or manifestations, including rectangular dwellings, maize horticulture, and associated traits paralleling in many respects those of the Central Plains (Lehmer, 1954). Here, however, fortifications are indicated, and there was a tendency toward orderly arrangement of the communities, with dwellings more or less in rows. In the Northwestern Plains hunting peoples were evidently responsible for extensive bison

2. Elsewhere I have discussed (Wedel, 1941, 1953) some of the environmental hazards to corn-growing in the Central Plains and the possibility that deteriorating climatic conditions may have forced abandonment of the Upper Republican habitat in late prehistoric times by semihorticultural peoples.

kills; and at a somewhat later time, perhaps, pottery-making groups from the Middle Missouri and Central Plains seem to have made their way into the eastern part of the area. Much further work is needed to clarify the distribution and nature of the complexes indicated and to determine more exactly their relationships to the Central Plains complexes.

COALESCENT VILLAGE COMPLEXES

In late prehistoric times notable population shifts took place in the Central Plains, and with these shifts came marked changes in the patterns of settlement. The many small, widely scattered, earth-lodge communities were abandoned, and horticultural peoples apparently withdrew for the most part from the region west of the ninety-ninth meridian. It has been suggested that much of the Central Plains was depopulated by a mid-sixteenth-century drought, followed by wholesale human emigration to the Middle Missouri and a subsequent movement back into east-central Nebraska. While there can be little doubt of the importance of the climatic factor in Plains prehistory, I believe there are serious chronological objections to this theory; and, before we settle on this or any other explanation that seems currently plausible, we should have more information on the archeology of the Loup and Elkhorn drainages southeast and east of the Nebraska Sandhills.

In any case, by the time contact had been established with white men in the mid-sixteenth century, the horticultural communities comprised a small number of large villages in relatively limited localities. The Pawnee were on the lower Loup and adjacent Platte rivers (Wedel, 1938), showing a decided preference for the larger stream valleys and their immediate borders in the selection of sites. Farther south, the Wichita were settled in large, though sometimes still discontinuous, communities situated sometimes on small creeks and sometimes on large streams (Wedel, 1942). Along the eastern margin of the Central Plains, Oneota sites, suggesting intensive and prolonged occupancy by large communities, probably represent Siouan peoples adjusting their economy and way of life to the eastern Plains village Indian pattern. In the western Plains the Dismal River sites of the Plains Apache, whose archeological progenitors still await recognition and definition, also indicate population aggregates of considerable size, in part corn-growing but doubtless more heavily dependent on the chase (Hill and Metcalf, 1942; Champe, 1949). The relation of the inhabitants of these sites to the "Querecho" and other strictly bison-hunting nomadic groups met by the first Spanish exploring parties in the Great Plains is still obscure; but the observations of Coronado and others furnish strong evidence of a prehorse, bison-hunting economy that was probably of considerable antiquity and may have been widespread throughout the area later taken over by the typical Plains hunting tribes of equestrian days. Numerous large village sites on the banks of the Missouri in the Dakotas also belong to the horizon here being considered.

Sites of the village Indians of this horizon frequently show refuse mounds and house remains scattered over areas of 20–80 acres or more; and occupational debris is usually much more abundant than at earlier sites. Some villages were fortified, in whole or in part; at others, the size of the zone of habitation and the topography are such that defensive works were not feasible or necessary. If the observed coalescence of population in the Central Plains reflected a need for greater security against hostile neighbors, achievement of its immediate purpose seems to have been sought initially through numbers rather than by fortification.

From central Kansas northward to the Dakotas, the sites from this time level, until perhaps a century or two after Coronado, generally yield the most varied, the most abundant, and, in many respects, the most advanced material culture remains yet found in Plains archeology. Much of the excavated material bearing on this horizon remains unreported, except perhaps in summary outline. There is evidence, however, of a well-developed and intensive maize-bean-squash horticulture; and the presence of numerous large cache pits—usually more abundant and often much larger than those of the Upper Republican and Nebraska cultures—suggests that this was on a much more productive basis than formerly. Whether this means new or improved crop varieties, better cultivation methods, increasingly favorable climatic conditions, or perhaps a combination of these and other still unrecognized factors is not clear. Undoubtedly, however, it was this improved food production, which would probably have been impossible on a comparable scale in much of the westerly Upper Republican habitat, that made life possible in large communities.

The abundance of animal bones, including those of the bison, indicates that hunting was also important. Since game in the vicinity of the large towns would have been quickly exhausted or driven away, large-scale hunts on a village or tribal basis must have been customary. Implied herein is the practice, characteristic also in later times, whereby for considerable portions of the year the permanent towns were largely deserted while the able-bodied population traveled westward in pursuit of bison, living meanwhile in temporary camps of skin tepees. The observations of Bourgmond among the Kansa in 1724, at a time when the great majority of the Indians were still afoot and dependent on dogs or their own backs for transport of baggage and meat, are directly relevant here; and they doubtless apply to most or all of the contemporary village peoples of the eastern Plains.

Concentration of the native population into a few large towns, whereby many hundreds or even thousands of persons dwelt more or less continuously within a few miles of one another, must have carried with it major sociopolitical and ceremonial changes. The problems of land use for relatively intensive horticulture with bone hoe and digging stick must have been serious. The food problem generally would have been vastly complicated, even though highly organized and effective large-scale community hunting practices could be developed. Stability of residence certainly sparked a notable florescence of culture and a more abundant life, as compared to the earlier days. Probably the intervillage and tribal rituals and institutions for which the Pawnee, for example, were so widely known in later days and the numerous societies which constituted such an important part of their life had their real development and growth in this period; and this was probably true also of other village Indian tribes.

DECADENT VILLAGE COMPLEXES

By the last quarter of the eighteenth century, still other changes were coming upon the Plains Indians. These involve historical phenomena, for the most part so well documented that they require only brief notice here. The horse had been taken over by tribe after tribe; and the elaborate militarily oriented bison-hunting culture based thereon was rapidly spreading over the entire region (Ewers, 1955). For the village Indians, the pressures from these mounted nomads plus diseases and increasing contacts with white men engendered cultural decline. It brought to completion the movement from loosely arranged communities, at first small and then progressively larger, to large, compact, fortified towns situated along the major streams. In the Central Plains the Pawnee illustrate what was happening everywhere. Their towns dwindled to three or four, usually within a few miles of one another, and finally to one. There was no regularity of arrangement, the circular habitations often being so closely crowded together—five to eight or more per acre—as to make travel through the village difficult. Contemporary observers (see, e.g., James, 1823; Oehler and Smith, 1851) credit these towns with 50 to nearly 200 earth lodges each, in which were housed from 250 to 900 families and from 1,000 to 3,500 individuals. The fortifications were evidently not impressive, since they are seldom mentioned, but they included sod walls and dry ditches. Outside the walled area, the grassy bottoms were occupied by herds of horses, unfenced but sometimes partially corralled at night within the village. Scattered widely over the bottoms, sometimes to a distance of several miles, were the garden patches from which a portion of the subsistence needs of the community were met.

On the Middle Missouri, the Arikara and Mandan (Will and Spinden, 1906) were likewise reducing markedly the number of their settlements and were surrounding those which survived with impressive log stockades and deep ditches. The Siouan tribes along the Missouri in Nebraska and Kansas similarly dwelt in large, compact villages, though here fortifications are apparently not mentioned.

There are suggestions that, despite the presence of horses and the more extended community hunts that took the village Indians into the bison plains for much of each year, the food quest was perhaps more strenuous than it had been a century or two earlier. Storage pits are frequently much smaller, perhaps reflecting less reliance on horticulture or a less productive pattern in pursuing it. The handicap under which the village Indians lived in this final stage of their existence is vividly illustrated in the story of the Pawnee for the decades preceding their reservation days (see, e.g., Hyde, 1951, pp. 112–212).

GENERAL COMMENTS

The archeological record for the Great Plains, as here briefly reviewed, suggests that environment exerted a stronger and more lasting influence on native settlement patterns in the semiarid western sections and among the earliest hunters, gatherers, and beginning horticulturists farther east than on the later semisedentary Indians of the eastern Plains. Largely for environmental reasons, the Northwestern Plains have always been predominantly a region of hunting or of hunting and gathering subsistence economies, with cultural development and population held to a relatively low level until the introduction of the horse two centuries or more ago.

Farther east, in the Central Plains and on the Middle Missouri, the environment permitted addition of a food-producing economy to the pre-existent hunting and gathering practices. This was a profoundly important step: with a surer food supply came increased populations in stable communities and, with this, a stimulus to social change. The Upper Republican house clusters, sheltering several families each, may represent unilateral lineages or small closely related bands. To what extent the environment might have limited the size of these communities we cannot say, but there are reasons for supposing that climatic uncertainties may have terminated native food-producing in this western section. At any rate, coalescence into larger aggregates, probably composed of several bands or even of tribes, apparently took place farther east, where a better environment and surer horticulture permitted life in large communities of several hundred persons or more. The decline of village Indian culture after 1800 reflects historical and cultural factors far more than it does natural environment.

Just what the changing settlement patterns in the Great Plains reflect in terms of specific social, political, and ceremonial change I do not venture to suggest at this time. I do suggest, however, that, when the archeological record has been expanded and its many gaps filled in, comparison with Steward's (1937, p. 101) formulation of the conditions which gave rise to southwestern society will reveal interesting parallels.

SETTLEMENT PATTERNS IN MESO-AMERICA AND THE SEQUENCE IN THE GUATEMALAN HIGHLANDS

By EDWIN M. SHOOK AND TATIANA PROSKOURIAKOFF

MESO-AMERICA includes regions of sharply contrasting topography, climate, and agricultural potentials. Since these factors are crucial in determining the location, size, and extent of settlements, no specific pattern characterizes the area as a whole. The cultural histories of its component regions also differ sharply, especially in so far as they were affected by population movements like the expansion and peregrinations of Nahua-speaking tribes. The area is united, nevertheless, by what Bennett called a "co-tradition," and its designation as a distinct culture area rests very largely on the nature of its settlements as distinguished from those of surrounding "lower" cultures.

These settlements were towns with nuclei of civic and religious buildings, which typically included pyramidal substructures of temples. Until recently, archeological work was concentrated on these nuclei or "ceremonial centers," and data on the extent of sites and on the arrangement of dwelling units within them are very scant. The widely held opinion that ceremonial centers, particularly in the Maya area, served scattered rural populations and had few permanent inhabitants has recently been challenged, and the question of the degree of urbanism achieved in the several regions of Meso-America at different times is far from being resolved. The issue is somewhat clouded by the uncertain meaning of "urbanism." Since the *civilization* of Meso-America is unquestioned, however, we can assume a general agreement that large public works and highly developed intellectual arts imply at least a significant stage of urban growth, without stating more precisely the degree of economic interdependence or the type of social organization that such a stage entails.

As recently as 1950, Wauchope postulated that preceding the civilized stage of culture there was a village formative stage, which he identified with the period of the earliest-known "Archaic," "Middle," or "Preclassic" cultures. Kidder's and Shook's (Shook and Kidder, 1952) work in the Guatemalan highlands, however, indicates concentrated settlement, the probability of large-scale temple construction, and even localized industry as early as ceramic remains have been traced. There is not now sufficient evidence to show distinct stages of progress toward an urban economy. So far as we can tell, in Meso-America we are dealing at the outset with patterns of town settlement rather than with purely agricultural village communities.

The character of the ceremonial centers of the towns, nevertheless, may reflect some general trends. For example, in the Maya area pyramidal temple foundations hold a more prominent place in the ceremonial centers in early periods. Later, there is a certain trend toward secular use of public buildings, indicated by the more spacious plans of long "palaces" and colonnades. There is reason to think that this is a reflection of a general trend throughout Meso-America. It is sometimes taken for granted that there was also a general trend toward increasingly dense centers of population, but this is not clearly supported by the evidence. The size and distribution of sites vary from region to region and fluctuate in time. Again turning to the Maya area, we find in the Puuc region of Yucatán many large sites crowded into a limited area. This arrangement is succeeded by such cities as Chichén Itzá and Mayapán in northern Yucatán, which were by far the most important settlements in a considerably larger district. This succession, however, is not duplicated in the highlands, where Teotihuacán, Monte Alban, and Kaminaljuyu were single dominant towns even in very early times. Similarly, choice of elevated positions and fortification of sites are characteristic in the Maya area of its latest unsettled period, but this does not seem to be the case in Oaxaca, where late Mixtec sites are situated in exposed low positions below the earlier elevated and protected position of Monte Alban.

We have chosen for discussion the sequence of settlement types in the region of Guatemala City, not because it can be presented as typical of Meso-America, but because this area is one of the few from which we have a good collection of surface data and an established sequence of ceramic assemblages by which we can approximately date remains.[1] The region forms a watershed between the valley of the Motagua River to the north and the Pacific slope to the south, at an elevation of about 1,500 meters. On the east and west it is flanked by mountain ranges forming the Guatemala valley, and beyond the western divide lie the valley of Antigua and the drainage of the Río Sacatapéquez. Kaminaljuyu, on the western fringe of the present Guatemala City, is much the largest assemblage of ruins in the valley and has been explored by a number of archeological excavations. For most of the other sites we depend on surface collections to estimate their periods of occupation.

The system of chronological reference is based on thirteen types of assemblages of remains representing sequent cultural "phases" (see Fig. 1). These in turn are grouped into periods which indicate distinct cultural stages. The dates suggested for these periods are rough estimates, as yet unconfirmed by independent criteria such as that of carbon 14 dating. The earliest period,

1. The data on sites mentioned here and the chronological sequence have been published by Shook (1952).

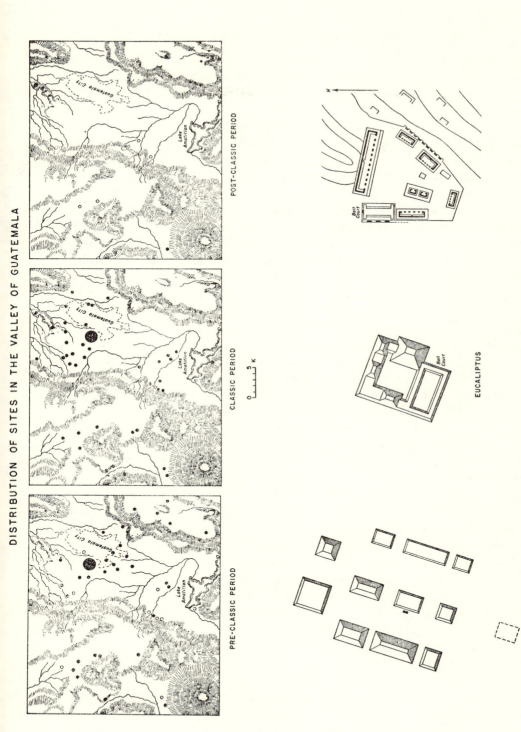

FIG. 1.—Distribution of sites in the valley of Guatemala and site types for the Preclassic, Classic, and Postclassic periods

termed "Preclassic" (or "Formative"), includes seven phases, beginning with Las Charcas and culminating with the Arenal phase followed by Santa Clara. It lasts from about 2000 B.C. to A.D. 200. The next period, the Classic, ends about A.D. 900. It is subdivided into the Early Classic period, which subsumes the horizon styles of Teotihuacán and of late Tzakol, and the Late Classic period, with its Amatle and Pamplona phases. The Postclassic period likewise has two divisions: an early phase linked to the horizon of extended trade in Tohil Plumbate ware, and a later phase, the Chinautla, which preceded the Spanish conquest.

The earliest Preclassic phase, Las Charcas, is largely obscured by later remains, but heavy deposits of pottery on the outskirts of Kaminaljuyu lead us to believe that this site held from the beginning a sizable aggregation of population and was the principal settlement in the Guatemala valley. Even in this early period, ceramic and lapidary arts were highly developed, and traces of basketry, matting, and other crafts indicate a variety of industries. Most revealing was the discovery of a concentrated group of obsidian workshops with large refuse pits that indicated a stable localized industry on the periphery of the ancient town. Although no ceremonial structure has been definitely identified as having been built in Las Charcas times, sherd material limited to this phase has been found in mound fill, and we believe that larger collections will demonstrate the existence of monumental architecture. We know that many later Preclassic towns were first occupied in the Las Charcas phase, and, finding no indication of radical change either in the character of sites or in their distribution during the Preclassic period, we have no reason to doubt that, in general configuration, the pattern of settlement was established in Las Charcas times.

Choice of location of Preclassic sites seems to have been dictated primarily by agricultural needs, from which we infer that each town was supplied principally from fields in its immediate vicinity. The sites are in open, undefended positions, and in most cases we do not know precisely their extent. Kaminaljuyu includes a number of mound groups, spreading out beyond its presently mapped area of 4 square kilometers. It has no clearly defined limits. Some of its several groups may have been at one time separate settlements, and, conversely, some adjacent sites, such as Ross, at its northwest corner, may have been merely outlying districts of the city. It is not certain that even intensive excavations could actually outline the metropolitan area of Kaminaljuyu in all the phases of its complicated history.

Most Preclassic sites were occupied for long periods of time and show successive phases in their surface collections. Moreover, many mounds in the Guatemala valley have been leveled, and the original site plans are not always clear. However, on the higher ground of the Canchon plateau in the southeast corner of the area is a number of large, well-preserved sites, which were abandoned before the beginning of the Classic period and which now exhibit a characteristic assemblage of mounds. The larger ceremonial structures are arranged to form long, narrow plazas, oriented slightly east of north. The most distinctive plans have two parallel plazas separated by a single row of buildings. All structures are built of puddled adobe, with no use of stone or of lime plaster. High pyramidal foundations sometimes contain elaborate tombs, but their primary function was to elevate temple buildings, which were of perishable material but which occasionally left traces in the form of large postholes and impressions of wooden wall poles on fragments of hardened adobe.

In a number of cases the principal pyramid faces east across the plaza toward a smaller structure with a plain, erect monument centered on its façade. The site of Naranjo, 4 kilometers to the north of Kaminaljuyu, is unusual in having a large aggregation of such monuments aligned on its plaza. Although we cannot trace in detail the development of the complex of high ceremonial structures and stone monuments so characteristic of the Classic period of the Maya lowlands, we can state with confidence that in the highland area of Guatemala it was already in existence long before the Classic era.

One gets the impression that the Preclassic period was one of steady growth and elaboration of pattern, reaching full maturity by perhaps 1500 B.C., at the beginning of the Providencia phase. Stable conditions apparently prevailed, and about 500 B.C. population and prosperity rose to a peak that was never equaled again. The remains of the Arenal phase are the most numerous in the valley and are the richest in the cultural elaborations characteristic of the region. The final Preclassic phase, the Santa Clara, judging on the basis of the comparatively small amount of material on hand, shows a degeneration of Preclassic traditions that precedes radical cultural changes.

The eclipse of the Preclassic culture in the Guatemala valley was clearly only one manifestation of a widespread change that was taking place throughout Meso-America, and the transition to the Classic period cannot be explained with reference only to local events. Radical changes even in household vessels and utensils imply at least some influx of new population into the valley, and changes in the character of settlements must also be attributed, if not to foreign settlers, at least to pressures and influences originating outside.

For some reason, the sites of the Canchon plateau, which had been abandoned even before the Classic period began, were not reoccupied, and the new distribution of towns also left vacant considerable areas of productive land to the southeast of Kaminaljuyu. At present we know of no change in natural conditions that may have disqualified these lands for settlement and can only suggest that historical or political factors may have been involved in the choice of new locations.

One difficulty in finding a reasonable explanation for the distribution of Classic sites is caused by the inconspicuous character of Early Classic remains, which are often overlaid by the typical building assemblages of the Late Classic period. We cannot, therefore, follow the resettlement pattern in sequence or identify the earliest towns. One very large site, however, San Antonio Frutal, which has yielded Early Classic material, shows a closely knit court arrangement of earth mounds, combining a Preclassic technique of building with an assemblage that later becomes typical. In the Esperanza phase, toward the end of the Early Classic period, a new masonry building technique was introduced, and the architectural style and artistic complex are so strongly tinged with the style of Teotihuacán that only the domination of the local culture by a people of foreign extraction can adequately account for it.

The new settlement pattern that emerges clearly only in the Late Classic period is radically different from the pattern of the Preclassic. The typical ceremonial center is now a compact group of structures on the order of the lowland Maya "acropolis" arrangement and almost invariably includes a rectangular ball court inclosed on all sides. At Kaminaljuyu, which remains the dominant town, no less than twelve such ball courts were built in this period. Sites vary considerably in size, but small sites with a single ball court are numerous not only in the valley itself but over a wide area beyond it. Settlements are still in open country and near to arable land, but, although there are many more of them than in the Early Classic period, their distribution still leaves a conspicuous gap in the southeastern part of the valley and on the Canchon plateau.

Pottery of the Amatle phase, found in thick deposits in and closely around the ceremonial centers, is mostly locally made utilitarian ware. Trade with adjacent regions is indicated by occasional imported pieces, but there was apparently no close contact with distant regions on the order of the connections with Teotihuacán that mark the previous Esperanza phase. The Late Classic period was an era of close regional integration rather than of far-flung foreign contact. It was also an era of great prosperity, surpassed only by the Arenal phase of the Preclassic, a millennium earlier. Subsequent developments appear to be in the nature of cultural decline. Pottery of the last Classic, Pamplona, phase is much less abundant, and the Ayampuk phase of the Postclassic appears only in occasional finds. No evidence of site occupation during the Ayampuk phase has yet come to light. Kaminaljuyu was apparently abandoned as a capital. Since this phase is linked to the horizon style of the Toltec, we may hazard a guess that their conquests may have been the cause of unsettled conditions in the valley, although cultural disintegration is evident even in the preceding phase. In view of historical suggestions that the Toltec instigated wars in the Guatemalan highlands, it is probable that they introduced the warlike political organizations that in Spanish conquest times controlled the region.

Military activities are well reflected in the choice of fortified locations which characterized the final Chinautla phase. Chinautla itself, for which the phase is named, is a site on a small mesa that can be approached only by a narrow neck of high land between two rivers and by several precipitous trails. It was occupied in Late Classic times, but its defended position was reinforced not long before the Spanish conquest by three small redoubts, set 1 kilometer apart along the ridge of approach. Site plans of this period are usually distinguished by so-called "twin-temples" placed on a single substructure, which also characterized late periods in the highlands of Mexico. There are long, open, "palace"-type buildings and ball courts with benches and an H-shaped plan. Such sites usually occur on high ground and most often on mountain spurs with a difficult approach. They could not have accommodated large aggregations of population for any extended period, and the notion that they represent a high stage of urban development is unfounded. There is, indeed, every reason to think that in Chinautla times the population of the Guatemala valley was either scattered widely through rural districts or considerably reduced, for no concentrated remains in the valley itself have been found. The raised land of the Canchon plateau, however, was reoccupied, and on one of its southern spurs is the important site of Mantaña, surrounded by deep barrancas and approached by a narrow neck from the plateau. This site, like Chinautla, seems to have a small outpost on its approach, about 1½ kilometers distant from the town. We do not know which, if any, of the late sites served as a capital for the region. None approaches in size the ancient city of Kaminaljuyu, which was abandoned at the end of the Classic period and was unoccupied in conquest times. Recently, when the city of Guatemala expanded its borders to engulf the *fincas* on whose lands the ancient city stood, the site is again reverting to urban settlement, at the cost of the destruction of its older buildings.

In summary, we can say that there were three successive patterns of settlement in the Guatemala valley: first, the Preclassic pattern, characterized by a distribution of sites over most of the arable land, with one very large, centrally located town, and by a typical open assemblage of large ceremonial buildings; second, the Classic pattern, with a limited site distribution in the valley and with more closely knit ceremonial centers, which in Late Classic times almost invariably include at least one ball court; and, third and last, the pattern of conquest times, of only small settlements in the valley and of towns strategically located on high ground and protected by outposts.

Although this brief account of the settlement history of one small region in Meso-America cannot be taken as representative of the culture area as a whole, the general settlement types described have parallels in many other regions. In building assemblages, in size, and in distribution, Meso-American settlements have great variety, but the fundamental unit of the town settlement, with its core of civic and religious buildings, is dominant in all periods and in all but the most remote and inaccessible localities. Landa's classic description of the town of Yucatán can be applied with only minor variations to most of the known archeological history within the area of high culture in Meso-America: "Before the Spaniards had conquered that country, the natives lived together in towns in a very civilized fashion . . . in the middle of the town were their temples with beautiful plazas, and all around the temples stood the houses of the lords and the priests, and then of the most important people. Thus came the houses of the richest and of those who were held in the highest estimation nearest to these, and at the outskirts of the town were the houses of the lower class."

The variations in this pattern are largely those of quantitative distribution and are determined by specific historical circumstances for each region. Perhaps some measure of withdrawal from the land and from religious function to a condition of greater military and commercial dependence may be interpreted as a general trend of development, but there is actually no clear evidence of progressive urbanization within the time span of known settlement. It remains to be proved that even the famed city of Tenochtitlán, with its ambition to dominate all Meso-America, was in fact and in any sense more "urban" than the great settlements of the earlier Classic and Preclassic eras.

SETTLEMENT PATTERNS IN THE GUATEMALAN HIGHLANDS: PAST AND PRESENT

By STEPHAN F. DE BORHEGYI

THE settlement patterns of pre-Columbian Meso-America, based on a study of archeological sites in the midwestern Guatemalan highlands, have been dealt with at length by E. M. Shook and Tatiana Proskouriakoff (this volume). There is relatively little that can be added to their well-rounded presentation. It would be of interest, however, to determine what correlations, if any, exist between the pre-Columbian settlement patterns and those of the present in the same area. The purpose of this paper is to examine whether such a correlation exists and, if so, what factors have been most influential in determining the settlement patterns of the highland Guatemalan Maya villages of today. This can be accomplished by carrying the investigation of settlement patterns from archeological times to the ethnological present.

In Meso-America, where, for the most part, the descendants of the people who lived in the pre-Columbian settlements still occupy more or less the same locality, I believe the job of the archeologist is twofold. His duty is only half-fulfilled when the excavation is completed. Since the landscape over which man has disposed himself in the midwestern highlands of Guatemala has changed relatively little in the last millennium, it follows that there must exist a strong correlation between pre-Columbian and modern settlement patterns. The archeologist can therefore infer much from the types of settlement in a region at any one given period to those of earlier or later times.

The settlement pattern of a village generally reflects the natural environment, the level of technology of its inhabitants, the density and composition of its population, and the elements of social interaction necessary to maintain the unity of the settlement. The next step is to examine how these factors operate and which are more important in the establishment and maintenance of a settlement. To illustrate the point in question, let us look at the present-day settlements in the Guatemalan highlands.

In the midwestern highlands of Guatemala the following three major types of Indian settlement patterns are in existence today: (1) compound villages, with well-defined plazas; (2) dispersed villages, with or without well-defined plazas; and (3) concourse centers, with well-defined plazas. Each of these villages, whether compound, dispersed, or concourse, represents a self-sufficient agricultural, social, religious, and political unit or entity (Tax, 1937).

101

In some localities the Maya inhabitants live close together in compact settlements, whereas in others they live in dispersed communities with the individual households scattered over the countryside. Still another type of settlement is that of the concourse center with a highly important plaza which serves to unite villagers from a large region on important secular or religious occasions. Some of these villages are almost exclusively agricultural, while others, although still basically agricultural, specialize in certain crafts, such as weaving, ceramics, etc. What factors operate to make one village compound, another dispersed, and another concourse? It would be logical to presume that the purely agricultural villages would be of the dispersed type, so that the inhabitants could be more directly in contact with their land, and that the craft centers would more likely be the compound settlements. This, however, does not seem to be the case in Guatemala. Santiago Atitlán (pop. 9,513, according to the 1950 census), San Pedro La Laguna (pop. 668), San Marcos La Laguna (pop. 516), and Santa Catarína Palopo (pop. 668), to mention a few of the villages in the Lake Atitlán region, are primarily agricultural communities; yet they are all compound villages. The farmers leave the villages early each morning and frequently must travel a distance of several miles to reach their corn plots or milpas. On the other hand, the nearby villages of Nahualá (pop. 18,511) and Santa Catarína Ixtahuacán (9,355) are equally devoted to agricultural pursuits, and yet they are of the dispersed type (McBride and McBride, 1942, pp. 255–59, Fig. 12). The *município* of Nahualá consists of close to 20,000 inhabitants; yet only a few dozen families live continuously in the village, the others live scattered over the countryside in houses near or on the respective landholdings. Besides the public buildings, there are only a few houses around the plazas of these two towns. There are no stores of any kind, and trading is limited to the weekly market, when the neighboring communities bring their wares to the public square.

Let us next turn our attention to settlements in which handicrafts play an important, if not a major, role in the village economy. The pottery center of Chinautla (pop. 1,672) is a dispersed village, in which there is neither a well-defined plaza nor a regular market. More or less the same situation exists in San Antonio Aguas Calientes (pop. 2,188), a famous weaving center. On the other hand, San Luis Jilotepeque (pop. 9,517) and Rabinal (pop. 11,857), pottery- and gourd-manufacturing centers, are compound villages. It seems, therefore, that neither the level of technology nor the size of the population is a deciding factor in the type of settlement pattern of a Guatemalan community.

An analysis of these same villages brings out the fact that the Indian composition, according to linguistic groups, has equally little bearing on the problem. Villages of both compound and dispersed types are found in relatively the same percentage in all regions of Guatemala (Goubaud, 1946). Whether the inhabitants of a village are of the Quiché, Cakchiquel, Zutughil, Mam,

Kekchi, etc., linguistic groups does not seem to determine the type of settle-ment. However, the percentage of inhabitants of non-Indian or mixed Indian and Spanish ancestry, commonly called "Ladino," does affect the character of the community. Villages where the Ladinos outnumber the Indians tend to be of the compound type (see 1950 Guatemala census data).

Undoubtedly, the local geography has some influence on the type of settle-ment. It would be virtually impossible to build a "gridiron" type of settle-ment in the narrow valley of Chinautla. However, this fact alone cannot ex-plain the lack of a well-defined community focal point or plaza in the vil-lage, especially since San Antonio Palopo, built on terraces on the side of a steep mountain slope, is nevertheless a compound settlement with a well-de-fined plaza.

We have eliminated the natural environment, the level of technology, and the density and composition of the population as major determining factors in the type of settlement of a Guatemalan community. What are the elements of social interaction necessary to maintain the unity of the population? These elements are generally of two types, religious and secular. Of these, the mar-ket pattern is perhaps the most important secular form of present-day com-munal gatherings.

In 1947 the Instituto Indígenista of Guatemala, under the direction of the late Antonio Goubaud, made an extensive survey of the various markets in the country (1947). Of the 311 *municípios* examined, 193 had regular mar-kets, 108 did not, and there were no data available on 10. The only positive conclusion reached was that the villages with predominantly non-Indian or Ladino populations were less likely to have regular markets. From their find-ings it is obvious that the market pattern seems to have no direct correlation with the type of settlement pattern. Markets were held in towns regardless of whether they were of the dispersed, compound, or concourse type. Strangely enough, the Guatemalan market pattern seems to have no relation to the size of the community, the number of other markets in the area, or the major occupation of the villagers.

Religious activities, which reach their peak with the celebration of the day of the patron saint of the village, are of about equal importance in both com-pound and dispersed settlements. Since these activities center about the church and the houses of the local *cofradías*, the type of village or the pres-ence or absence of a well-defined plaza does not seem to be of great impor-tance.

Is it possible, then, that the factors determining the settlement patterns of the present day have their origin in the pre-Columbian past? Could it be that the prototype of the compound village was probably the "compound village" or agglutinated hilltop village of preconquest days, while the origin of the dispersed village was the "scattered or agglutinated small-house village"?

It is a well-known fact that many of the present-day communities in Central America represent the end-result of the Spanish colonial program of *re-ducción* or "civil congregation," by which means the colonial government sought to gather together the scattered Indian elements of a pre-Columbian settlement into what would correspond to Spanish towns (Simpson, 1934; Kubler, 1942). It was thought that such human concentrations would bring the Indian populace under a stronger influence of church and civil authorities and thus would discourage revolts or organized uprisings against Spanish rule. The colonial authorities attempted to settle the Indian population in most cases around well-defined plazas, usually dominated by a massive church and surrounded by public buildings. As there is no record of any mass displacement, it is conceivable that the modern towns were built either on the site of the pre-Columbian settlements or very close to them (see the latest findings of Roys, 1952, in Yucatán). The success of this concentration in colonial days depended, I believe, upon the types of settlements from which these people were drawn. That is, where compound settlements exist today, we can feel fairly sure that the ancestors of the present population lived originally in a compound village or an agglutinated hilltop village. We know, for example, that this was the case with Santiago Atitlán, which was formed of the population of the nearby Zutughil stronghold of Chuitinamit. Where the colonial authorities were unable to maintain a compound village, in spite of the nucleus of a well-defined plaza, the people undoubtedly reverted to the same scattered village pattern in which they were accustomed to live before the conquest. In the latter case the result today is a well-defined but largely non-functional plaza in the center of an almost non-existent town, such as is the case in Nahualá and Santa Catarína Ixtahuacán. The third type of present-day settlement pattern, the concourse village or "vacant town," may reflect the concept of the pre-Columbian ceremonial center. Santo Tomás Chichicastenango is an example. In the *município* there are 27,718 people, according to the 1950 census, although only 1,622 people live in the actual town. The greatest part of the population lives in houses widely scattered over the neighboring cornfields, although many families maintain "town houses" in which they live while holding public office and during feast days and use as headquarters for the Thursday and Sunday markets. Only 697 Indians live in the town continuously. The fact that the people habitually congregate in Chichicastenango and even bother to maintain special houses for use during ceremonial and market occasions suggests that it was perhaps the locale of a pre-Columbian ceremonial center. Another present-day settlement pattern of the same sort is that associated with a pilgrimage center. A good example of this type of village is the town of Esquipulas near the Honduras border in eastern Guatemala. The town itself has a population of 2,844 inhabitants. On the feast day of the Black Christ of Esquipulas, on January 15, the pilgrims crowd into town from all parts of the country and number occasionally as many as 100,000. After the fall of the ancient Maya ceremonial center of

Copan in southwestern Honduras in 1530, the postconquest town of Esqui-pulas, which was on the ancient trade route, replaced Copan as the pilgrimage center (Borhegyi, 1954b).

Since the visible core of the settlement pattern of most of the present-day Maya villages is the town plaza, its relative importance may also reflect the pre-Columbian situation. According to the findings of Foster (1951, p. 317), the small villages of Spain, with the possible exception of those in Old Castile and Extremadura, more often than not have no plazas, and, if one is present, it is not at all well defined. Consequently, the feeling of a central focal point for town life in Spain is not well marked. Although the Spanish introduced the "gridiron" type of town with a centrally located plaza into New Spain in the sixteenth century (Stanislawski, 1947), the plaza, as such, seems to be more an indigenous feature of the Meso-American settlement pattern than a European element. Its importance, more than its presence in the present-day Indian community, therefore, probably represents a pre-Columbian vestige. On the basis of the importance of the plaza as a unifying element in the community, we can differentiate the following three types of present-day settlement patterns in the Guatemalan highlands:

a) Dispersed villages, where there is a plaza but with little or no function. This represents a type of town set up by the colonial authorities which was never really accepted by the inhabitants. The pre-Columbian counterpart of this type of settlement probably was the scattered or agglutinated small-house village, which had no well-defined plaza. The inhabitants were more than likely accustomed to frequent the plaza of a nearby ceremonial center on religious and secular occasions and continue this pattern to the present day.

b) Compound villages, where the plaza is the focal point of village activities. This represents a successful reducción by colonial authorities primarily because in preconquest days the ancestors of these people lived in settlements where the plaza was an important center of communal activities. The pre-Columbian counterpart of this settlement pattern would be the compound village or agglutinated hilltop village.

c) Concourse centers, where the plaza is of considerable regional importance for markets and for religious communal gatherings. The pre-Columbian counterpart would be the ceremonial or pilgrimage center, in which only a small group of people connected with the ceremonial activities lived continuously around the plaza.

From the foregoing evidence it appears that the most important factors in determining the type of settlement patterns of today in highland Guatemala lie buried in the pre-Columbian past. In villages where the relationship between the plaza and the type of settlement pattern cannot be clearly defined, it may be due to more recent factors, such as degree and intensity of acculturation, size and influence of non-Indian groups, and proximity to modern trade routes, highways, or non-Indian commercial activities.

While there seems to be a rather definite correlation between types of pre-Columbian and present-day settlement patterns in the Guatemalan highlands, the ultimate validity of this theory must await further investigation. It is hoped that, when other communities in this hemisphere are subjected to similar scrutiny, we shall be able to learn more about the structural relationship between pre-Columbian and present-day Indian settlement patterns. A good start was made by Stanislawski in his study (1950) of the anatomy of eleven towns in Michoacán, Mexico. However, he assumed that the anatomical differences in the structure of his villages reflected regional differences due to environment, level of technology, and density and composition of the population. He made no attempt to relate these with the pre-Columbian settlement patterns of the region. Perhaps if this factor had been taken into consideration, he would have been able to find explanations for the unexpected lack of correlation between regional differences and settlement patterns.

PROBLEMS CONCERNING PREHISTORIC SETTLEMENT PATTERNS IN THE MAYA LOWLANDS

By GORDON R. WILLEY

SETTING AND PROBLEMS

MAYA civilization had its most brilliant rise and dramatic decline in the lowland jungle regions of the Guatemalan Petén, adjacent Mexico and Yucatán, British Honduras, and the western fringes of Honduras. An estimated date of 1500 B.C. does not seem excessive for the first evidences of a pottery-making, agricultural people inhabiting the forests of the Petén during the Mamom phase of the Maya Formative period. The Formative period is terminated at about A.D. 300,[1] the date at which fully developed forms of Maya architecture, art, and the Initial Series calendrical dating appear. These traits mark the Maya Classic period (Tzakol and Tepeu phases), which lasted from A.D. 300 to approximately 900. The cessation of the Initial Series system of dating and the desertion of the great sites of the southern part of the lowlands provide a break in the sequence dividing the Classic and Postclassic periods. The Postclassic, a time at which nearly all lowland Maya activity was focused in northern Yucatán, is the final period, ending with the Spanish conquest of 1519–40. Throughout this entire time span of Maya prehistory, life was based essentially upon the cultivation of maize by jungle farming. With this background in mind—a 3,000-year history of agricultural civilization in a forested, tropical environment—we turn to settlement patterns.

A great many problems surround the matter of Maya settlements in the lowlands, but the two which we shall consider in this brief essay seem most fundamental at the present stage of research. The first problem, or question, is a double-barreled one, but it is impossible to treat the two halves separately because their interrelationship is obvious. What were the size and composition of the Maya living community, and what was the relationship between the living community and the ceremonial center? As will be evident in the ensuing discussion, this question cannot be answered satisfactorily at the present time, but it is basic to all research into prehistoric settlement in the area. The second question is a demographic one: What changes, if any, occurred in population size and grouping throughout the full run of Maya prehistory?

1. Dates for the opening and close of the Classic period follow the 11.16.0.0.0, or Goodman-Thompson, correlation of Mayan and Christian calendars.

THE FORMATIVE PERIOD

Most of the accumulated knowledge of field archeology in the Maya lowlands derives from investigations of major sites, where large pyramids, platform mounds, and imposing architectural remains (hereafter referred to as "ceremonial centers") have attracted attention. This has resulted from the difficult conditions of tropical vegetation cover—in which small mounds and building foundations are extremely hard to locate and examine—rather than any lack of interest on the part of the archeologists. Well over a hundred large ceremonial centers have been surveyed and explored in the lowland area (see Morley, 1946; Thompson, 1954), and, undoubtedly, there are a great many more which are smaller and unrecorded. Most of the ceremonial centers, at least as far as their principal edifices can be dated, belong to the Classic period; however, we know that platform mounds, pyramids, and temple or palace-type buildings make their appearance in the latter part of the Formative. The A-I structure at Uaxactun in the Petén clearly dates from the late Formative, and the E-VII-submound may be this early (A. L. Smith, 1950; Ricketson and Ricketson, 1937). To the north, in Yucatán, the mound at Yaxuná is Formative, as may be others at Santa Rosa Xtampak (Brainerd, 1951).

Concerning the nature of the living community during the Formative period and its relationships to these ceremonial or large mound centers, Brainerd (1954, pp. 15 ff.) states that all or part of Maya settlements at this time may have been of substantial size but that there have not been sufficient excavation and survey to prove this. On the other hand, Shook and Proskouriakoff (this volume) contend: "So far as we can tell, in Meso-America we are dealing at the outset with patterns of town settlement rather than with purely agricultural village communities." The data are too limited to resolve this difference of opinion, but what evidence there is from the lowlands does not indicate large Formative period settlements. At Uaxactun the early Formative, or Mamom, period occupation of that site appears to have covered little more than the top of the knoll of what later became E Group, an area about 200 meters in diameter. For the late Formative, or Chicanel, phase there is again evidence that the E Group knoll was occupied, as was the somewhat larger A Group hill (about 350 meters in diameter). On the latter location the previously mentioned small ceremonial mound, A-I, was constructed. A Chicanel house mound was also discovered at a distance of about 800 meters from the Group A section of the ceremonial center (Wauchope, 1934). These Uaxactun data give the impression of very small villages or hamlets rather than towns. Such small villages became the seats of special or ceremonial buildings in the late Formative, and at this time at least some houses were occupied as much as a half-mile away from what may have been the "main" or "parent" community.

Recent work in the Belize Valley, at Barton Ramie (Willey, Bullard, and

Glass, 1955), affords some additional information on this question of the size of Formative living communities. No ceremonial mounds have been identified with the Formative period at the Barton Ramie site, but several house-mound locations have been dated, tentatively, as of this period. These mounds are rather widely spaced over a square mile of alluvial bottom land, with the implication that Formative period settlement at that site was in small hamlet clusters or isolated houses rather than in a densely occupied town.

Turning to the second problem, that of changes in population size, there are only occasional clues from the Formative period. Shook and Proskouriakoff (this volume) have noted that there is no valid case for increasing populations throughout the Formative period in the Guatemalan highlands. For the lowlands there are some few suggestions that such an increase may have taken place. The Uaxactun excavations reveal more extensive occupational and architectural debris for Chicanel than they do for the earlier Mamom phase; and at Barton Ramie the stratigraphic digging in house mounds gives us three or four times as many Chicanel house occupations as those dating from Mamom. Moreover, lowland sites and ceramic materials of a late Formative or Chicanel-like identification are reported in greater numbers than those for the early Formative.

THE CLASSIC PERIOD

Although there is considerably more knowledge of Maya sites of the Classic period than for the Formative, the question of the size and form of the living community and its relationships to the ceremonial center is still a matter for dispute. Both Morley (1946, pp. 312–13) and Shook and Proskouriakoff hold that the ceremonial centers, with their temple and palace mounds grouped around rectangular courtyards, were nuclei of true cities or towns, with dwellings clustered in or closely around them. In this view they seem to be strongly influenced by Landa's sixteenth-century accounts of Yucatecan town or city life:

Before the Spaniards had conquered that country, the natives lived together in towns in a very civilized fashion . . . in the middle of the town were their temples with beautiful plazas, and all around the temples stood the houses of the lords and priests, and then most of the important people. Thus came the houses of the richest and of those who were held in the highest estimation nearest to these, and at the outskirts of the town were the houses of the lower class.

Brainerd (1954, pp. 70 ff.) disagrees that this Yucatecan town pattern of the conquest time can be projected back into the Classic. It is his feeling that the town, as both a reality and a concept, was a Toltec-Mexican introduction into Yucatán and a phenomenon of the Postclassic period. He visualizes the Classic settlement pattern as that of scattered single houses or hamlets, with the inhabitants of these dwellings gathering together to support, or celebrate in, the ceremonial centers. In this he is supported by Thompson (1954, pp. 43 ff.).

In this argument it is interesting that Brainerd and Morley each quote the Uaxactun house-mound survey to bolster their respective points of view. The former is of the opinion that the Uaxactun data indicate a dispersed, rural population, while the latter feels that they demonstrate a loosely compacted urbanism. This Uaxactun house-mound survey (Ricketson and Ricketson, 1937) revealed a total of seventy-eight house mounds in an area totaling 0.3 mile of the habitable terrain surrounding the ceremonial precincts at the site. This is a dense occupation on a house-per-acreage basis even if one follows Ricketson's assumption that only one-quarter of the house mounds were in use at any one time; however, it must be kept in mind that the actual distribution of the seventy-eight mounds extended over an area of 2 miles in both north-south and east-west diameters.[2] Perhaps the difficulty here is a matter of definitions: What is a village? A town? What is "densely settled"? My own thinking tends to coincide with Brainerd's in seeing the Uaxactun settlement as scattered rural rather than as an urban concentration.

Another lowland region where house-mound surveys have been carried out, the Belize Valley, presents a picture of ceremonial-center–dwelling-site relationships that differs somewhat from either of the two afore-mentioned conceptions, although it is somewhat closer to the Brainerd interpretation (Willey, Bullard, and Glass, 1955; Willey and Bullard, n.d.). In this valley the house mounds are found along the alluvial terraces in groups varying in size from five or six up to three hundred. Such house-mound groups may lie immediately adjacent to a ceremonial center, as at Baking Pot (Ricketson, 1929), or may be as much as 7 or 8 miles from any important center. It is a logical possibility that the inhabitants of several such dwelling groups may have acted in concert to build and maintain a religious and political center on the order of the nearby centers of Baking Pot or Benque Viejo (Thompson, 1940). In this case the settlement could hardly be considered to be a "city" but rather a series of near-contiguous villages, or even towns, focusing upon a major ceremonial center. It is interesting to note that in each group of a dozen or more house mounds there is at least one mound, or mound-plaza unit, that is appreciably larger than the others and whose presence suggests that some local and small-scale politico-religious activities were carried on within the small dwelling groups as well as in the great centers.

In attempting to sum up this problem of ceremonial-center–dwelling-site relationships for the Classic period, there seem to be three logical and abstract settlement-type possibilities: First, there is the one in which (Type A) the ceremonial center is surrounded by dwellings which are so closely spaced that their inhabitants could not have farmed immediately adjacent to them (Fig. 1). This is nearest the conception of Morley, Shook, and Proskouria-

2. The Uaxactun house-mound survey was made in a great cruciform zone, each arm of the cross being 400 yards wide and 1 mile long. The ceremonial precincts were situated near the center of the cross.

koff. In the second type (Type *B*) the ceremonial center is without dwellings, and houses of the sustaining population are scattered singly over a wide
surrounding area. The extent of such a sustaining area is unknown, but Ricketson offered an arbitrary estimate of a 10-mile radius for Uaxactun. This
seems reasonable, particularly in regions where foot transportation was the
only means of going to and from the ceremonial center. This type would
seem to be closest to Brainerd's views. The third idealized type (Type *C*) is
similar to *B* in that there is no appreciable population concentrated in the

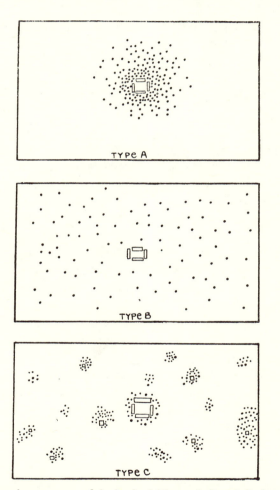

Fig. 1.—Idealized settlement types of the lowland Maya, *A*, *B*, and *C*, showing relationships of
ceremonial center to house mounds or locations. Major ceremonial centers indicated by small rectangles in plaza arrangement, houses by dots. There is no exact scale for these diagrams. In Type *A*,
houses are packed in close to the ceremonial center; in Type *B* houses are dotted over the landscape at
a half to a quarter of a mile apart; in Type *C* houses are grouped in hamlet or village clusters, with some
near the major ceremonial center but many others in outlying hamlets. The small rectangles in some
of the larger hamlet clusters of the Type *C* pattern represent small ceremonial constructions whose
importance is assumed to be local and subsidiary to that of the major center.

ceremonial center, but the sustaining populations are spotted through the surrounding country in hamlets or small villages rather than in individual houses. It is further suggested that some of these hamlets maintained small ceremonial buildings in their own midst. This may be the type of settlement in the Belize Valley, with, however, the significant modification that the hamlets and villages are distributed "ribbon-wise" along the river. In such a case river travel would have been the obvious means of transport.

It should be emphasized that these are only projected ideal types for prehistoric settlement in the Maya lowlands. There is no reason why combinations of these types might not be nearer actuality, nor need any type have prevailed throughout the entire area and Classic period. Thompson (1954, pp. 43 ff.) and others have described the modern Maya pattern of a town center with church, plaza, and market, around which were the houses of its citizenry. These houses were occupied seasonally, on market days, or during fiestas, while several miles distant from the town were the scattered bush houses in which the same people lived while working their milpas. Such would be a combination of Type A with Type B or C. For the present, however, these types are but working hypotheses. The task facing the archeologist is to check house concentrations, or lack of same, in the immediate environs of ceremonial centers and to plot their occurrences and spacings in the miles of jungle that surround these centers—no mean chore!

The question of lowland Maya population increase between Formative and Classic or within the Classic period is also a moot one. The fact that many more Classic ceremonial centers are known than are reported for the Formative is by no means conclusive as to population growth. Ceremonial-center construction was undoubtedly greater in the later period, but it is also a strong probability that many of these sites were also occupied in the earlier period. As to house-mound counts, only five of the Uaxactun small mounds were excavated and are, therefore, datable by their ceramic contents (Wauchope, 1934); one of these was Formative, the other four Classic. In the Belize Valley, at Barton Ramie, we have sampled the pottery in thirty-nine house mounds (as of 1955) out of a group which numbers over three hundred. A preliminary appraisal of these ceramics shows an increase of about four-to-one between Classic and Formative house occupations. Further, late Classic occupations by far outnumbered those of the early Classic. The stability of the community is attested to by the fact that many of the mounds had been used as house platforms continuously from Formative to Classic times. This is very limited evidence upon which to base any generalizations as regards population changes in the Belize Valley as a whole, let alone the entire Maya lowlands; still the trend revealed in this sampling is that of steady increase.

THE POSTCLASSIC PERIOD

One of the most startling settlement phenomena of Middle American prehistory occurs with the change from Classic to Postclassic. This is the apparent abandonment of the southern Maya lowlands. This abandonment is noted in all the southern ceremonial centers, where construction and stelae dates cease after about A.D. 900. And, from the data available, the events of the ceremonial centers appear to be paralleled in the domestic sites. Ceramics or other materials datable as Postclassic are rare in the Petén and the Belize Valley. As is well known, the only great Postclassic sites of the lowlands are in the plains of northern Yucatán. Chichén Itzá is an old Puuc Classic ceremonial center, considerably enlarged under Toltec influence. The urban quality of the site is not fully known, but there are many house mounds in the immediate vicinity. Mayapan, which reached its zenith somewhat later than Chichén, is an urban zone. Three by 2 kilometers in extent, it is encircled by a great wall within which are some four thousand house mounds (Jones, 1952). The houses are arranged in random fashion, but at the center of the site is a ceremonial center with plazas and pyramid mounds. There is, then, some indication that the Postclassic Maya of northern Yucatán were urbanized and that the concept of the city or town as a fortified position had come into vogue. This, as Brainerd and others have suggested, may well be the result of Toltec and Mexican influences. Yet the walled city is not common in Yucatán. Tulum (Lothrop, 1924), on the east coast of Quintana Roo, is the only other notable example, and the wall inclosure here does not appear to embrace the great house-mound concentrations found at Mayapan.

There is no information on population size change between lowland Classic and Postclassic. Chichén Itzá and Mayapan appear larger than the Puuc ceremonial centers which preceded them in the northern lowlands, but nothing has been reported upon the size or form of Puuc domestic settlements. Populations may have been more densely concentrated in the Postclassic, but there is nothing to indicate that they were, in an over-all sense, larger.

COMMENT

Prehistoric settlement in the Maya lowlands is still a matter for speculation and debate rather than for statement of fact. Ceremonial centers, with temple and palace mounds, were obvious nuclei for the ancient populations of these regions from the latter part of the Formative period, if not earlier. The question as to just how the population grouped itself around these centers—whether in concentrated town fashion, in a dispersed rural manner, or in scattered hamlets—cannot be answered without extensive field surveys and excavations. There are some indications that the population increased more or less steadily from early Formative to late Classic times; but this trend needs checking in many different localities. Following the desertion, or near-desertion, of the southern part of the lowland area, building activity was concentrated in northern Yucatán, a region which also came under strong Mexican influence after A.D. 900. The concept of the town, as a tight population grouping around a ceremonial center, sometimes fortified, may have been introduced into Yucatán from Mexico. Or this concept, as reported upon by the early Spanish, may have been the final expression of an old and deep tradition of the Maya lowlands.

Until we have more real knowledge of Maya settlement, the archeologist will be in no position to attack the problems of demography or of prehistoric agricultural techniques and productiveness. Arguments of milpas versus intensive farming (Ricketson and Ricketson, 1937) will remain insoluble until we can pin down the facts of habitation.

THE CENTRAL MEXICAN SYMBIOTIC REGION
A STUDY IN PREHISTORIC SETTLE-
MENT PATTERNS

By WILLIAM T. SANDERS

INTRODUCTION

THE study of settlement patterns is a study of the ecological and demographic aspects of culture. Settlement pattern is, in effect, human ecology, since it is concerned with the distribution of population over the landscape and an investigation of the reasons behind that distribution. In this paper I shall outline the basic ecological factors of importance to human settlement in the defined region and discuss the effects of such factors on the form and character of modern and prehistoric populations.

One of the reasons why complex civilizations developed in Meso-America is that the area is broken up into scores of climatic and topographic subzones. This has meant an extraordinary complexity of products and specialization of production. What is of even more importance is the fact that these subzones are in extremely close proximity; very often a trip of 30 or 40 kilometers means a complete shift in climate and agricultural products. In this situation a considerable volume of trade and a consequent development of urbanism were possible even with the limitations of primitive transport. In an unpublished manuscript I have divided Meso-America into component geographical regions which are based upon an internal economic symbiosis. These "symbiotic regions" consist of several parallel subdivisions of differing climates and productions, which, because of these differences, formed mutual trading units. One such unit is termed the "Central Mexican symbiotic region."

The Central Mexican symbiotic region is one of the key archeological areas of Mexico. It may be divided into two subregions, a northern and a southern. The northern subregion is a broad belt of elevated tableland running from the Michoacán-Mexican (state) borders on the west to the Vera Cruz–Puebla border on the east. To the north (except for a narrow strip of southern Hidalgo) the border is defined by the state border between Mexico and Hidalgo and that of Puebla-Tlaxcala with Hidalgo–Vera Cruz. Practically all communities in this subregion are situated above 2,000 meters and below 2,600. This subregion is typical "Tierra Fría" in the traditional sense. The southern subregion is a parallel belt formed by the southern escarpment

115

of the plateau to the north. It includes the middle and lower courses of the Balsas River tributaries plus the upper and middle courses of the Balsas River itself. The bulk of this subregion is "Tierra Templada," or intermediate in climate between the elevated plateau and the hot coastal lowlands of Meso-America; products characteristic of the coast were produced in this belt in prehistoric times. At the time of the Spanish conquest these two subregions formed a close, interdependent economic trading union.

Aside from its symbiotic basis, our defined region has a unity in one other aspect. Within the heavily populated zones the rainfall never exceeds 40 inches a year. A long, almost rainless dry season extends from October to May, and this is followed by a moderately heavy rainy season from June to September. The country ranges from truly arid in the lower altitudes to semiarid or subhumid in the southern Valley of Mexico. As a result of the limited precipitation and moisture, the plant cover for the region is thin and easily controlled even by the most primitive agricultural tools and techniques.

In most of the region intensive agriculture of either naturally humid bottom lands ("Tierra de Jugo") or artificially irrigated flatlands and terraced slopes is the only certain way of insuring a stable food supply. In some parts (especially the "Tierra Fría") rainy-season crops yield well and have a high degree of security, while in others rainy-season agriculture is impossible. In all cases, however, the utilization of irrigation results in at least 50 per cent production increase, and often this may be raised to 200 or 300 per cent. Because of this, from the earliest period of occupation of the region by agricultural populations there has been a premium on those techniques usually subsumed under the term "intensive agriculture," that is, those techniques which emphasize a maximum of production and labor per unit of land. The effect of this economy upon the personality and development of civilizations in the region has been enormous.

The Central Mexican symbiotic region is distinguished from all other symbiotic regions of Meso-America in that both its subregions were populated by peoples practicing intensive agriculture. I believe that this resulted in the most intensive development of urbanism and commerce in Meso-America.

In our discussion of settlement patterns the data naturally fall into two separate categories. First, we have "community settlement patterns," which are the individual units of population, including such data as types of communities, organization of public buildings, street and population distribution and form, density of community population, and character of the resident population. It would also include house types and solar organization. Second, we have "zonal settlement patterns," which are concerned with the distribution of community sizes, distances between communities, density of population, and the symbiotic interrelationship between communities—societal, economic, or religious.

CONTEMPORARY SETTLEMENT PATTERNS

In our region we find three basic community types. (Practically all the rural population lives in nucleated communities, with a very low percentage dwelling in haciendas or ranchos.) One of the three types is the village. We define a village as a nucleated community with populations running at least into the hundreds and in which at least 75 per cent of the population derive at least 75 per cent of their income from agriculture or some other extractive activity. Villages in the region run from 100 inhabitants up to approximately 6,000 (the latter figure achieved at San Gregorio Atlapulco in the Valley of Mexico—a chinampa community). Theoretically, there is no fixed population limit to a village; actually, it is closely determined by agricultural production.

The second type of community is the town. The town may be defined as a rural community in which the bulk of the population is still dedicated to farming but in which trade and craft specialization are added as secondary activities, reducing the percentage of population dedicated to agriculture to below 75 per cent. In our region, towns in general are collection centers for agricultural produce and *municipio* centers for aggregations of villages. In the Valley of Mexico we could include under this category such communities as Texcoco, Zumpango, and Xochimilco. Some of the smaller towns have smaller populations than the larger villages; but, as was pointed out, the difference lies in mode of life, not in size. Most of the towns range from 3,000 to 10,000 inhabitants, with one monster—Xochimilco—passing 20,000.

The third type of community is the city, in which over 75 per cent of the population is non-agricultural in way of life. In the Central Mexican region all communities of this type are also of considerable size. They usually run from 15,000 to 40,000 persons, with Puebla registering 200,000 and, of course, the huge metropolis of Mexico City with over 2,000,000 inhabitants.

The basic form of the Central Mexican community, whether village or town, varies slightly. We have, as universals, the presence of a central plaza with church and public buildings; around this in all directions the streets are laid off on a checkerboard grid, with the blocks broken up into rectangular house lots. Important differences between villages and towns are the presence of large open-air markets in the latter and closely packed, wall-to-wall houses and shops along the central streets. Even in villages, however, house lots are small, and space is at a premium. Aside from the theoretical checkerboard street pattern, the blocks in many communities are broken up by winding alleys into irregular-sized and shaped parcels. This is a reflection of the extreme scarcity of land and overpopulation of communities in this region. When new families form, the general procedure is to divide up family house lots rather than form new ones. The villages grow more in population density than in gross size. This is especially true in the chinampa area, where every square meter of farmland is precious.

In most modern communities the ancient division into barrios has been maintained. There is no apparent separation today. One side of a street may pertain to one barrio, while the other side is part of another. The number of village barrios ranges from two at San Gregorio up to four at Tláhuac. Towns may have from six to a dozen.

To discuss zonal settlement patterns we shall select a small test area within our symbiotic region, the southern Valley of Mexico, including the modern *delegaciones* of Xochimilco, Tláhuac, Milpa Alta, and Tlalpan in the Distrito Federal and the area embraced by the former district of Chalco of the state of Mexico. This is undoubtedly the most productive agricultural area in the entire northern subregion of our Central Mexican symbiotic region, being the center of chinampa agriculture and terrace agriculture for the Valley of Mexico.

The congestion of population within the community in this area is truly extraordinary. A study of ten communities in the *delegaciones* of Tláhuac and Xochimilco indicates a population density within the community ranging from approximately 6,000 to 10,000 inhabitants per square kilometer. The total area embraced by our test zone measures approximately 2,000 square kilometers and in 1950 had 180,000 inhabitants. The population density varies considerably within the area. In the chinampa *delegaciones* of Tláhuac and Xochimilco it runs from 240 to 360 per square kilometer. In the *delegación* of Milpa Alta and the district of Chalco, where rainy-season agriculture is practiced, it drops to 64.

Our test zone is overwhelmingly agricultural in economy, with but five communities which can truly be called towns (Xochimilco, Milpa Alta, Chalco, Amecameca, and Tlalpan). Aside from this, there are no less than one hundred and five villages. Grouping towns and villages together, approximately 50 per cent of the population live in communities with over 2,000 inhabitants, and 75 per cent of the population live in communities of over 1,000. It is an area of big villages. The towns range in size from 4,000 to 20,000.

Sociologically and economically, the communities of the southern valley may be grouped into three, possibly four, definite clusters. This clustering is based upon two principal factors, one political and the other economic. Xochimilco is the political center for the *delegación* of the same name, which includes the town plus fourteen villages. Xochimilco possesses a huge open-air market, used heavily by its dependent villages. For example, women from the nearest villages make several trips a week. The rural bus traffic along the stretch of highway from Tulyahualco to Xochimilco is really extraordinary; there is a bus passing through the villages every 15 or 20 minutes, and it never has less than thirty or forty passengers—at times it reaches seventy—almost 100 per cent rural villagers traveling to the big Xochimilco market or returning. In the villages themselves there is almost no formal commerce.

The southern valley may be divided roughly into two parallel, symbiotic zones. To the north and paralleling the ancient lakes of Chalco-Xochimilco, are the chinampa and coastal-plain communities, which are centers of specialization in truck-garden crops, maize, *huauhtli* (*alegría*), tomatoes, and chili. To the south lies a band of mountain communities which specialize in beans, pulque, and forest products. Today there is an intense commercial relationship between the two subzones which probably goes back to prehistoric times. As recently as forty years ago, one could add a third band on the other side of the Sierra de Ajusco—that of northern Morelos, which was a center for hot-country products from the Amacusac drainage system. And to the north of the chinampa strip was a fourth zone, which included the villages of Tláhuac and Santa Catarína, which were fishing communities.

PREHISTORIC SETTLEMENT PATTERNS

ETHNOHISTORIC SOURCES

Of necessity, a considerable portion of our data on prehistoric settlement patterns is documentary in nature. Archeological settlement-pattern surveys have never been carried out in the Central Mexican region. This is especially true of zonal settlement patterns; we know somewhat more about community or site patterns.

There is a considerable literature, dating principally from the years 1560–80, which offers excellent data on community and zonal settlement pattern. A thorough review of published and unpublished material would give us a nearly complete idea of the distribution and types of communities for that period in the Valley of Mexico. The principal difficulty is that we cannot always be sure of the applicability of such data for the pre-Spanish period.

The data indicate clearly that the basic pattern of nucleated settlements was characteristic of sixteenth-century Central Mexico and that the three modern communities—city, town, and village—were all well-established types. Also, the basic plan of a central plaza dedicated to religious and political activities, along with the modern street pattern, was in existence in most communities at the time period indicated. Community population-density data are, as one might expect, absent;[1] but estimates based on the sixteenth-century sources indicate an approximate population of 500,000 for the Valley of Mexico for the 1560–80 period. This figure is about that of the modern rural population. Perhaps one-fifth of these were dedicated to non-agricultural, urban activities.

The typical sociopolitical unit during the period was the "pueblo," which was not a settlement unit. For example, take the "pueblo" of Cuauhtitlán. In 1570 the population was distributed as follows: at the *cabacera*, or central community of Santa Buenaventura, we find a population of 1,666 *vecinos*;

---

1. My observations on modern population densities were made by comparing air photographs with contemporary census figures.

and in the *estancias*, or dependent villages, we find Santa María with 347; San Francisco, 70; Visitación de Nuestra Senora, 170; San Miguel, 180; San Mateo, 88; Santa Barbara, 359; San Lorenzo, 36; San Juan Evangelista, 103; San Pedro, 149; Los Reyes, 66; San Martín, 130; and Santiago, 80, with a grand total of 3,398 *vecinos*. The term *vecino* here refers to adult married males, and we can calculate the total population by multiplying these figures by 4. The data may be analyzed in the following way. Cuauhtitlán was a sociopolitical unit which had a total population of approximately 13,000 inhabitants. Slightly over 6,000 of them resided in smaller, satellite, nucleated communities ranging in population from 150 to 1,500, with a mean population per dependent community of slightly over 500. The data are of special interest, as Cuauhtitlán was an important center during the Aztec period and probably held the status of town rather than village, as it does today.

A second example is Huehuetoca, with a population distribution as follows: in the *cabacera*, 917 *tributarios* (a term equivalent to *vecino*); *estancia* of San Miguel, 315; *estancia* of Santiago, 223; and *estancia* of Tlachco, 150— a grand total of approximately 6,400 inhabitants, of which 3,600 lived in the central community and the rest in the three dependent communities.

Although the greater percentage of the rural population of the Valley of Mexico resided in nucleated settlements during the sixteenth century, there were notable exceptions. An interesting variation was the case of Tepoztlán in the northwest. We find that in this "pueblo" the population consisted of two distinct ethnic groups—the Mexicans, who resided in the nucleated *cabacera*, and the Otomi, who lived in a scattered, rancheria-type settlement pattern, each house being separated from its neighbors by milpas and ravines. This scattered settlement pattern seems to have been characteristic of the Otomi, whereas most Mexican or Nahuatl-speaking peoples resided in nucleated communities.

In general, the *cabacera* with its *estancias* formed a tight geographical unit, with most *estancias* lying within 10 kilometers of the *cabacera*. During the sixteenth century these were the "pueblos" or administrative units of the Valley of Mexico. Each *cabacera* was a religious and political center. A cluster of geographically contiguous "pueblos" formed a larger administrative unit called a *partido*, which again had religious and political functions. One of the pueblo *cabaceras* served as the administrative center of the *partido*, and this center was almost always a large community of several thousand inhabitants. Above the *partido* existed a larger unit called *provincia*, or province, of which there were six in the Valley of Mexico (Cuauhtitlán, México, Texcoco or Acolhuacan, Teotlalpan, Chalco, and Xochimilco). The centers of these provinces were all towns, with the exception of México, which may be classed as a true city. All were especially important as market centers.

Economically, all communities were interlocked into a tight trading system based on periodic markets and formalized exchange. It is safe to say that no community was truly self-sufficient. Today the bulk of this intervillage trade and village industry has been replaced by shops and factory production, but traces of it are still abundant. As we shall see, urbanism had sharply declined from the Aztec period level, and we find most of the trade in the sixteenth century of the intervillage type. The only city in the valley during the latter period was Mexico City itself, and there were few towns.

Our documentary data which refer to preconquest settlement patterns concern strictly community patterns, with very few data on zonal settlement. Most of such data, unfortunately, refer to communities which fall into our classification of city or town, with very little concerning villages or other types of rural communities. Especially good accounts are given of Tenochtitlán-Tlatelolco, Texcoco, Cholula, Tlaxcala, Huaquechula, Izucar (the ancient Itzoccan), and Ixtacamaxtitlán. The Spanish descriptions of these centers leave little doubt as to their urban character. They were centers of political and religious administration and of commercial and manufacturing activities. Cholula, for example, was a holy center, of the type of Mecca, for the entire Central Mexican highlands, as well as a pottery-manufacturing center and the home of a large class of professional itinerant merchants. In the case of Cholula we have a definite statement from Salazar to the effect that it was a community of narrow streets and closely packed houses. Space prohibits going into detail on the degree and character of urbanism at these Central Mexican centers; we can only state that the data seem conclusive. Motolinia and Ixtlilxochitl state that centers were divided up into numerous craft-specializing barrios or *calpullec* (a native lineage group which had numerous functions) (60 at Tenochtitlán, 30 at Texcoco). The larger centers possessed huge open-air markets which met daily—a sure sign of full-time specialization—along with restaurants, cantinas, and hotels, all features of fully urbanized centers (Sanders, n.d.). In at least two cases (Tenochtitlán and Tlaxcala) we find mention of numerous secondary barrio markets, like modern neighborhood grocery stores, a certain indication that the bulk of the population was non-food-producing. One of the best proofs of the non-agricultural character of these larger centers was the simple fact that Cortez was able to starve the Aztecs into submission by simply cutting off the canoe traffic from Tenochtitlán during the famous siege of Mexico.

One of the most interesting documents from the sixteenth century which has been carefully studied in recent times (Toussaint, Gomez de Orozco, and Fernández, 1938) is the famous "Plano en Papel de Maguey." It is evidently a sixteenth-century map of the colonial city of Mexico, drawn in native style on native paper. It covers only one thirty-first of the total of the ancient urban area, and the authors place the section in the northeast part of the city. The map shows approximately 400 houses, each placed on a rectangular solar or house lot. This lot, in turn, is split up into narrow rectangular parallel bands, which almost surely represent chinampas. The total size of the house lot was 500 square meters. The over-all pattern is very regular, almost as much so as a modern village of checkerboard pattern. If we calculate community population density based on the average size of the house lots, we get an interesting result. It is almost exactly that of modern rural villages in the chinampa area.

The presence of chinampas in the house lots raises a crucial problem. Were the inhabitants of sixteenth-century Mexico City really urban in their way of life, or were they part-time farmers? The answer lies, first, in the size of the plots. Five hundred square meters, even with the extraordinarily productive chinampa agriculture, would provide a negligible fraction of the family income. Second, the sixteenth-century document "Descripción del Arzobispado de Mexico 1570" (Pimentel, 1897) indicates that the basis of life of the Indian population of the city was trade and handicrafts, with agriculture playing a very minor role. There seems to be no doubt that chinampas were held by a high percentage of the population of the city, but the total effect on community economy must have been slight.

The total area of Mexico City at the time of the conquest is estimated by the authors of the "Maguey" map study at 7.5 square kilometers (750 hectares or 2,000 acres); and they, assuming the population density of the pre-Spanish city to have approximated that of the colonial, estimated the population at 62,000 inhabitants. We probably will never be able to prove that the settlement pattern and population density of Tenochtitlán were the same in 1519 as in 1570, but the probability seems quite strong. One of the Spanish conquistadores estimated the population of the city at 60,000 inhabitants (Anonymous Conqueror, 1917), very close to the estimate of Toussaint. Most of the sixteenth-century writers give the figure of 60,000 houses, a certain exaggeration. Centers like Cholula, Tlaxcala, and Texcoco certainly had nucleated urban populations running into the scores of thousands.

Some of the smaller communities, by the accounts, were probably equivalent to modern towns in function. The descriptions, brief as they are, suggest true nucleated centers, but we cannot be sure. A number of Spanish writers make blanket statements, or statements referring to individual communities, that "pueblos," in the Spanish sense, did not exist; or they state that, whereas the late-sixteenth-century population lived in large nucleated planned centers, the ancient population lived scattered through the countryside. These statements, however, are misleading. In the first place, the term "pueblo," as we have seen previously, was applied not to single communities but to a cluster of communities, including a *cabacera* and several *estancias*. Second, the Spaniards often used the term "pueblo" with a tight legalistic definition based on Spanish standards. In Spain it was a strong social, as well as a settlement, unit and possessed a certain plan or form. None of these conditions were met in aboriginal Mexico. In native usage the local group corresponded to a town-state rather than a single community and comprised a central settlement, where the lord (who symbolized the unity of the state) resided and in which was located a large religious plaza, often along with an open market. The central community was made up of a number of barrios or *calpullec*. The rest of the population lived in numerous small rural villages, a single village, in general, made up of one *calpulli* which had landholding functions. These villages had populations running into the hundreds.

What seems to have happened in postconquest times is suggested as follows. First, the area was hit by epidemics which cut the population to half or less of its former size. To facilitate conversion, the Spanish padres tried to combine the remnants of the population of the *estancias* and resettle them at the *cabaceras*, forming large nucleated communities. The program was, in general, successful, and on modern maps the bulk of the *estancias* listed in late-sixteenth-century documents as still existent have now disappeared. In many cases the new nucleated community was not much larger than the ancient *cabacera*, owing to the over-all decline in population. Many of the ancient *cabaceras* had populations running from 3,000 to 6,000 inhabitants. The rural villages or *estancias* usually had between 300 and 500 inhabitants, to judge from those communities in the valley which survived Spanish resettlement policies.

One distinction, however, between the settlement pattern of the ancient and modern rural communities lies in community population density. Several sixteenth-century writers state that each house was surrounded by a milpa. We find the same situation in modern villages in Guatemala and northeast Puebla. In these cases each house has a small adjacent milpa which is cultivated more intensively than the larger holdings outside the village. My own studies of native agriculture indicate that the approximate limit of milpa size cultivated by this more intensive agricultural system is ¼ hectare. Ancient communities were less densely populated than modern ones in our region— probably approaching modern Yucatecan communities, in which the average density runs between 1,500 and 2,000 inhabitants per square kilometer.

PREHISTORIC SETTLEMENT PATTERNS
ARCHEOLOGICAL DATA

Archeological studies of settlement patterns for the area in question are almost unknown. I have made extensive but brief surface examinations of numerous sites in the region, with special attention to settlement, but all but one such survey have been superficial. Published data (other than that concerning formal architectonic planning of civic and religious centers) is almost non-existent, with the exception of Linné's (1934, 1942) work at Teotihuacán. The purpose of Linné's excavations was chronological, the settlement-pattern data being incidental to the main objective. Armillas (1950) was the first to note the significance of these incidental data, and, utilizing them as a beginning, he initiated studies to establish the basic settlement pattern of the site. The data presented later on Teotihuacán are based on his brief publication, personal discussions, and my own field observations.

One of the interesting facts about the settlement of Teotihuacán is the presence of a main street as the orientation axis of the site. This is the so-called "Camino de los Muertos," which runs the length of the government archeological zone. Most of the principal civic and religious structures are lined up along this street, together with scores of residential buildings of what was obviously a wealthy upper and middle class. Of further interest is the presence of side streets intersecting at right angles to this main street. These side streets usually separate large residential structures, but the exact pattern and spacing are unknown. Large residential buildings are not restricted to the main-street area but are also scattered throughout the site, as in the Tepantitla and Xolalpan sections. These residences consist of numerous rooms situated on various levels and surrounding open patios.

Linné, after excavating the residential palace at Xolalpan, excavated what appeared to him to be a similar structure at Tlamimilolpa on the eastern outskirts of the site. He ran into a complex of rooms, corridors, and patios, as at Xolalpan, but there were fundamental differences. At Xolalpan the structure had an over-all plan, with central patios, and had a defined limit. At Tlamimilolpa, Linné was constantly puzzled over the fact that this "building" seemed to have no obvious plan, nor was it limitable. Apparently, he was excavating in an extensive urban barrio and his "corridors" were narrow alleys. The density of population in this barrio must have been exceedingly heavy, probably greater than that of a modern chinampa village. My own surveys of the site have convinced me that a very high percentage of the area delimited by Armillas as the urbanized zone (750 hectares or 2,000 acres) was characterized by the settlement pattern discovered by Linné at Tlamimilolpa. This is based upon pottery and construction distributions. We may picture the aboriginal community as follows: a central zone of large religious and civic buildings and luxurious residential palaces aligned along a wide boulevard with numerous narrow, but well-planned, cross-streets. This was surrounded on all sides by an urban population living in almost continuous clusters of rooms separated by small patios and narrow, winding alleys.

One of the interesting features of civic planning at Teotihuacán is a vast and complex drainage system which is conducted through underground channels, collects in a central canal along the main street, and empties into the Río de Teotihuacán. Possibly the Aztec barrio organization goes back to the Teotihuacán period. One finds scattered throughout the site, in areas of very heavy ceramic concentration, single isolated pyramids which may have been barrio temples like those mentioned for the Aztec capital. Also, several huge, open plazas north of the Sun Pyramid and west of the Moon Pyramid may have served as markets. One of the plazas west of the Moon Pyramid is not surrounded by religious structures, and sections of it are characterized by surface concentrations of obsidian, suggesting workshops.

There is no doubt whatever as to the urban character of the settlement pattern at Teotihuacán. Assuming a population density comparable to Tenochtitlán and the modern chinampa villages, we compute at least 50,000 inhabitants. The archeological evidence suggests an even denser population, possibly double that of the Aztec capital as analyzed by Toussaint and coauthors.

The surface surveys which I carried out suggest that the settlement pattern of Teotihuacán is in no way unique for the Central Mexican region. The same degree of urbanization seems to have been characteristic of such major sites as Tula, Texcoco, Tlaxcala, Cholula, and Xochicalco. Unfortunately, with the exception of the first and last of these centers, the architectonic features of the sites have been almost destroyed by postconquest building activities; however, the density and distribution of pottery sherds are clues as to settlement size. None of the settlements is as large as Teotihuacán or Tenochtitlán, but all must have had populations in the scores of thousands. A six-week survey at Xochicalco indicated an estimated urbanization of 250 hectares. There is a main street at this site similar to that of Teotihuacán. But the Xochicalco pattern varies somewhat from the other named sites, in that it combines the function of urban center with fortress. The major zone is situated on the artificially leveled top and terraced slopes of a large hill. Hillside terraces evidently were occupied by urban folk under very congested living conditions. Houses must have been of perishable materials, probably similar to modern pole and thatch dwellings in the same area. The approaches up the hillsides are defended by a series of walls and moats (we have this type of center described in the documentary centers—Ixtacamaxtitlán, Huaxtepec). To the east of the Xochicalco Acropolis, as the main hill is called, is a second hill called the "Cerro de la Bodega," which combines the function of a religious center with that of a fortress. The slopes of this hill appear not to have been occupied. To the north of these two hills stretches a flat, extensive plain with concentrations of pottery refuse. The intensive settlement zone of the plain, which was probably occupied by an urban population and contiguous to the urban population of the Acropolis, covered at least 100 hectares. Beyond this zone are remains of small village sites scattered over the entire plain.

A principal problem of archeological settlement-pattern surveys in the Central Mexican region is the character and mode of organization of rural settlements. What few sites I have seen seem to indicate nucleated communities of similar density of population as modern villages but smaller in size. In preconquest times a community the size of San Gregorio Atlapulco almost always was partly urban in function.

SUMMARY

In Central Mexico we are dealing with a region of complex internal micro-geography and intricate zoning of natural products; but it is also a region in which we have an over-all unity in those factors which affect agricultural techniques and types of land utilization. It is a country of intensive agriculture and extremely dense population. This may have been more pronounced in aboriginal than in recent times. There is no doubt that the modern rural population has not yet reached the level achieved during the final phase of the archeological record. In 1519 the Valley of Mexico had at least double the population that it has today (subtracting, of course, the huge urban center of Mexico City), reaching a million inhabitants. What we have termed the Central Mexican symbiotic region had an approximate population of 2½ million at the date of the conquest. Two conditions of complex zoning of agricultural products in a small area (approximately 50,000 square kilometers), along with intensive agriculture, permitted this dense population; and this provided, in turn, a basis for an extraordinary development of commerce on an intervillage level as well as the growth of huge urban centers. At least twice in the history of the region urban settlements passed the 50,000 population point (Tenochtitlán and Teotihuacán). These great centers were religious and administrative centers, with large, resident, non-food-producing, economically specialized populations and completely urban settlement patterns. Population density within these centers was at least 8,000–9,000 inhabitants per square kilometer.

In the case of the smaller communities our data are not conclusive, but they suggest that the modern types of nucleated settlements—the town and the village—were well-established types in prehistoric times. However, community population density was considerably less than in the modern chinampa communities. The towns were probably centers of much part-time specialization, with populations of a size comparable to modern communities of the same category. Villages, on the other hand, appear to have been smaller than modern villages in the same region.

The precise form of ancient communities was probably quite distinct from modern ones, especially that of the smaller rural settlements. Instead of the regular block street and solar pattern, the organization was probably one of irregular land parcels and winding, narrow alleys. A certain continuity between ancient and modern patterns does exist in the presence of a central plaza flanked by religious and civic structures and in the open-air markets.

We might also see a certain amount of continuity in general zonal patterns. At the time of the conquest, the valley was divided into scores of semiautonomous city- or town-states, which in general organization of population were not very different from the late-sixteenth-century "pueblo" and the modern *município*—especially the larger *municípios*. Within these town- or city-states we find a large central community of several thousand inhabitants, with a number of smaller dependent villages. The central community was often made up of several barrios or *calpullec*, while the rural community was, in fact, a single *calpulli*. This *calpulli* was a landholding unit as well as a sociopolitical and spatial unit. Clusters of such city- and town-states occupied by people speaking the same dialect and possessing a common name and often politically unified, as well, provided the basis for the late-sixteenth-century administrative *provincia*.

As can be seen, settlement-pattern studies are in their infancy in the Central Mexican region, and there are many lacunae in our knowledge. We need a thoroughgoing reappraisal of all documentary data plus extensive surface reconnaissance and selected excavation to fill those gaps. This paper is meant to point out these lacunae and to formulate test hypotheses as working concepts.

SETTLEMENT PATTERNS IN NORTH-CENTRAL MEXICO

By J. CHARLES KELLEY

THE purpose of this paper is to discuss briefly what is now known of aboriginal settlement patterns in the north-central Mexican plateau, specifically in the states of Zacatecas, Durango, and Chihuahua. Only the sedentary archeological cultures will be discussed, and the meagerness of archeological research completed in this area further restricts the study. Settlement patterns of historical ethnic groups will receive little or no consideration, since in most instances there is considerable doubt regarding their relationship to the archeological cultures.

THE LA QUEMADA–CHALCHIHUITES OCCUPANCE IN ZACATECAS AND DURANGO

A relatively narrow tongue of sedentary occupation, culturally Meso-American, extends through Zacatecas and Durango approximately to the southern boundary of Chihuahua. This narrow corridor of settlement follows the foothills which lie adjacent to the Sierra Madre Occidental on the west and the interior desert plateau on the east. Known habitation sites are found principally at elevations ranging between about 6,000 and 7,500 feet. They lie at the edge of the juniper-oak-pine vegetational complex and follow the eastern edge of a belt of Cw climate.

Within this archeological zone, the best-known site is that of La Quemada, located southwest of the city of Zacatecas at an elevation of some 6,500 feet.[1] The site itself covers most of a large hill rising some 500 feet or better out of a fertile valley. This hill is covered, fortress-like, with a complex assemblage of stone-masonry pyramids, halls, courts, and rooms and a great wall. Other structures occur on a high hill range to the south, and small sites are reported in the valley itself.

In actual plan, La Quemada resembles a combination fortress and ceremonial center. On the lowest level of the main hill, a sort of sacred way, possibly a ball court, partially paved and walled, joins a steep-sided, non-truncated pyramid on the east, with a large stone-walled court and an adjacent masonry building filled with great masonry columns on the west. On the hill above are complicated mazes of great walled courts surrounded by rooms. There is at

---

1. This site is the anchor point for the pattern but is in many ways atypical. See Batres (1903), Hrdlicka (1903), and Noguera (1930).

least one walled court with a central masonry altar and, to one side, a small terraced pyramid. This site is very large, recalling in general situation and proportions that of Xochicalco, west of Cuernavaca, while the pyramid–sacred way–walled-court assemblage is highly suggestive of Teotihuacán in the Valley of Mexico.

Some 90 miles due northwest of La Quemada is the archeological zone of Chalchihuites. Here excavations have been made at the site of Alta Vista (Gamio, 1910; Noguera, 1930; Ekholm, 1940). This site is represented by a series of ruin mounds closely clustered on a hill ridge overlooking the Suchil Valley. Other sites are reported in the same vicinity. To the west the land rises in a series of rolling upland plains to the main foothills of the Sierra Madre a few miles away. Altitude, physiographic situation, and vegetational associations repeat the La Quemada situation, although the Chalchihuites hilltop is low. Again, reportedly, there are small sites in the main valley.

But here the resemblance ceases. Chalchihuites is no fortress-like, towering mass of masonry structures. The excavated sections include one masonry hall, with several alignments of crudely made tapering masonry columns and an associated complex of walls, rooms, and one stairway leading to a platform. No true pyramids are visible, although they may exist.

About 65 miles northwest of Chalchihuites is the modern city of Durango, situated at an elevation of 6,400 feet in an open valley in the eastern foothills of the Sierra Madre. To the east extend the basins and isolated mountain ranges of the northern interior plateau with hot, steppe climate and vegetation. The Durango Valley was a center of aboriginal occupance (Mason, 1937; Kelley, 1953). Almost every major hill in the valley has the ruins of an Indian settlement.

The largest settlements, however, occur on the foothills along the south side of the Río Tunal and on the adjacent lowland, south and slightly west of the city of Durango. Here are almost continuous occupation sites extending 3 or 4 miles along the river.

The largest of these, the Schroeder site, lies on two hills and an intervening "saddle," adjacent to the Río Tunal. One truncated terraced pyramid occupies the eastern hill, while two structures on the western hill may be the remnants of small pyramidal structures. The hills themselves, which are very rocky and covered with nopal thickets, are terraced all along the northern side. The terraces are artificial, made by constructing masonry walls on the downhill side and filling the area above with rubble, capped with dirt. Their purpose or usage is not clear. Around the foot of the pyramid on the eastern hill are the ruins of a rather elaborate complex of rooms, probably ceremonial structures. In the "saddle" itself and along the northern flanks of the hill at the valley edge and on the hill slopes above are the ruins of many masonry structures. Two of these were excavated in 1954 by an anthropological field session of Southern Illinois University and the Instituto Nacional de Antropología e Historia.[2]

The general plan of the excavated structures is that of a central court or plaza, around which rooms and elevated platforms have been constructed. Structure No. 1 at the base of the "saddle" on the east was a more complex assemblage, with several large house platforms attached to a central area of rooms around a court. Also, the whole assemblage was tied together by a raised masonry banquette on the east, joined at right angles to a similar paved terrace on the north, which was reached from below by a stairway ascending to the largest house platform at the western end. Partially shaped or well-shaped, horizontally placed stones and monolithic building stones (often 4 feet or more in height, 2 feet in width, and 1 foot or more in thickness) were used in the construction of the walls of rooms or courts.

Thus the general pattern of occupance in the Durango Valley was characterized by settlements, perhaps ceremonial centers, on the foothills, and, as usual, smaller sites, perhaps farm villages or outlying farmsteads, are reported in the valley.

About 135 miles northwest of the Durango Valley is the archeological zone of Zape, first reported as a ruin area just after 1600 (Brand, 1939).[3] The ruins are situated at an elevation of 6,400 feet in the valley of the Río Zape and on the adjacent hills. Zape lies in the margin of the juniper-pine-oak zone, while hot-steppe vegetation lies to the east and extends up the Zape Valley. Climatically, Zape lies at the contact of *Cw* (mesothermal savanna) and *BSh* (hot-steppe) regions.

There has been very little excavation at Zape, but once again there is a complex of ruined masonry structures evidenced by *cimientos* of vertical stone slabs. These stone "walls" outline central courts, and some appear to have an isolated masonry structure within the court. This vaguely recalls the masonry structures at the Schroeder site, but intensive excavation will be required to provide sufficient architectural data to make valid comparisons possible.

In the region between Zape and the Durango Valley a few isolated sites of a related culture have been found. The general pattern is a familiar one. The sites lie on the top of isolated hills, with farmland below, in the foothills at the edge of the Sierra Madre, and at the western margin of the interior

2. The 1954 expedition of the Southern Illinois University and the Instituto Nacional de Antropología e Historia was directed by J. Charles Kelley and Ramón Piña Chan, representing the parent institutions, assisted by W. J. Shakelford, Howard Winters, and Esther Bennett, of the Southern Illinois University staff, and fifteen students from various American universities. The expedition was financed by the Southern Illinois University and by a grant-in-aid from the Wenner-Gren Foundation for Anthropological Research, Inc. Studies of the specimens and data obtained are now in progress.

3. According to Brand, the Zape archeological sites were first described in the manuscript source: "Anuas del Año de 1604 y del Año de 1612," quoted in the works of the Jesuit historians Perez de Ribas in 1644 and Alegre in 1767–80 (Brand, 1939, p. 85).

desert plateau. Such recorded sites between Zape and Durango are generally quite small. The house ruins appear to be small, rectangular structures outlined by rows of vertically placed stone slabs. In the high sierra to the west of Durango and Zape are other small isolated sites, observable principally as sherd areas with occasional rectangular structures of vertical stone slabs.

On the Weicker Ranch, about 30 miles west of the city of Durango, an anthropological field session of the Southern Illinois University in 1952 excavated two low mounds lying on a small natural terrace of a steep hillside, overlooking a forested valley and a clear mountain stream (Kelley and Shackelford, 1954, pp. 145–50). Excavation of the mounds revealed two long, rectangular structures with hard-clay floors outlined by one or more rows of vertically placed stone slabs on one side (structure No. 1) or three sides (structure No. 2). Within the "compounds" thus formed were single or double rectangular floor areas, in most instances paved with stone slabs and outlined by vertical stone slabs in three instances. Between the small floors (or rooms) within the compound were stone-lined fire hearths set in the floor. The terrace itself was protected from erosion on the downhill side by a crude wall of rough field stone.

From La Quemada to Zape there are certain fundamental similarities in culture. Red-on-buff wares in tripod and hemispherical non-legged bowl forms, together with rare engraved tripod "cloisonné" vessels and a variety of plain red and brown wares in bowls, ollas, small jars, etc., make up the ceramic complex. Associated trade wares often include pottery from Sinaloa on the west coast of Mexico. In addition, engraved and plain spindle whorls in conical and spherical forms, metal bells, obsidian blades, and a variety of stone artifacts make up the general complex.

Peripheral to the central area and culture are the sites with isolated structures of stone slabs placed vertically around a rectangular area, such as those of the Weicker site and others lying between Zape and Durango. These appear to have a somewhat simpler associated material culture. Here plain red or buff wares, occasionally decorated with a fugitive red paint, dominate the ceramic complex. Tripod bowls are rare or altogether missing, and the pottery is characteristically poor in construction. Other elements of the complex give it the appearance of a sort of "back-country" version of the material culture of the large sites situated in the foothills. As a guess, the culture represented by these small sites exemplifies a crude adjustment by the foothill dwellers to a new and different life-zone in the high sierra.

The closest relations of this general culture pattern, for convenience termed the "La Quemada–Chalchihuites culture," seem to lie with the Tula-Mazapan cultures of the Valley of Mexico, although some elements of the northern cultures appear to have been derived from the earlier Teotihuacán horizon, and at the Schroeder site one potsherd, identified by Ramón Piña Chan as Teotihuacán II or III in origin, was found in the lowest level of one of the stratitests. The period of principal development of the La Quemada–Chalchihuites complex would seem to lie within the limits of the era *ca.* 900–1350, with some possibility of earlier beginnings. The entire development certainly was terminated well before 1600.

To recapitulate, the La Quemada–Chalchihuites cultural pattern developed in a long, narrow, geographic belt, oriented southeast-northwest, following the eastern foothills of the Sierra Madre Occidental at elevations between 6,000 and 7,500 feet on the eastern periphery of a vegetational belt dominated by a juniper-oak-pine assemblage in a *Cw* climate and at the western edge of a desert or hot-steppe climate and an associated vegetational belt. The cultural pattern was Meso-American in origin, with closest ties to the Tula-Mazapan horizon, and was best developed *ca.* 900–1350. The basic settlement pattern involved areas of intensive settlement, perhaps colonies, spotted at distant intervals along the occupied zone and sparse occupation in the intervening areas.

Within the zones of heaviest occupance, which must certainly have been supported by intensive agriculture, the settlement pattern included one or more central villages or ceremonial centers, usually located on hilltops and slopes, and a number of neighboring smaller dwelling areas on lower hills or in the valleys. Masonry structures of a permanent nature, including pyramids and courts in at least two centers, point up the importance of the hilltop centers, while the architectural remains at the smaller—and generally lower—sites are much less impressive. A subpattern, apparently evolving peripherally from the major pattern, emphasized small settlements on hills or hill slopes in the high mountains, and the associated material culture was aberrant and crude.

UPPER RÍO CONCHOS, THE LOMA SAN GABRIEL OCCUPANCE, DURANGO, AND CHIHUAHUA

Just north of the La Quemada–Chalchihuites archeological zone, in extreme northern Durango and southern Chihuahua, on the headwaters of the Río Florido and other upper branches of the Río Conchos, is a transitional and very poorly known archeological zone. This occupance is best known at the Loma San Gabriel site (found in 1952) situated on a high "hog back" or narrow mesa top astride the Río Florido a few miles above Villa Ocampo on the Durango-Chihuahua border (Kelley, 1953). Here the Río Florido has cut a steep canyon through a long, narrow, high mesa. Along the top of the mesa section lying south of the river are the ruins of structures outlined by horizontally and vertically placed stones. Along both steeply sloping sides of the mesa throughout its entire length are artifical terraces supported by crude masonry walls.

Pottery found at Loma San Gabriel was plain red and buff ware, showing occasional traces of red decoration. No vessel legs were found, and only one sherd of the characteristic La Quemada–Chalchihuites red-on-buff ware from the south was found. The stone complex identified from surface collections is a simplified version of that occurring in the great sites to the south and is also familiar from sites found along the lower Río Conchos, with some differences.

In this Loma San Gabriel zone the pattern of the ceremonial (or civic) center situated on a high hilltop, with farmland and a running stream below, seems to have been carried over from the La Quemada–Chalchihuites zone to the south. But elaborate masonry structures, pyramids, legged vessels, cloisonné ware, and other items of Mexican culture have now been lost. In 1952, William J. Shackelford was able to trace the Loma San Gabriel zone into southern Chihuahua, where he found several similar sites in the upper drainage of the Río Conchos. Just how far north this settlement pattern of terraced hillsides below groups of small crude masonry structures situated on high hilltops, with an associated simple non-Mexican material culture, extends is not known, although crude masonry house remains with associated pottery are reported from northwestern Chihuahua (Sayles, 1936).[4]

Climatically and vegetationally the region occupied by the Loma San Gabriel culture, superficially at least, does not differ notably from the La Quemada–Chalchihuites zone to the south. However, in general, the upper Río Conchos is "chopped up" physiographically into a great number of more or less isolated occupation areas; the terrain is often very rough, the canyons usually deep. And that there may actually be significant differences in the natural habitat is perhaps indicated by the personal observation that the nopal thickets are small and thin in the upper Río Conchos, while the plants are large and the thickets frequent and extensive in Durango, where they almost serve as reconnaissance indicators of the location of La Quemada–Chalchihuites sites. Also the Loma San Gabriel sites are located at lower elevations (as a guess, running between 5,000 and 6,000 feet) and in the margin of the hot steppe climatically.

In general, Loma San Gabriel is transitional, the cultural pattern reduced and modified, possibly through incomplete adaptation to changing physiography and other natural factors. Northward along the eastern margins of the sierra and extending eastward into the desert basin country is the Chihuahua culture of purported southwestern origin, which will be discussed briefly later in this paper. Northeastward, down the Río Conchos, settlements of the Bravo Valley culture are found.

THE RÍO CONCHOS–BRAVO VALLEY
SETTLEMENT PATTERN

Beginning in the upper Conchos and Río Florido, in the same area as the Loma San Gabriel occupance just discussed, and extending to the south of

4. These sites apparently belong to the Carretas Phase (Sayles, 1936, pp. 16, 17, 31, and Table 1).

the Río Conchos, there is another cultural pattern related to the Loma San Gabriel culture but having a distinctly different settlement pattern. This settlement pattern is one of small occupation sites situated at intervals along the river and directly upon its terraces. The preferred situation is a low terrace remnant located at a point where a tributary stream, or dry arroyo, enters the main stream. In the mountainous section of the middle Río Conchos there are many small valleys formed along the river where it flows through deep canyons across a series of parallel ridges. Sites of this occupance characteristically are located against the mountain ridge at the head of the valley and adjacent to the outlet of the canyon above.[5]

Consistently, these little Conchos sites are found eroding from the surface of the alluvial valley fill, which usually forms a low terrace or high flood plain along the river. Buried deeply in the alluvium beneath these sites are fire hearths and flint chips, representing an earlier and as yet unidentified occupation.

Plain red and brown pottery in simple forms and sparse sherds of a similar ware with red-line decoration are characteristic of these sites, as is a quite simple stone complex made up principally of flint chopping tools, knives, arrow points, scrapers, and such pecked stone artifacts as grinding stones and end-notched pebbles. Nothing is known of actual house structures or village plans of the Bravo Valley settlements located above the vicinity of the junction of the Río Conchos with the Río Grande.

The extreme lower section of the Río Conchos and the adjacent portions of the Río Grande Valley is a region of somewhat higher aboriginal culture. Here three sequential cultural stages, representing foci of the sedentary Bravo Valley culture, have been identified. These are, from early to late, the La Junta, Concepción, and Conchos foci. The La Junta Focus has been dated by intrusive southwestern pottery to the period *ca.* A.D. 1150 or 1200 to about 1400 or 1450, while the Concepción Focus survived from the latter date into the early historic period, and the Conchos Focus represents the full historic period at La Junta (Kelley, 1939, 1949, 1951, 1952, 1952–53; Kelley, Campbell, and Lehmer, 1940; Shackelford, 1955).

The Bravo Valley Aspect has origins which can be traced, at least in part, to the Jornado Branch of the Mogollon on the Río Grande near El Paso, Texas, and Las Cruces, New Mexico (Lehmer, 1938). The culture was a sedentary one, with a primary dependence on agriculture. During the La Junta Focus, to about 1400, there was apparently a continuous zone of settlements from southern New Mexico to the La Junta region. This occupance was terminated above La Junta at *ca.* 1400, but the settlements around La Junta were occupied through the mission period.

5. I worked the mountainous section of the middle Río Conchos, between Julimes and Falomir, in 1951, on burro back, under a grant from the American Association for the Advancement of Science.

The settlement pattern of the Bravo Valley Aspect at La Junta was, on the evidence, much like that of the middle and upper Río Conchos. Sites were characteristically located on the first terrace above the low flood plain and directly upon the terrace edge, usually adjacent to the river or its former channels. Occasionally, higher terraces were occupied when they lay adjacent to the stream and no suitable low terrace was available nearby.

In the older La Junta Focus sites excavation reveals small, shallow or deep pit houses, which are rectangular and have adobe floors and often plastered adobe blocks (altars?), with attached firepits, at the south end. These pit houses, which had adobe or jacal superstructures, were placed in east-west rows, separated by the space of one or more houses, across the flat surface of the river terrace. Houses themselves were oriented north and south, and on occasion a secondary structure was attached to the north end of the house. Entrance to the houses was probably through the roof, although the evidence is inconclusive.

In a site on the lower Río Conchos near the town of Ojinaga, although only one house was excavated, the general village plan was evident. Here there was a central east-west street with rows or double rows of carefully spaced pit houses running along both sides. At the eastern end of the street there was a large mound of fire-cracked stone. This may have represented a communal hearth or an artificial refuse heap made by deliberately dumping there the residue of the village fires over a period of years.

In the following Concepción Focus, houses were built three or four times as large as those of the La Junta Focus. Less care was shown in manufacture. Floors were made of tamped refuse, and there were no adobe curbs or altars. Huge posts in varying arrangements supported a roof which was probably either flat or slightly pitched, and again roof entrances seem indicated. Houses were built side by side in east-west alignments, but, in practice, long structures of many rooms sharing intervening walls developed. Streets or rough irregular plazas lay between these long house rows. Within the houses there were no regular fire hearths, but concentrations of ashes on the floor imply that several fires were maintained within each structure, thus perhaps indicating a change in residence habits or social organization from that of the earlier La Junta Focus.

The Concepción Focus occupance survived into the Spanish contact period, and we have good descriptions of houses, villages, and settlement patterns, which continue with only slight modification through the full historic Conchos Focus, and locally to the present day (Kelley, 1952–53). Villages were compact, with one or more plazas, village walls in some instances, and regular village entryways. Where there were more than one plaza, the villages were divided into sections, which apparently housed diverse ethnic groups. Houses were large, with jacal superstructure, and, by 1715, if not earlier, they faced on the plaza and hence must have had side entrances rather than entryways through the roofs. The fields were located in the nearby river flood plain, where the crops were irrigated by natural river flooding. In 1747 the Indians explained to the Spaniards that La Junta pueblos must be located on a hill (terrace remnant) near the river so that they might have materials for building their houses and the necessities for their households close at hand and yet not be exposed to destruction by the annual floods.

The Bravo Valley occupance coincides with the distribution of the mesquite-grasslands of the Chihuahua Desert (Brand, 1936) along the Río Conchos–Río Grande and lies in a *BWhw* (hot desert, dry winters) climatic zone where ten years out of every twenty are desert years (Russell, 1932). The riverine type of agriculture which the Bravo Valley people practiced was possible only on the river lowlands and hence was severely restricted spatially and directly dependent upon the volume and regularity of the annual floods. Documented population shifts within the area have been explained partially in terms of such factors and their fluctuation with minor cycles of climatic change (Kelley, 1952). Although the archeological evidence seemingly indicates a peripheral southwestern origin for the Bravo Valley Aspect, there are peculiarities in the pattern that appear non-southwestern and which may trace back to an origin in the Loma San Gabriel pattern of the upper Conchos and, remotely, southward in the La Quemada–Chalchihuites pattern. In any event, the cultural pattern represents a rather radical adaptation to stringent restrictive factors in the geographic habitat of the culture.

THE CHIHUAHUA CULTURE

Northward from the headwaters of the Río Conchos along the eastern flanks of the Sierra Madre Occidental and extending out into the desert basins of northwestern Chihuahua are the archeological sites of the Chihuahua culture. This culture has been known for a long time, and there are many field reports and discussions of it in the published literature (Kidder, 1916; Noguera, 1930; Carey, 1931; Brand, 1935, 1943; Sayles, 1935, 1936). Nevertheless, it is difficult to obtain a clear idea of the settlement patterns and their relation to the geographic habitat from the published sources.[6]

Certainly, two principal patterns of occupance are at once visible. To the west in the canyons of the sierra and the outlying hill chains are large cliff dwellings of stone masonry and adobe, while in the valleys of the Casas Grandes, Santa María, and Carmen rivers, in the adjacent mountain valleys, and extending eastward in dilute form into the desert basins are house ruins of adobe and locally of stone masonry. An agricultural basis for the economy seems certain in both instances.

The cliff dwellings of the west resemble those of the southwestern United States. They vary from single-room structures to large community houses

6. Unfortunately, actual excavation reports on Chihuahua culture sites are few, and I have had no personal field experience in northwestern Chihuahua.

of more than eighty rooms. Some are located low in the canyon walls near streams, while the western sites occur high in the cliffs of the deep gorges which cut through the sierra and are characterized by their relative inaccessibility. The cliff dwellings are single- or multiple-storied and consist of compact masses of living and storage rooms with entry and connecting doors (often T-shaped), conforming in general plan to the natural shape of the rock shelter in which they were built. In the nearby valleys are artificial terraces (*trincheras*), supposedly agricultural in function, and associated single-room masonry structures.

In the open valleys to the east, ruins appear to be located on low hills or slight eminences on the valley floor near the streams. A variety of house forms is reported, ranging from small compact groups of a few rooms to larger L-shaped and shallow U-shaped clusters of either stone masonry or puddled adobe construction, and some large community houses, of puddled adobe construction only, such as Casas Grandes, where the rooms are grouped around a central court to form a hollow square of dwellings.

While the general evidence seems to indicate a southwestern origin for the Chihuahua culture, several investigators seem to think that some of its elements may have been derived from the Meso-American cultures to the south. In view of recent additions to our archeological knowledge of Durango and southern Chihuahua, the possibility of a basically Meso-American origin for the culture needs re-examination.

Some outstanding factors in the geographic environment should be noted. Here in northwestern Chihuahua is the northern terminus of the Sierra Madre Occidental. Except on the extreme west and south, the fretted mountain front of deep canyons and barrancas, so characteristic of southwestern Chihuahua and the Río Conchos headwaters, is lacking. Here the "top-of-the-mountain country" of the high sierra is simply an easily accessible upland plateau. It is in this country and in the gorges on the west and south that the cliff-dwelling and *trinchera*–single-house settlement patterns prevail, in the northern extremity of the Cw (mesothermal savanna) climate and the juniper-oak-pine vegetational association.

But on the eastern flanks of the Sierra Madre in northwestern Chihuahua the foothill belt with a hot-steppe (BSh) climate becomes very narrow, and in effect the desert belt of BWh climate and mesquite-grassland (Chihuahua Desert) vegetation borders almost directly upon the upland Cw climate and the juniper-oak-pine association. Notably, the main Chihuahua culture settlements appear to be distributed along the BSh-BWh margin, extending out into the interior basins of the latter belt, rather than along the Cw-BSh margin, as is the case with the La Quemada–Chalchihuites pattern far to the south. Here any wave of sedentary occupation following the Sierra Madre foothills out of the south would be forced to adapt to the BWh climate and the associated vegetation and soils, and just such a cultural pattern as that of the Chihuahua culture might well have evolved. Obviously, much more work on both the archeology and the ecology of the Chihuahua culture needs to be done before this possibility, as well as others, can be checked. In the meantime, most of the evidence does indicate a southwestern origin for both the cultural complex and its ecological basis.

SUMMARY AND DISCUSSION

Thus four cultural complexes and their associated settlement patterns have been identified in north-central Mexico. The La Quemada–Chalchihuites culture represents a northward extension of an authentic Meso-American pattern through the states of Zacatecas and Durango, almost to the Chihuahua boundary. Pyramids, stone-masonry buildings, columns, tripod vessels, red-on-buff and cloisonné decoration, copper bells, spindle whorls, obsidian blades, and other items characterize the culture itself, while the settlement pattern involves dispersed small sites, presumably farmsteads, around a central ceremonial or civic center located on a hill. This culture, probably best developed between ca. 900 and 1350, followed a narrow ecological zone—the margin of hot-steppe and mesothermal savanna belts—northward along the eastern foothills of the Sierra Madre Occidental at an elevation between 6,000 and 7,500 feet, into northern Durango, where it gave way to the Loma San Gabriel culture.

The poorly known Loma San Gabriel culture represents, in all probability, an attenuated form of the La Quemada–Chalchihuites pattern. The concept of the hilltop ceremonial or civic center, presumably in association with small farm sites in the valleys, was retained, but pyramids and elaborate stone masonry are missing, as are such Mexican items in the material-culture inventory as tripod vessels, cloisonné decoration, and presumably spindle whorls, metal bells, and obsidian blades. The material culture is simple and reduced. The life-zone occupied is similar to that of the pattern to the south, although sites lie at slightly lower elevations and more nearly in the steppe climatic belt and vegetation, but the regional physiography is characteristically rugged and fragmented. This cultural pattern could well be transitional to the Bravo Valley culture, which developed along the Río Conchos to the north and east, and to the Chihuahua culture, which developed along the terminal northern flanks of the Sierra Madre Occidental in northwestern Chihuahua.

The Bravo Valley culture found along the Río Conchos from its headwaters to the Río Grande and in the adjacent valley of the latter stream appears to be an aberrant southwestern culture of ca. 1150–1450 based on riverine agriculture in a *BWhw* climate and a mesquite-grassland association. Settlements of pit houses grouped into streets and around plazas, with pottery and other artifacts closely related to sedentary cultures of southwestern origin farther up the Río Grande, were situated on low hills or terraces immediately adjacent to the river. Hilltop settlements, civic or ceremonial centers, tripod ware, cloisonné decoration, spindle whorls, obsidian blades, and copper artifacts are characteristically missing. Nevertheless, the pattern shares certain traits with the Loma San Gabriel culture, and the possibility that it originated, at least in part, from the latter cannot be completely disregarded.

The Chihuahua culture also is a late sedentary development, *ca.* 1100–1400, under similar environmental conditions at the foothill margins of the Sierra Madre Occidental in northwestern Chihuahua. Here the settlement pattern is primarily one of cliff dwellings in the far west and compactly grouped masonry and puddled adobe houses situated on low hills in the valleys in the east, with an associated material culture that is basically southwestern but which shows some putatively Meso-American elements. Its focal location is also the geographic point where the Sierra Madre Occidental has its northern termination and where the life-zone along which the La Quemada–Chalchi-huites and Loma San Gabriel cultures developed to the south also ends.

The general picture is one of Meso-American cultures advancing north-ward along a restricted corridor representing a unique ecological zone and meeting and mingling with a similar extension southward into the Chihuahua Desert and along the Río Grande–Río Conchos corridor of a basic south-western pattern of architecture, material culture, and settlement. But there appears to have been a virtual continuum of sedentary cultures from the Cen-tral Mexican area into the southwestern United States early in the second millennium A.D.; the hypothesis of a cultural hiatus separating the Meso-American cultures from those of the Southwest no longer appears tenable or, at best, must be shifted backward in time. All these cultures appear to have disappeared almost coincidentally around 1350–1400, except for the Bravo Valley culture at the junction of the Río Conchos and the Río Grande, which survived into the historic period under exceptionally favorable envi-ronmental conditions. The close correspondence of cultural complex and settlement patterns with ecological areas, together with the local survival of the Bravo Valley culture under uniquely favorable environmental conditions, suggests that ecological changes triggered by comparatively minor climatic fluctuations may have brought about the disappearance of the sedentary cul-tures described and, perhaps, on an earlier time horizon may have encouraged and supported their original development and expansion.

In this paper, settlement patterns of the preceramic horizon have not been considered, although they offer much valuable information supplementary to that here discussed, and certain minor patterns have been ignored, largely because of lack of space, on the one hand, and the paucity of available data regarding them, on the other. Also the cultural patterns discussed here should not be considered alone but should be viewed against the background of con-temporaneous cultural developments along the Pacific Coast of Mexico and in the Huasteca of northeastern Mexico, regional patterns which could not be included here.

PREHISTORIC SETTLEMENT PATTERNS ON THE NORTHEASTERN PERIPHERY OF MESO-AMERICA

By RICHARD S. MAC NEISH

ARCHEOLOGICAL reconnaissance and excavations have been undertaken in the south and east portions of the state of Tamaulipas and adjacent parts of the states of Veracruz and San Luis Potosí, Mexico, for five seasons: 1941–42 (Ekholm, 1944), 1945–46 (MacNeish, 1947, 1948), 1948–49 (MacNeish, 1950, and MS, n.d.), 1953–54 (MacNeish, 1955), and 1955. Materials have been collected from 346 sites in Tamaulipas and about 40 sites from Veracruz and San Luis Potosí. Three major excavations and two testings occurred in Sierra Madre in southwestern Tamaulipas, three large digs and stratitests in ten sites were made in the Sierra de Tamaulipas, test trenches were sunk in six sites in east-central Tamaulipas, while in the Tampico-Pánuco region of northern Veracruz, Ekholm and MacNeish have extensively tested five sites.

Although all these archeological materials have been analyzed, many of the results are still not in print. Therefore, before discussing the sequential settlement patterns of these areas, it is necessary to outline briefly the stratigraphic information which is the basis for the sequence of cultural complexes of the various regions of northeastern Mexico.

The first region to be examined is the northern edge of the "Humid Lower Tropical Biotic Subzone" (Goldman, 1951) in the flat lands of the drainages of the Tamesi and Pánuco rivers in northern Veracruz and southeasternmost Tamaulipas. Here Ekholm dug two stratified sites in the 1941–42 season (Ekholm, 1944), and MacNeish excavated the Progresso site in 1948 (MacNeish, 1954). On the basis of the pottery and figurine changes, they established a sequence of ten phases or periods. Table 1 summarizes their excavations.

The excavated sites and the other sites known from survey of the region may be assigned to these outlined phases. However, both the total artifact complexes and the exact type of subsistence of each phase are very poorly known.

The second region comprises the dry, rugged mountain and canyon country of southwestern Tamaulipas. Here yucca, small oaks, mesquites, aguaves, and pines occur together in an area of limited rainfall that seems to be transitional between the "Lower and Upper Austral Biotic Zones" (Goldman, 1951). Excavation and survey were undertaken by P. W. Grant, D. A. Kelley, and R. S. MacNeish in 1953–54 and 1955. The three stratified caves excavated and the two ruins tested are the basis for a sequence of eight cultural complexes (see Table 2).

In this region the artifact and subsistence complexes of each phase are well known, but our survey was not complete enough to give adequate data on settlements for all the phases.

TABLE 1

Progresso Site	Pavon Site	Tancol	Phases
Level 1..........	Levels 1–3 Levels 4–6 Levels 7–10 Levels 11–12 Levels 13–17	Upper levels	Pánuco (VI) Los Flores (V) Zaquil (IV) Pithaya (III) El Prisco (II)
Levels 2–5........	Levels 18–19	Lower levels	Tancol Chila (I)
Levels 6–13.......			Aguilar
Levels 14–20......			Ponce
Levels 21–22......			Pavon

TABLE 2

Romera Cave (Tm c 247)*	Portales Cave (Tm c 248)	Ojo de Agua Cave (Tm c 274)	Phases
Occupations 15–16....		Layers 1–2	San Antonio
Occupations 13–14....	Levels 1–2	Layers 1–2	San Lorenzo
Occupations 11–12....		Layers 3–5	Palmillas
Occupations 9–10.....			Mesa de Guaje
Occupations 5–8......			Guerra
	Level 3	Layers 6–12	Flacco
Occupations 2–4......	Levels 4–5		Portales
Occupation 1........	Levels 6–8		Infiernillo

* "Tm c" = Tamaulipas cave.

The third region is the canyon-cut country of the Sierra de Tamaulipas. In terms of flora and fauna, it seems to be transitional between the "Arid Upper Tropical" and "Lower Austral Biotic" zones, and one finds oaks, cacti, ojite, mesquites, palmitos, cypresses, sycamores, occasionally pine, and a wide variety of thorny bushes (Goldman, 1951). Three seasons, 1946, 1949, and 1954, have been spent here, and five caves and a number of open sites or ruins have been dug (MacNeish, MS, n.d.). Though nine sequential artifact complexes have been uncovered, all did not occur in any one excavation, nor is there a total artifact or subsistence complex for each one, and there are still some bad gaps in the sequence. However, survey has revealed a number of examples of settlement patterns for each of the archeological phases. Table 3 shows the correlation of the excavated stratified site and the phases.

The final area is the arid coastal plain and dissected peneplain of eastern Tamaulipas from the Soto la Marina River to the Río Grande. This has been called the "Lower Austral Biotic Zone" (MacNeish, MS, n.d.). Though much surveying has been undertaken in this region and four sites have been excavated, only one was stratified, and it had a very inadequate sample (MacNeish, 1948). However, recent excavation in the Falcon Dam area along the Río Grande in northwest Tamaulipas reveals a very similar sequence (Stevenson, 1952; Cason, 1954) (see Table 4). However, before one can speak very confidently about the sequence of phases of coastal Tamaulipas, there should be considerably more investigation.

TABLE 3

Tm c 81	Tm c 174	Tm c 82	Tm c 315	Tm c 314	Tm c 85	Tm c 79	Phases
Layer 1......		Layer 1 Layer 2		Layer 1			Los Angeles
				Layer 2		Layers 1–2	La Salta (III)
Layer 2......					Layers 1–3	Layers 3–4	Eslabones (II)
	Layer 1	Layer 3			Layers 4–7		Laguna I
			Layer 1				
		Layer 4	Layers 2–3	Layer 3			Almagre
	Layers 2–3	Layer 5	Layer 4				La Perra
Layer 3......		Layers 6–7					Nogales
Layer 4 (mixed)....	Layer 4						
Layer 5......	Layers 5–6						Lerma
Layer 6......							Diablo

TABLE 4

Tm c 29	Possible Sequence Based on Excavation and Seriation
Level 1	Catan-Brownsville–Los Flores and Pánuco (Mier?)
Level 2	
Level 3	Abasolo (Late Falcon Focus in 40-ft. terrace)
Level 4	{Repelo (Early Falcon Focus in 90-ft. terrace) {Nogales

Tentatively, on the basis of similarity of artifact types as well as actual trade items, the sequence of each of the four regions may be correlated. Unfortunately, the knowledge of each phase is not equal for each area, nor are all the temporally comparable phases known. However, even without complete knowledge of every horizon in all localities, it seems possible to make some generalizations about settlement patterns on the northeastern peripheries of Meso-America. The settlement patterns of this area may be divided into seven classes. Not all these classes have been found in any one region, but an attempt will be made to present them in their rough chronological order. In the presentation of each class the phases that belong to it from each region, the subsistence, the mode of life, the estimated size of settlements, the kind of settlement, and something about the material culture will be considered.

Class I.—The only well-defined example of this class is the Lerma Phase (though the poorly defined Diablo complex may also be of the same class). These materials represent the earliest found in the Sierra de Tamaulipas region and may be earlier than all others from the region. Components occur at two excavated cave sites and one surface site. In the cave the two refuse layers in Tm c 174 and the one in Tm c 81, as well as the three refuse strata seen in cross-section at site Tm c 309, were all less than 2 inches in maximum thickness. From this it may be inferred that occupations were of short duration and that the Lerma people were probably nomadic. The area covered by the Lerma refuse ranged from 50 to 250 square feet. From this it may be estimated that groups were small, consisting of one or two nuclear families (four to ten people?). In the Lerma refuse there were proportionally more bones than in any other phase, and most of the tools seem to have been used for hunting (projectile points), skin scraping (snub-nosed, plano-convex, and stemmed end-scrapers), splitting of bones (choppers), or cutting of meat (square-based knives). This evidence certainly leads to the conclusion that Lerma subsistence was based primarily on hunting.[1] Thus, in summary, Class I—represented by the Lerma Phase of the Sierra de Tamaulipas—seems to have represented a people with a hunting subsistence pattern, a nomadic mode of life, who lived in small groups in temporary camps or caves and had a series of crude tools, such as choppers, plano-convex scrapers, square-based knives, stemmed and snub-nosed end-scrapers, and large, thick, lentoid projectile points.

Class II.—This type of settlement pattern is represented by a number of phases. The Infiernillo Phase of southwestern Tamaulipas and the Nogales Phase of eastern Tamaulipas seem to be fairly early, but the Repelo, Abasolo, Huastec camps, Catan, and Brownsville phases or complexes of northeastern Tamaulipas seem to be later, and the latter two were in existence in historic times. The Infiernillo Phase is represented by four excavated components, while artifacts of the Nogales Phase were found in three excavations and on eleven open sites. Repelo and Abasolo are known from one excavated component, in addition to the former being represented at thirty-one open sites and the latter at eighteen open sites. The very late Catan Phase occurred in two excavated components, as did the Huastec camps, while there were five Catan surface sites. Collections were made from the surface of three Huastec camps, while the Brownsville complex is represented by adequate surface collections from fifty-two sites. The deepest refuse layers of

---

1. In cave Tm c 174, a La Perra strata level with preserved food remains, appeared above a Lerma level with only bone preserved. However, when the amount of bone per cubic foot of refuse from these two components was compared, it was found that there were five times as many bones in the Lerma level as in the La Perra level. If this number of bones had been found in the La Perra level, it would have been considered not a layer laid down by food-gatherers but one by hunters who did some food-gathering. Therefore, it is reasonable to conclude that the Lerma levels are those of a group primarily dependent on hunting.

any of these components were 6 inches, and one of the layers with preserved vegetable materials from Tm c 248, Infiernillo Phase, seems to represent a collection of spring food plants. Thus these peoples seem to have been
seminomadic, that is, they changed their location seasonally. Sites range
from ones that cover 100 square feet to others spread over 12,000 square feet.
A rough comparison with ethnological data from the Basin-Plateau concerning the number of families with a food-gathering economy and the area
occupied by them allows one to estimate that the size of band population of
Class II ranged from ten to sixty people (perhaps varying with the seasons).
The preserved food remains from the Infiernillo Phase reveal that they (and
perhaps all the others) were primarily dependent on wild-food plants and
only secondarily on game.[2] The Brownsville, Catan, and Huastec complexes, that are more or less concentrated along the coast, may have been
more dependent on shell food than on wild plants, but nevertheless all were
primarily food-collectors. Since this class is represented by a number of
phases of different horizons, there is considerable range in the kinds of artifacts used, but characteristically they have projectile points (early ones are
possibly atlatl points and the later ones arrow points), scraping tools, large
blades, and mortar fragments, and all are lacking locally made pottery. Thus
Class II is represented by seasonally nomadic (or semisedentary), food-collecting bands who lived in seasonal camps of from ten to sixty people and had
a simple material culture.

Class III.—This class is represented by eleven excavated components and
two open sites in the Sierra Madre of Tamaulipas belonging to the Portales,
Flacco, and Guerra phases, while in the Sierra de Tamaulipas six excavated
sites and five found on the surface are assignable to the Almagre or La Perra
phases. Refuse of these phases covered about the same range as those of
Class II, so the size of settlements was probably about the same. Fortunately,
refuse from all but the Almagre Phase was well preserved, giving us a very
full knowledge of the subsistence pattern. Basically, all these groups seem
to have been wild-food collectors but did practice some squash and/or corn
and/or bean agriculture. Since the refuse is a little thicker than that of the
previous horizon in caves in both the Sierra Madre and the Sierra de Tamaulipas and since it seems likely that they would remain in the immediate locale
of their planted crops during a growing period of several months, they may
be considered to have been semisedentary. In summary, then, Class III characteristically has semisedentary, incipient agricultural bands who lived in

2. These early Infiernillo layers from Portales cave were most interesting, as they contained
abundant stone tools in conjunction with food remains and feces. The stone tools consisted of
a large series of heavy scrapers, choppers, knives, and projectile points. All were artifacts normally thought of as being connected with the chase, and there is not one tool that could be
connected with food-gathering. However, an examination of the preserved food remains revealed that less than 2 per cent were animal bones and the remainder were wild-food plants.
In reality, then, these people were food-collectors. Thus one must be particularly cautious in
making estimates of ancient subsistence patterns based on only the artifact complex.

camps or caves and who had a simple material culture characterized by large (dart) points, mullers, large amounts of chopping or pounding tools, nets, baskets, and twined blankets.

Class IV.—This class is found only at Pánuco and is poorly represented by the Pavon and Ponce phases. The people seem to have been sedentary farmers living in small villages, with a number of material skills such as weaving cotton cloth, making pottery and figurines, and building wattle-and-daub houses.

Class V.—This class is represented by the many components of Laguna, Eslabones, and La Salta phases in the Sierra de Tamaulipas, the numerous ruins of the Aguilar, Chila, Tancol, El Prisco, Pithaya, and Zaquil phases of northern Veracruz, as well as the Mesa de Guaje and Palmillas of southwestern Tamaulipas. Numerous metates, as well as preserved food from caves in the mountains, reveal that they did intensive farming of beans, squash, corn, manioc, tobacco, and cotton. A survey of sites discloses that they are of two types: small villages represented by house mounds or house platforms and larger villages represented by house platforms associated with truncated pyramids, with or without plaza and with or without ball courts. In the Sierra de Tamaulipas there is a tendency for the templed villages to be on hilltops, possibly for defense, but this is not always true and may not have any cultural significance but merely be due to the fact that hilltops are clearer of vegetation and have a less rugged terrain. A rough counting of house platforms reveals from 2 to 600, so I have estimated that settlements may have ranged from 10 to 5,000 inhabitants. Thus Class V seems to be groups of sedentary, intensive agriculturists living in hamlets associated with ceremonial centers. Artifacts and architecture reveal a host of skills, and one cannot but wonder whether there were not, besides full-time priests, a few full-time craftsmen.

Class VI.—This class occurs only in the Huasteca of northern Veracruz, southernmost Tamaulipas, and northeast San Luis Potosí and is represented by the Los Flores and Pánuco phases. The period is not well studied, nor is much of the pertinent data concerning the Huastecs at the time of the conquest generally available. However, there is little doubt that these people, like their predecessors, were sedentary, intensive agriculturists. Sites range from camps along the coast through villages around ceremonial centers to huge ceremonial centers with large populations that must be considered cities. Two of the larger "cities" at Tamuin and Pánuco have not been mapped carefully but appear to cover an area of at least 5 square miles, while one site, on Ranch El Toro near Nuevo Morelos, Tamaulipas, covers about 6 square miles, and about 900 house platforms were counted in about one-quarter of the site. Material accomplishments are extremely numerous, and such complex items as metallurgy, writing, sculpture, and weaving of double cloth on a complex loom occur. Certainly, there were full-time specialists at this time.

Class VII.—This type of settlement pattern occurs only in the Sierra Madre of southwestern Tamaulipas and the Sierra de Tamaulipas. It appears to be very late, lasting into historic times, and is in part contemporaneous with the urban centers just south of it and the simple food-gatherers to the north.

TABLE 5

Northeast-ern Tamau-lipas	Southwest-ern Tamau-lipas	Sierra de Tamaulipas	Pánuco-Tampico	Class	Subsistence	Mode of Life	Size of Settlement (Popula-tion)	Type of Settlement
Catan and Browns-ville	San Antonio .... San Lorenzo	Los Angeles .... ?		VII	Agriculture and food-gather-ing	Sedentary	50–200	Small villages
			Pánuco (VI) .... Los Flores (V)	VI	Intensive agri-culture	Sedentary	50–25,000	Camps, villages, and cities
?	Palmillas .... Mesa de Guaje	La Salta Eslabones .... Laguna	Zaquil (IV) Pithaya (III)	V	Intensive agri-culture	Sedentary	10–5,000	Camps and hamlets near ceremonial centers
....	.... Guera	.... ?	El Prisco (II) Tancol .... Chila (I) Aguilar					
Abasolo	Flacco	Almagre	Ponce .... Pavon	IV	Agriculture	Sedentary	10–500	Camps and vil-lages
Repelo	Portales	La Perra	?	III	Food-gather-ing with in-cipient agri-culture	Semiseden-tary	10–60	Camps and caves
Nogales	Infiernillo	Nogales		II	Food-gathering	Seasonally nomadic	10–60	Camps and caves
		Lerma (Dia-blo?)		I	Hunters	Nomadic	4–10	Temporary camps and caves

In the Sierra de Tamaulipas the Los Angeles Phase, found in the excavation of five caves and at six open sites, is an example of this class, as are the San Antonio and San Lorenzo phases of the Sierra Madre, represented in three caves and three open sites. Foodstuffs from the caves reveal that they were basically corn, bean, and squash farmers who did some food-collecting and hunting. It may be inferred from this type of subsistence, as well as from their relatively thin layers of refuse, that, though sedentary some of the time, they were occasionally on the move in search of game and wild-food plants. Open sites range from ones covering 500 to 60,000 square feet, and wattle

and daub, as well as postholes, reveal that they had permanent house structures. From the foregoing data, they appear to be much like Class IV found
at the lowest level at Pánuco. However, their material culture is far less complex than at Pánuco. Flint tools and particularly arrow points are more
prevalent, and there are no figurines. Thus this final class is characterized by
sedentary agriculturists with a simple material culture who did some food-
gathering and lived in small villages.

In Table 5 the regional sequence of phases is correlated with the classes
of settlement patterns and their characteristics: subsistence, mode of life, size
of settlements, and kinds of settlement.

As is obvious, full data from every region about all classes of settlement
patterns are still not available. However, even from the meager data now
available it appears that we have three regional developments of settlement
patterns in northeastern Mexico—one in the region north of the Soto la Marina River, one in the mountains of southern Tamaulipas, and one in the lowlands of southern Tamaulipas and northern Veracruz and San Luis Potosí.

SETTLEMENT PATTERNS—PERU

By ALFRED KIDDER II

WHEN Peruvianists consider very broadly what has been learned during the last twenty years about the linked cultures comprising what Wendell Bennett called the "Peruvian co-tradition," they can congratulate themselves for having so enlarged our perspective of one of the two major New World civilizations that it can now be studied in comparison with similar developments anywhere. It is inevitable, however, that, in so relatively short a time and with so comparatively little time and money actually spent in the field, there should be numerous gaps in our detailed knowledge of many regions and periods. We have, indeed, not yet passed the stage of exploration in a number of localities, and regional chronologies have not been sufficiently developed to relieve us from major dependence on the one worked out for the north coast in generalizing about Peruvian culture growth as a whole.

In this field of interpretation and comparative study we are still handicapped by the lack of enough data to raise our ideas from speculation to logical inference in large areas of both space and time. This is especially true in such related matters as population, settlement pattern, social structure, and the history of the nature of political institutions and of conflict between them. It was for these reasons that Bennett, in listing the major characteristics of the Peruvian co-tradition in 1947, could say no more on the subject of settlement pattern than: "The population is concentrated in villages or larger aggregates" (Bennett, 1948, p. 2). This was perfectly true in the most general way; the point is that, at the time, he could hardly have been much more specific, particularly in presenting a brief outline of changing patterns within the co-tradition.

Today, we find ourselves in a somewhat better situation, thanks largely to the work of the Virú Valley Expedition and particularly to the part of that co-operative project carried out by Gordon R. Willey. His work illustrates what can be done when the history of settlement pattern is regarded as a research goal. It also demonstrates that it is not easy to produce such results for a long range of time without a great deal of work, even under relatively excellent conditions.

In Peru generally, both on the coast and in the highlands, conditions for the study of pre-Columbian settlement patterns are comparatively good, especially for late periods. In both regions plant cover is either absent or very

148

light. This makes aerial photographs most useful on the desert, as Willey discovered. They could also be used to advantage in many parts of the highlands, although the great altitude of some of the highland basins makes the photography more difficult and expensive. It seems curious that more work has not been done on the very numerous coastal sites that show up so clearly from the air. I suppose it is attributable to more pressing concern with stratigraphy and grave excavation and that it is only a question of time before a much greater use of aerial survey will be made to supplement our increasing knowledge of the association of sites and parts of sites with pottery sequences.

Willey's Virú study (Willey, 1953; subsequent references to Virú, unless otherwise specified, are drawn from this work) stands as the pioneer work on the settlement pattern for the central Andes and, as such, provides a history to which the little information we have from elsewhere can be compared. In so doing, it must be kept in mind that Virú is a coastal valley of only medium size and hence cannot be expected to be entirely comparable to the larger valleys. It is also quite unlikely, although unproved, that highland settlement patterns would parallel those of the coast, save in the most general way.

No brief summary can possibly do justice to Willey's detailed analysis of Virú, in which dwellings, politico-religious structures, fortified sites, cemeteries, and public works are considered both separately and in conjunction as they form community patterns. These are then considered in relation to population and sociopolitical organization, with a final section, considerably longer than this paper, in which Virú patterns are compared to others in Peru and Bolivia. I do not intend, therefore, to summarize Willey's monograph but to consider the major periods of Peruvian history with constant reference to Willey's work as the single fairly complete history of settlement pattern known to us. Whether treated in this way or by any of a number of possible regional divisions, it will be apparent that the highlands are not so well known in this respect as is the coast.

Virú Valley did not produce any remains of early hunters, whose presence in the central Andes is to be tentatively inferred from some pressure-flaked points and scrapers from the north coast (Larco, 1948), the Nazca region (Strong, 1954, p. 216), and the Huancayo district of the central highlands (Tschopik, 1946). If these remains should prove to be clearly prehorticultural, we can probably safely infer a seminomadic camping pattern, as the rock shelters found by Tschopik in the Jauja Valley seem to indicate. Nothing further can be said at present about settlements of this virtually unknown period.

Peruvian prehistory really begins with the preceramic fishermen and at least part-time farmers, best known to us through Bird's work at Huaca Prieta (Bird, 1948) and that of Strong and Evans at Guañape in the Virú Valley

(Strong and Evans, 1952, pp. 17–46). These early north-coastal people, who lived at Huaca Prieta for over a thousand years (on the basis of carbon 14 dating), were oriented toward seashore and lower-valley life. I have always thought it amazing that no remains of deer turned up in the thousands of square feet of rubbish excavated by Bird at Huaca Prieta, a fact which tends to strengthen the opinion that these people were isolated near the river mouths and hence unusually static in terms of culture change. Settlements consisted of clusters of simple underground houses, as at Huaca Prieta, or conjoined, simple, above-ground houses with mud walls that follow underground houses in Virú. Although the rubbish mounds, in and on which these villages were built, are of considerable size, they were occupied for many centuries, as at Huaca Prieta, indicating a stable, well-adapted, but probably quite small population, unexposed to innovation and lacking the need for specialized structures. This pattern probably exists in other coastal spots where net fishing is good close to the beach but has not been found as such. I should expect it to appear, perhaps with variations in house type, in the shell heaps of the Ica Valley mouth and to the south of Nazca at Chavinia and Lomas, recently reported by Strong (1954, p. 216).

For this period we have absolutely no evidence from the highlands.

In view of the introduction of pottery, followed by maize, in the next major coastal period, one is tempted to postulate for the highlands, during the coastal preceramic periods, a more developed technology, correspondingly larger population, and larger villages, perhaps with simple ceremonial structures, foreshadowing those at Chavín de Huantar, for example. Until the highlands are well enough known to rule out this possibility, I shall continue to believe that the remains of some such culture will be found.

The transition from the Preceramic to full Formative, marked by the achievement of the major traits of the Peruvian co-tradition, is known only from the north coast. In Virú and Chicama valleys there was little change in settlement pattern from the lower-valley, beach-oriented life of Preceramic times. Pottery appears on the north coast at this time, but it is not until the advent of maize and the development of decorated monochrome wares of the full Chavín horizon style that the true Formative can be said to have begun. In Virú and Chicama at this time no great advance in domestic architecture had been made; the underground house probably persisted in some places near the coast but was largely supplanted by small, scattered dwellings, both round and rectangular, made of conical adobes. Small villages in groups, still mostly in the lower Virú Valley, suggest to Willey the beginnings of what he calls the "Nucleated Community," in which two or more villages support a "Capital." Specialized buildings, which can probably be called "temples," first appear at this stage. For other areas covered by the Chavín horizon we have little or nothing from which to determine a full settlement pattern. There are, however, striking regional differences when ceremonial structures are considered. Although pottery types from Ancón are virtually the same as those of Chavín itself and are very closely related to those of Virú, Ancón seems to lack large, specialized structures of any kind. At Supe a simple, rectangular, stone-and-adobe, altar-like platform may date from this period or even from the Preceramic. Farther north, in Casma and Nepeña, the elaborately painted clay reliefs of platform and temple buildings suggest the platform buildings of Chavín. In Virú, much simpler, rectangular, stone inclosures date from this general period. Willey has called them "community buildings" because they appear to have been integral parts of villages rather than special shrines removed from midden areas and dwellings. Llamas apparently were sacrificed in them, but they lack any indications of ever having been elaborately decorated. In Chicama true pyramid mounds of conical adobes may also have been built in Chavín times. We are thus faced with the problem of whether elaborate structures were present in all north-coastal valleys and have been too deeply buried for easy recognition, in Virú, for example, or whether only the people of the larger and richer valleys were able to afford them. This is important in assessing the general nature of the Chavín culture, since Bennett and others have called attention to the beginnings of a pilgrimage pattern at this stage. Sites like Chavín, Bennett believed, were not the centers of large communities but the ceremonial centers of regions from which their builders were drawn and to which people came from considerable distances to join in celebrations of the Chavín cult (Bennett and Bird, p. 136). This would accord well with the general impression, made more explicit by Willey, that Chavín sites are generally found near the seashore, in small side valleys, and in the smaller highland basins. Chavín art has a grandeur that was never quite equaled in Peru; but it apparently sprang from a relatively small and apparently rather scattered population, drawn together periodically by a religious force that did not yet require the addition of political and military power for wide acceptance and for the recruiting of labor.

The Late Formative period, marked by the white-on-red pottery horizon style, foreshadows many of the developments we think of as typically coastal Peruvian. Most of our evidence is from Virú, but there is some from the central coast, and more may be expected as a result of Stumer's work (Stumer, 1954, which presents a preliminary account of his continuing explorations in the Rimac Valley). In Virú canal irrigation was almost certainly being practiced, which would basically account for the obviously increasing population, the spread of villages to all major parts of the valley, and warfare, attested by hilltop forts. The older, "scattered-house" village pattern was largely replaced by conjoined groups of room or house units (Willey's "Agglutinated Type"). Large pyramid-platform mounds probably indicate politico-religious control. The "nucleated community" is still present but is more tightly spaced physically and, presumably, more tightly organized socially. A similar dwelling cluster is known from the Chancay Valley, apparently associated with a mound, but elsewhere in Peru, at what is considered to be the same general time period, there is no clear evidence of pattern, although underground houses have been reported from the northern highlands and the southern coast. Strong found rectangular wattle-and-daub houses of late Paracas date in Nazca, but their arrangement is not known (Strong, 1954, p. 216).

There is one highland site in Bolivia, at Chiripa in the southern Titicaca Basin, that has produced what may prove to be a village pattern characteristic of that region in pre-Tiahuanaco times (Bennett, 1936, pp. 413–36). There Bennett found fourteen rectangular houses of adobe on stone foundations, closely grouped in a circle around a central court. Unfortunately, we have nothing from the southern highlands with which to compare this arrangement of houses until much later. At Chanapata, near Cuzco, Rowe (1944, p. 14) found evidence of stone-house construction, as did I at Pucara, but, except for the fact that in neither case were rooms conjoined, we are ignorant of pattern. Apparently there were no specialized structures at Chiripa. Although only two of the fourteen houses were excavated, they were all of about the same size. If we take this as evidence, it would indicate that the introduction of the ceremonial inclosure of the Tiahuanaco-Pucara type, which is related to that of Chavín in general layout, and by the presence of sunken central inclosures, did not appear in the southern highlands until post-Chiripa times. This would be a dangerous assumption, however, since it is quite possible that Chiripa and its sister site of the same period on Pariti Island were small villages within the orbit of a center of pilgrimage as yet unknown. They would thus be comparable to my hypothetical pre-Chavín highland sites and to the villages from which it is believed pilgrims came to Chavín.

Following the white-on-red horizon, we are on the threshold of the Classic, or Florescent, stage of Peruvian history and have far more information to compare with that from Virú. Consequently, I shall have to speak in more general terms.

On the north coast and probably all along the coast, the valleys were fully exploited by irrigation. Large, agglutinated villages, with hundreds of rooms, often associated with pyramid mounds and large rooms or courts with decorated walls, are well exemplified by Bennett's Gallinazo excavations (Bennett, 1950). The largest pyramids, of the "castillo" type, and the famous Moche pyramids were built at this time. The same pattern is found on the central coast at Chancay and in the Rimac, and there is some evidence that it extends farther south to Chincha. In Nazca (Strong, 1954, p. 217) the wattle-and-daub tradition of house building persisted, in the form of compounds of rooms associated with platforms, mounds, and walls; we shall have fuller data when Strong's recent excavations are fully published.

We know little about highland settlements of this period. Recuay villages of the Callejon de Huaylas are smaller than the coastal villages and have underground rooms. Whether these were permanently used dwellings is not clear to me. In the southern highlands the large ceremonial centers, such as Tiahuanaco, Pucara, and others, are full of refuse, but houses are unknown except for the single Pucara example that consists simply of a rough outline of foundation stones. It is perfectly clear, however, that there was a village or town of considerable size near the Pucara temple structures. The quantity of refuse at Tiahuanaco, therefore, may in part be the product of the visitations of pilgrims and of sacrifices of llamas, but I believe the site was permanently occupied by more than a few nobles and priests and their retainers. This does not preclude, however, a much more scattered occupation of the Titicaca Basin or of any of the highland basins. In such regions arable land is to be found over a much wider area than it is in the irrigated coastal valleys, and herding would keep some of the population at considerable distances from the large centers. Speculatively, I should say that it is likely that in Tiahuanaco-Pucara times many Indians lived in scattered farmsteads of a few closely grouped buildings, as many of them do today. They may also have built small villages, like the one at Chiripa. My point is that, with farmland less restricted than on the coast and with herds to care for, the Titicaca highlanders, at least, were probably widely dispersed at this period. I also believe that this continued until fairly late, when large villages and towns begin to appear.

Perhaps the most interesting of the many new ideas to be found in Willey's monograph is that urbanism, which reached its peak in Chimu times on the north coast, may be of coast Tiahuanaco inspiration. The detailed studies made in Virú showed clearly that, with the coming of Tiahuanaco style and the probable military overthrow of the Mochica kingdom by its bearers, there were important changes in both domestic and "politico-religious-military" architecture, to use Willey's term. To quote him further: "Outstanding among the changes in site types are the decline of interest in the great pyramids or Pyramid-Dwelling-Palace ceremonial centers, the abandonment of the castillo-fortifications and the appearance of the planned enclosure or compound community." As he states, these trends have generally been associated with the Chimu culture—Bennett's last major pre-Inca epoch, which includes the Chimu kingdom, he called "City Builders" (Bennett and Bird, 1949, p. 201). Inclosures containing conjoined houses had been used in Virú from the Late Formative but never were so popular as the unwalled, agglutinated village. Willey believes that large inclosures, with symmetrically planned interior rooms, courtyards, and corridors, some with small platforms or mounds, were brought to Virú with the influx of Tiahuanaco ideas. They did not immediately displace all the agglutinated villages, but in Chimu and

Inca times several of the original ones, in Virú at least, continued to be used, and others were built.

Willey also makes a very convincing, if not conclusive, case for the introduction of the inclosure compound at Chanchan on the Tiahuanaco horizon. It is less probable, as he implies, that the same type of urban layout was introduced so early into the valleys north of Chanchan. These northern sites, surveyed by Schaedel (1951), are on the same grand scale as Chanchan and can be classified as "urban elite," with dwelling-palace-temple complexes within inclosures, and "urban lay" centers, lacking decorated rooms, mounds, and other refinements presumably limited to the nobility. This distinction in site types is mentioned because it stresses the obvious class distinction apparent in Peruvian society since at least the Early Classic and shows that, by Chimu times, it had been applied to whole urban populations. I do not know of any parallel situation in the New World.

Urbanism in Peru was essentially coastal, most highly developed in the north. Central coastal sites like Cajamarquilla and Pachacamac and as far south as Chincha, however, are of the same kind. All have been presumed to be very late, but in some cases there is reason to suspect that they, too, were of coast Tiahuanaco inspiration.

The suggestion of a Tiahuanacoid origin of the planned inclosure compound and of coastal urbanization as one of the results of its forced adoption raises the question of Huari, near Ayacucho. This large site, at which Bennett (1953) procured a pottery sequence in 1950, has high, walled inclosures, generally less regular and less obviously planned than those of the coast. In spite of Bennett's excavations, the main inclosures cannot be definitely ascribed to the Huari period, that of greatest Tiahuanaco influence. There does, however, seem to be a very real possibility that coastal inclosure compounds may be derived from Huari, since Strong (1954, p. 218) reports from Nazca "great towns or even cities . . . characterized by great rough stone enclosures and thousands of rooms." These are clearly on the Tiahuanaco horizon. It was Bennett's opinion that Huari influence on the coast was greatest in the Nazca region.

If we pursue this idea, we may perhaps conclude that the ultimate inspiration came from Tiahuanaco itself, with its great stone inclosures like Calasasaya. It is an intriguing possibility and one that it may be possible to explore further in the Cuzco region, where, according to recent word from Rowe, Tiahuanacoid sites are now being found.

While the coast developed urban centers, perhaps from an ultimate highland source, a more open pattern was retained in the highlands, even in Inca times. Cuzco was not a city in the sense that Chanchan was, for it consisted of a central imperial and ceremonial area separated from surrounding villages by fields. Towns and large villages did grow up in the Jauja Valley and the Titicaca Basin. Some of the former are very large, said to contain over five thousand round stone houses (Bennett, 1953, p. 16). They were fortified, in contrast to Titicaca towns, which had defensive forts on nearby hilltops. Many of these are probably pre-Inca, but this is often difficult to determine, at least in the Titicaca area.

We know, however, that the Inca built many new towns in their process of relocation of peoples. These were ideally laid out in square blocks, each containing one or more inclosures. Rowe (1946, p. 228) suggests that this idea may have returned to the highlands from the Chimu, which would complete a hypothetical circle of diffusion. By the time of the Spanish conquest, the town pattern was well established and was retained, in spite of heavy depopulation, since it was well suited for control of the Indians. With increased population since colonial days, many Indians live in scattered house clusters in the Titicaca area, perhaps resuming a pattern that goes back to Tiahuanaco times or even earlier.

Although there is still a great deal to be done on the coast, there is even more to be done in the highlands before the history of their settlement patterns can be compared to produce a reasonably complete picture of the society of prehistoric Peru as a whole.

THE RECONSTRUCTION OF SETTLEMENT PATTERN IN THE SOUTH AMERICAN TROPICAL FOREST

By BETTY J. MEGGERS AND CLIFFORD EVANS, JR.

THE Tropical Forest area of South America is unusual among the archeological areas of the New World, in that it is predominantly associated with a single level of cultural development. The non-pottery-making groups that were the first settlers rarely left any trace, and advanced cultures never gained a permanent foothold. The typical site thus represents the relatively simple level of culture still observable in living Tropical Forest groups. Under these circumstances the analysis of settlement patterns cannot be expected to provide the insight into the evolutionary development of culture that it does in other parts of the New World. From the point of view of the archeologist working in the Tropical Forest area, however, there is another equally important role: elaboration of the description of the extinct cultures so that they can be compared with living groups. Identification of the type of culture represented by the archeological sites is a prerequisite to any attempt to establish the relative antiquity of the Tropical Forest pattern in different parts of the culture area. Reconstructions of the place of origin of this type of culture and the direction and rapidity of its spread also depend for evidence on the ability to recognize the archeological version.

The attempt to describe and interpret archeological settlement patterns in Tropical Forest South America suffers from two severe handicaps. First, the building materials were of a perishable nature, leaving no direct evidence of house construction or village composition. Decomposition of vegetal products is so rapid and complete that even post molds do not remain. Hence interpretation of the prehistoric settlement pattern must rely on generalized features of the site itself and on inferences stemming from correspondences with the ethnographic situation. It is here that the second handicap appears. There is an almost complete absence of detailed information on the location and extent of archeological sites in the greater Amazon area, and similar information is rarely to be found in ethnographic reports. However, although the ensuing discussion depends specifically on evidence collected at the mouth of the Amazon and in Brazilian and British Guiana, the general problems and interpretations are probably applicable to the Tropical Forest area as a whole.

The deficiencies in the archeological record, stemming from the simple level of development of the culture involved and the lack of survival of perishable materials under tropical conditions of climate, make it essential to draw upon ethnographic data in making interpretations of settlement pattern. In order to do this, it must first be established that the past and present cultures are similar in general type or level of development. This can be done by comparing certain features. If these show a similarity, the functional interdependence of cultural traits makes it seem probable that other aspects of the culture were also similar. In the Tropical Forest area the archeological remains consist principally of the pottery complex and the location and area of the site. The first is too slightly known on the ethnographic level to be of much use in making a cultural correlation, but the second serves the purpose very well.

Marajó Island in pre-European times was occupied by five different groups, distinguishable not only ceramically but also in village location. The Ananatuba Phase avoided the coast and navigable streams, selecting a place at the edge of the forest adjacent to open savanna (Fig. 1, *a*). The succeeding Mangueiras Phase also preferred the forest and avoided the coast but typically settled on or close to a navigable stream (Fig. 1, *c*). The Formiga Phase differed from both these in choosing a site on the open savanna, as did the Marajoara Phase (Fig. 2). The villages of the Aruã Phase were situated in the forest on the bank of a stream not far inland from the coast (Fig. 1, *b*). The distinctive character of these settlement patterns reinforces the judgment based on ceramic evidence that we are dealing with separate and independent cultures, although it is not possible to identify them as tribes. On the adjacent mainland, where the terrain is more uneven, sites are along stream banks on land high enough to escape annual flooding in the rainy season. The area covered by sherd refuse is variable but generally small, and the site seriations do not suggest a large number of contemporary villages. It can be inferred that both village size and population density were low. In the later phases the shallowness of the refuse deposits suggests that villages were of short duration.

An examination of the ethnographic evidence on village size and location shows that advantages of defense, comfort during the rainy season, and proximity to gardens or fishing grounds are differently weighed by living Tropical Forest tribes. Some select high banks along a large stream, others the headwaters of a creek, still others the depths of the forest. While high land is most often chosen, some settle on islands or lowlands likely to be inundated in the rainy season. Villages are usually of short duration, with five years being an average period of occupation. Population is typically small, although some Tupinambá settlements are reported to have numbered more than a thousand individuals.

The settlements of living and extinct groups in the Tropical Forest thus fall into a single range of variation in village size, location, and permanency. The quality of the ceramics, including technique of manufacture, variability

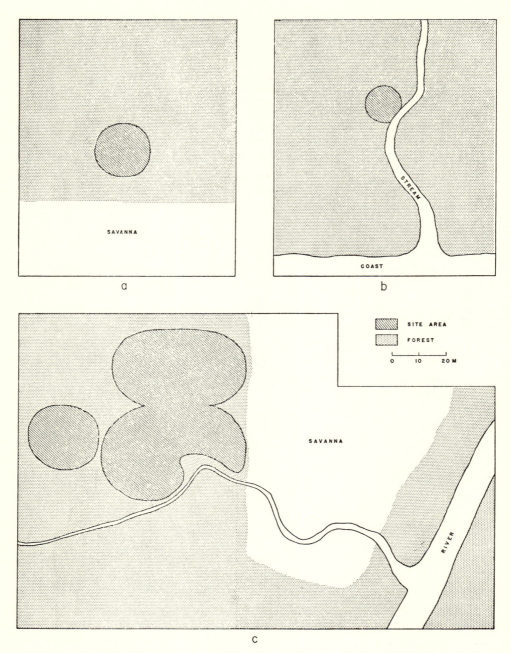

Fig. 1.—Typical settlement patterns of the Tropical Forest archeological cultures on Marajó Island. *a*, Ananatuba Phase (J-9: Ananatuba); *b*, Aruã Phase (J-11: Carmo); *c*, Mangueiras Phase (J-5: Croarí).

of vessel form, and simplicity of decoration, is also comparable. This evidence leads to the conclusion that the majority of the archeological cultures on Marajó Island and the adjacent Guiana mainland are extinct representatives of the ethnographically defined Tropical Forest pattern of culture.

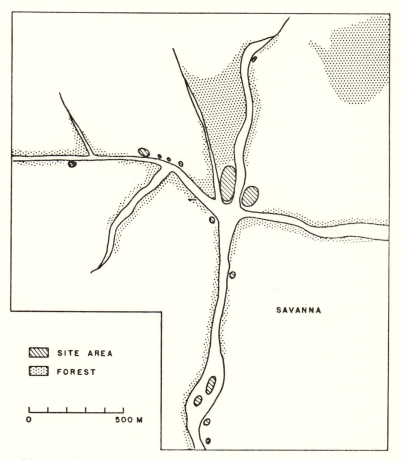

SAVANNA

▨ SITE AREA

▒ FOREST

0   500 M

Fig. 2.—Marajoara Phase settlement pattern: mounds of the Fortaleza group after a field map by Farabee (1914).

This being the case, it is possible to draw upon ethnographic evidence to reconstruct the house type of the extinct cultures. Among living Tropical Forest tribes, both communal and single-family houses are constructed, with communal houses being the more frequent. These vary from structures housing three to eight families (Omagua, Tapirapé) to immense dwellings sheltering several hundred people (Apiacá, Tupinambá). Measurements range from 4 by 10 meters or less to structures 150 meters long. The floor plan may be circular, rectangular, or elliptical. Village composition is also variable between tribes, the alternatives being a single communal house, several communal houses, or several single-family houses. Multiple dwellings may be arranged around a central plaza, in a row or rows, or scattered about the clearing.

In attempting to apply this information to the archeological situation, the first thing to be determined is whether there is any general consistency in site area within each phase and whether this differs between phases. Since no physical remains of the houses exist, the area of the site offers the most promising clue. In this respect there are distinct differences between the archeological cultures. On Marajó Island, sites of the Ananatuba Phase are circular or oval, with an area of between 500 and 770 square meters. Mangueiras Phase sites are much larger, covering an area frequently ten times as great as those of the Ananatuba Phase (Fig. 1, a and c). Formiga Phase sites are intermediate in area, and those of the Aruã Phase are the smallest of all, typically covering less than 300 square meters (Fig. 1, b). In Brazilian Guiana, habitation sites are very large. Those of the Mazagão Phase range from 4,160 to 6,600 square meters, while those of the Aristé Phase cover 7,854 square meters.

If these cultures are extinct representatives of the Tropical Forest pattern of culture, then the house types reflected in these differences in site area are of three sorts: a single communal house, several communal houses, or several single-family houses. In the case of the Aruã Phase, it is readily apparent which of these alternatives represents the village composition. Aruã Phase sites are much too small to have been produced by anything but a single communal house of the type still used by many unacculturated tribes in the Guianas, where the Aruã lived before moving to the islands. Sites of the Ananatuba Phase also fall within the dimensions recorded ethnographically for a single communal house. Since the Ananatuba Phase communal house is larger than that of the Aruã Phase, we may conclude that there was a comparable increase in village population. Mangueiras Phase sites differ considerably in area, and, although some are small enough to equate with a single communal house, others are much too large. One of the latter, however, is differentiated into three approximately circular mounds of refuse that suggest three communal houses (Fig. 1, c). If this analysis is correct, Mangueiras Phase villages are more variable in size than those of the other Tropical Forest cultures on Marajó Island, being composed of one communal house or several houses arranged in a cluster. The village composition of the archeological cultures of Brazilian Guiana cannot be decided so easily. The site area corresponds to that in the Mangueiras Phase, but the sherd density is considerably less. This could be explained equally well by two alternatives: (1) a number of single-family houses or (2) several large communal houses. This ambiguous situation and the lack of consistency in size and composition between sites of the Formiga Phase on Marajó Island illustrate the limitations that surround the attempt to interpret village composition on the basis of site area and comparative ethnographic evidence. Only where the solution is reasonably clear cut, can this kind of approach be used with any degree of confidence.

The interpretation of non-material aspects of a culture on the basis of settlement pattern has limited possibilities. Having identified the majority of the archeological phases as extinct representatives of the Tropical Forest pattern of culture, we can reliably assume that social organization was based on kinship, as it is among living tribes, and that there was little, if any, occupational specialization or institutionalized leadership. The only site differentiation that exists in these archeological cultures is between habitations and cemeteries. The absence of cemeteries in some of the phases does not, of course, argue against a belief in an afterlife and a systematic method of disposal of the dead. However, the concept of a cemetery, which was used over a longer period of time than any single village and probably by several contemporary villages, is a more complex idea. Whatever its origin, there is no evidence that this trait was developed independently in the Guianas or at the mouth of the Amazon. It is not present among the early cultures here and makes its appearance only a few centuries before European contact, associated with cultures that are clearly intrusive from the north and northwest.

Some of the archeological Tropical Forest cultures deviate from their modern counterparts in one significant respect. The two earliest ceramic cultures on Marajó exhibit considerably greater village permanency than do the later ones and represent a duration far in excess of any recorded ethnographically. This indicates that none of the explanations for frequent moving of the villages cited for living groups were applicable at that time, including the conclusion that abandonment of the village at the death of a member was not a trait of these early cultures. On the other hand, questions arise about the subsistence of these early Tropical Forest–like cultures. Marajó Island is notoriously poor for agriculture, and it does not seem probable that villages of several hundred people could have been supported in a limited region for several hundred years if agriculture were a major source of food. However, there is the possibility that the initial agriculturalists may have found the soil more fertile than they left it to their successors or that the facilities for hunting, fishing, and gathering may have been abundant enough to compensate for this deficiency. Whatever the cause, it should be determined whether a decline in village permanency is widespread in the Tropical Forest area or whether it is unique in this instance.

One culture to occupy Marajó Island in pre-European times does not present a settlement pattern of the Tropical Forest type. The groups of artificial mounds, up to 255 meters long and 10 meters high, that comprise the Marajoara Phase villages are public works of a scope not associated with a Tropical Forest level of social organization. The number and size of these mounds presuppose a well-developed leadership and an occupational division of labor, so that food production was carried on by a segment of the society instead of being a universal occupation as it is in the Tropical Forest level of culture.[1] The fact that the cemetery mounds are an integral part of the village, rather than set apart in remote and isolated spots, implies a different attitude toward the dead than pertained in the Tropical Forest level cultures where cemetery burial was practiced. Although evidence is incomplete, there is the suggestion that the burial mounds, which contain quantities of beautifully decorated pottery, the majority of the fragments not associated with any particular burial, may have functioned as ceremonial centers or, at the least, that the burial of an important person was accompanied by a funeral of considerable elaboration in goods and ritual. The fact that the cemeteries represent secondary burials (except in the late period when cremation was adopted) makes the situation especially interesting.

The Marajoara Phase is intrusive at the mouth of the Amazon. Detailed analysis of its affiliations (Meggers and Evans, 1957) indicates its probable derivation from the northwestern part of South America. The archeology of the latter region is almost completely unknown, and proof of this hypothesis will not be forthcoming until the situation is remedied. In the meantime, certain aspects of the Marajoara Phase settlement pattern are suggestive of the type of environment to be sought. First, the sites are found on the savanna half of the island, and none are reported from the western, forested part or from the vicinity of the coast. Further, no Marajoara Phase sites have been found along the Amazon, the route that the culture presumably followed from its point of origin to Marajó Island. Whether this was because the culture, unused to coping with a forest environment, did not find the situation congenial or simply because the banks were already occupied, we cannot positively decide. However, the fact that the presence of inhabitants of the Tropical Forest level of culture on Marajó Island did not hamper settlement of the invaders there suggests that the environmental explanation may be valid. If this is so, the point of origin should be sought in more open terrain, in the forested lowlands in the northwestern part of South America. The second clue from settlement pattern exists in the construction of earth mounds as house foundations and burial spots. This may be a secondary adaptation to the rainy-season inundation of much of the island rather than a trait belonging to the ancestral culture. On the other hand, artificial mounds are more characteristic in northwestern South America than in other parts of the continent. Since people tend to prefer an environment that resembles that of their homeland, the choice of an open terrain as opposed to a forest habitat may be the best clue to derivation. It is at least the most specific in narrowing the beginning of the search, since evidence from comparative material culture

1. Social differentiation and occupational specialization are also suggested by ceramic development and by differential treatment of the dead.

is almost equally suggestive over a wide expanse, including Ecuador, Colombia, western Venezuela, Panama, and Central America.

A critical evaluation of the role of settlement-pattern data in archeological interpretation will differ from area to area. It is our opinion that such evidence is invaluable in the reconstruction of the past in the Tropical Forest area of South America and, in fact, is almost the only means by which something approaching a well-rounded description of the past cultures can be attained. The paucity of other evidence means that, if this possibility is not utilized, archeology is confined almost entirely to the description and manipulation of pottery types and ceramic sequences. While these will always provide the basic distinction between phases and the chronological framework, details of settlement pattern bring out strong contrasts between the archeological cultures of the Tropical Forest pattern on Marajó that are not revealed in the details of the pottery. Compare, for example, a brief sketch of the Ananatuba Phase with that of the Aruã Phase and note how much of the description is inference based on settlement pattern:

Ananatuba Phase: A single communal dwelling large enough to house between 100 and 150 individuals constituted a village, which was located in a clump of forest at the edge of the savanna. All evidence derived from village location and duration (estimated as typically 100 years) points to a quiet, peaceful existence, uninterrupted either by exhaustion of the food supply or by raids from belligerent neighboring tribes. Two comments can be made about burial practices, both negative ones: (1) surface or mound urn burial was not the method of disposal of the dead, and (2) abandonment of the house at the death of an occupant was not a custom of the culture. Ananatuba Phase ceramics are of good quality and include the only well-developed decorated type (Sipó Incised) present in the Tropical Forest archeological phases. No figurines or other objects of possible ceremonial use were found, suggesting that concepts of the supernatural were not well developed.

Aruã Phase: These people lived in very small communities probably typically composed of a single communal house sheltering a dozen or less families, located near the coast on the shore of a navigable stream. This proximity to a ready route of travel and the extremely short duration with which the majority of the sites were occupied give an impression of mobility to the Aruã culture that contrasts strongly with the sedentariness of the earlier phases. There is a possibility that abandonment of the village was customary at the death of an occupant, a practice frequent in the Guianas today. Aruã dead are given a secondary burial in urns set on the surface of the ground in isolated cemeteries, which must have served several villages and probably continued in use when the villages were moved. Aruã pottery is sherd-tempered and rarely decorated. Crude pottery figurines and the existence of well-defined cemeteries are evidence of simple religious development.

In making interpretations of this sort, archeologists are handicapped not only by the limitations of their own evidence but also by the paucity of data available on comparable aspects of the living cultures. In the Tropical Forest area, this is partly because of the scarcity of complete ethnographies and partly because the importance of information on settlement pattern as a link with the past has not been emphasized. Since settlement pattern is not haphazard but bears a functional relationship to many of the non-material aspects of the culture, a better understanding of what this relationship is in living cultures would make it easier for the archeologist to interpret his data fully and accurately.

While it is possible to carry this sort of interpretation too far, it seems probable that, as long as the inferences are labeled as such, the risk of too much speculation is more than compensated for by the advantages of achieving at least a minimal reconstruction of the culture, especially of its non-material aspects. Such an achievement makes it possible to relate the present and the past and produces archeological evidence applicable to the solution of general anthropological problems. While the procedure outlined in this paper may not be useful or desirable in other areas of the New World, where the archeologist has a more complete "skeleton" of the once-living culture available to him, it is our feeling that the fullest possible interpretation of settlement-pattern evidence is essential for an understanding of prehistoric adaptation in the Tropical Forest region of South America.

SETTLEMENT PATTERNS IN THE CARIBBEAN AREA

By IRVING ROUSE

THIS paper is concerned with the West Indies, the coastal sections of Venezuela and northeastern Colombia, and the islands off the coast, such as Aruba, Curaçao, and Trinidad. Central America and Yucatán, on the western side of the Caribbean, are excluded, on the grounds that they are culturally divergent.

In eliminating the latter regions, we implicitly reject Steward's (1948) conception of a Circum-Caribbean culture area. We are inclined, instead, to agree with Kirchhoff (1952, p. 25) when he incorporates the main part of the Caribbean in his Amazonian superarea and divides the rest of it between his Chibchan and Meso-American superareas. We shall here discuss only those sections of the Caribbean which are neither Chibchan nor Meso-American in Kirchhoff's terminology.

One of the characteristics of the Caribbean area, as here defined, is that it was occupied by tribes on different levels of cultural development, who sometimes lived side by side. In the time of Columbus these included (1) Indians who subsisted by hunting, fishing, and gathering without the practice of agriculture and who generally also lacked pottery; (2) tribes which practiced agriculture and made pottery but which had a relatively simple social organization and religion; and (3) agricultural, pottery-making Indians with chiefs, social classes, and rather elaborate forms of religion, characterized by the presence of priests, temples, and idols. It has become customary to call the Indians of group 1 "Marginal"; those of group 2, "Tropical Forest"; and those of group 3, "Circum-Caribbean" (Steward, 1947).

An example of the coexistence of these three groups of Indians may be drawn from Venezuelan ethnology: the Warrau, who inhabited the delta of the Orinoco River, were Marginal; their closest neighbors, at Araucay (now Barrancas) just above the delta, had a Tropical Forest type of culture; while the tribes around Cumaná, farther to the west, may be classified as Circum-Caribbean (Rouse, 1953b, pp. 25, 78–80; MS). The situation in Cuba provides another example: the Ciboney on the western tip of that island were Marginal; the so-called sub-Taino in the center were Tropical Forest; and the Taino in the east were Circum-Caribbean (Rouse, 1948, pp. 542–43).

While it is manifestly difficult to apply an ethnological classification like this to archeological remains, where, for example, there is no direct evidence

165

of chieftainship and social class and the temples and idols may have been made of perishable materials which have left no traces, nevertheless it would seem reasonable to assume that those sites which contain no traces of agriculture or of pottery were inhabited by Marginal Indians. The sites which have pottery and agricultural utensils (particularly griddles used to bake cassava) may be presumed to have been occupied by Tropical Forest Indians, unless there is appreciable evidence of ceremonialism in the form of special religious or burial structures, amulets, idols, etc., in which case the occupants can be identified as Circum-Caribbean (Rouse, 1953a, pp. 194–95). We shall proceed on the basis of these assumptions.

Recent stratigraphic excavations have made it possible to set up a series of four periods in the Caribbean area, numbered from I to IV. Period I appears to have been a time of settlement of the Caribbean by Marginal Indians; we now know sites of these Indians throughout the Greater Antilles (except for Jamaica) and along the eastern and western coasts of Venezuela. Period II is marked by the arrival of Tropical Forest Indians, who first settled on the mainland and then expanded out into the Antilles as far as Puerto Rico. It is probable that these Tropical Forest newcomers took over the more fertile land from the Marginal tribes, pushing them aside into the poorer terrain. During Period III the Tropical Forest people continued to expand at the expense of the Marginal tribes, from Puerto Rico into the rest of the Greater Antilles. At the same time, we find the beginnings of ceremonialism in Puerto Rico and the Dominican Republic; and it is probable that similar developments were taking place on the mainland. These developments reached their climax during Period IV with the appearance of true Circum-Caribbean culture in three widely separated parts of the Caribbean: (1) the Greater Antilles, centering again in Puerto Rico and the Dominican Republic; (2) the central part of Venezuela; and (3) the Santa Marta region of Colombia. This apparently produced the coexistence of Marginal, Tropical Forest, and Circum-Caribbean tribes which occurred ethnologically, as noted previously.[1]

MARGINAL SETTLEMENT PATTERNS

The Marginal sites along the north coast of South America have been so recently discovered and are still so poorly known that they cannot yet be profitably discussed from the standpoint of settlement patterns. Those in the Greater Antilles will be dealt with descriptively, but lack of chronology makes it impossible to fit them into the sequence of four periods which has just been outlined. It is customary to identify all these sites as "Ciboney," on the assumption that they were occupied by the Marginal tribe of that name which existed in Cuba and Haiti at the time of Columbus; but one should not

1. It should be pointed out that no evidence of Circum-Caribbean culture has been found in the Cumaná region, although it is known there ethnologically, as stated above. This exemplifies the weakness of our archeological classification, but it is the only such instance known to us.

conclude from this that the sites were inhabited only during the later periods and only by the Ciboney or their direct ancestors.

Harrington (1921, II, 385–86) was the first to characterize the Ciboney settlement pattern, as follows:

In eastern Cuba, particularly in Baracoa, the characteristic habitat of this culture is the rock shelters and cave mouths along the coast, and in the stream gorges near it; but sometimes open-air village-sites of these people may [also] be found in these places. On the western end of the island open-air village-sites are frequent and large in places where good fresh water could be obtained convenient to the coast, and caves showing occupancy are abundant, not only near the coast but near streams far inland.

To this may be added our impression that the Ciboney sites are situated without regard for the availability of cultivatable land. More often than not, especially along the south coast of the island, where there are large concentrations of sites, the open-air sites lie on small islands in or adjacent to swamps and along channels in which fishing could most profitably be carried out (Cosculluela, 1951, p. 139).

These statements apply not only to Cuba but also to Hispaniola and Puerto Rico, where caves are again a favorite place of habitation and open-air sites likewise occur on high land along the shore, often near marshes. The only known concentration of interior sites—and this is still on the coastal plain—is in northern Haiti, where the sites of the Couri culture are located in a former savanna region, which contrasts sharply with the forested regions in which the nearby Tropical Forest and Circum-Caribbean sites are found (Rouse, 1941, p. 51).

Detailed surveys of sites have been made in the Maniabón Hills of north-central Cuba and in Puerto Rico (Rouse, 1942, 1952). In both cases the number of sites is small, indicating a relatively sparse population. As suggested elsewhere (Rouse, 1942, p. 134), the sparsity of population in the Maniabón Hills may have been due to the scarcity in that region of the marshes and caves which the Ciboney preferred as places of habitation, but this can hardly have been true of Puerto Rico. It seems probable that the size of the Ciboney population was limited by its primitive means of subsistence.

Most sites, whether in caves or in the open, consist simply of deposits of refuse and are quite small and shallow. Rather than term them "village sites," as in the statement of Harrington cited above, we have speculated that they are the remains of camps, occupied only briefly by small, independent bands of Indians (Rouse, 1941, pp. 50–52). The refuse almost invariably contains large amounts of shells, which testify to the importance of shellfish in the diet of the Indians.

There are no traces of dwellings or ceremonial structures. In the absence of references to houses in the historic sources, García Valdes (1948, p. 504) has suggested that the Ciboney probably constructed no "more than the simplest windbreaks of brush or palm thatch." Burials have been found in the cave

sites of Cuba; some are primary, some secondary, and some apparently crema-
tions (e.g., Harrington, 1921, II, 336–42). While the evidence is not clear, it
seems likely that these burials were placed directly in the refuse, with or
without grave objects.

A special problem is provided by a series of mounds in the marshes along
the south coast of Cuba, which are known locally as *caneyes*. These are considerably larger than the usual Ciboney sites, measuring as much as 40–50
meters in diameter and 3 meters high. Some are composed only of shell refuse,
but others consist of alternate layers of earth and refuse, which have apparently been artificially constructed. Most seem to be places of habitation, but
several have been called burial mounds because they contain the same forms
of burial as those found in the caves and rock shelters (Pichardo Moya, 1945,
pp. 61–63; Cosculluela, 1951, pp. 139–47). Remains of pile dwellings occur at
one place and may or may not be Ciboney (Cosculluela, 1951, pp. 147–50).

These mounds raise a number of questions, which cannot be answered at
the present time. Were they originally inhabited during Period I or II, when
the sea level was probably lower than at present, to judge from the evidence
in Florida (Rouse, 1951, pp. 21–34)? If so, the layers of earth might have
been added gradually to keep the settlements above the rising water. Or were
the mounds constructed at a later date, after the Tropical Forest Indians had
arrived in Cuba? In such a case they might represent a socially more advanced
group of Indians who were pushed back into the marshes by the newcomers.
It has also been suggested that the custom of erecting these mounds may have
diffused from Florida, where similar structures occur (Rouse, 1949, p. 127).

TROPICAL FOREST SETTLEMENT PATTERNS

The Tropical Forest sites of the West Indies are likewise concentrated
along the shores, although some occur inland as well. In Puerto Rico, for
example, our survey has showed that the Tropical Forest Indians inhabited
only the coast when they first arrived during Period II but that they pene-
trated into the interior in increasing numbers during Period III, i.e., during
the time of transition from Tropical Forest to Circum-Caribbean culture
(Rouse, 1952, pp. 566–68). Both Fewkes (1914, p. 663) and De Hostos (1941,
pp. 50–53) have noted that more sites occur on the south or west shores of the
islands than anywhere else. As De Hostos (1941, p. 51) explains this,

The south coast . . . is more protected than the north from the prevailing winds. . . .
The more exposed portion of the coast, the eastern, was the less populated. Whenever
the conditions of habitability concurred on any point of the southern coasts—water and
food supply, accessibility, defensibility and soil fertility—the place was occupied. . . .
Of course, settlements were principally made on the shores of tranquil bays, bordered
by wide sandy beaches or on or near the mouths of rivers.

All this suggests that, while the Tropical Forest Indians of the islands did
practice agriculture, they still relied upon fishing to such an extent that it
influenced their choice of sites.

On the mainland, by contrast, the sites are as common inland as along the shore. They occur most frequently along streams and around lakes, where there is fertile land and a good water supply. While the evidence is not conclusive, the Tropical Forest Indians seem to have had a preference for low land in the alluvial valleys; and they took advantage of natural eminences, on which they lived so as to escape from damp and flooded ground (Osgood and Howard, 1943, pp. 134–35).

Information as to the size of population is available only on the islands. Our survey of Puerto Rico has shown a steady increase in the number of sites during the Tropical Forest periods (II and III) to an estimated density of 2.5 people per square kilometer (Rouse, 1952, pp. 566–71). For the Maniabón Hills of Cuba, we similarly estimated a density of 1.6 people per square kilometer (Rouse, 1942, pp. 154–55). These figures indicate a relatively large population; they compare favorably, for example, with Kroeber's estimate of 0.5 person per square kilometer for America north of Mexico (Kroeber, 1934, p. 4).

The Tropical Forest dwelling sites are exclusively in the open air except in the Greater Antilles, where the Marginal custom of living in caves was followed in some cases (e.g., Rouse, 1952, Part 3, pp. 417–19). The sites consist of refuse deposits with or without shells, depending on the availability of shell food. No traces of structures are known, and it can be inferred from the historic sources that the Indians built huts of perishable materials (Lovén, 1935, p. 344). To judge from the sources, some were single-family houses and some were inhabited communally, but these two patterns cannot be distinguished archeologically, except that the relatively small, separate middens which occur at some sites probably mark single-family dwellings. They indicate an irregular arrangement of the houses (e.g., Rouse, 1952, Part 3, Fig. 17).

Studies of the distribution of pottery in the refuse show that the Indians moved their houses frequently from one part of the site to another (e.g., Rouse, 1952, Part 3, pp. 412–13). Because of such movements, it is difficult to estimate the size of the settlements, but they were certainly villages, in contrast with the camps of the Marginal Indians, and were occupied for a much longer period. It has been suggested that each village or group of contiguous villages was ruled by a chief or headman, as in historic time (Rouse, 1941, pp. 109–10).

For the most part, burial was directly in the refuse of the villages. Primary inhumation was the general rule, although there are some instances of urn burial as well, both on islands and on the mainland (e.g., Rainey, 1940, pp. 190–97). It was customary, throughout the area, to bury in caves apart from the places of habitation (e.g., Reichel-Dolmatoff, 1954c, p. 356).

Ceremonial structures are excluded by definition from the Tropical Forest sites. There are no burial mounds, such as the *caneyes* of Cuba, or religious buildings of any kind. Petroglyphs do occur, however, both along streams and in caves (e.g., Osgood and Howard, 1943, p. 135); and a few caves have yielded idols, suggesting the beginning of the use of caves for ceremonial purposes which reaches its climax in the Circum-Caribbean cultures (e.g., Rouse, 1942, pp. 149–50).

CIRCUM–CARIBBEAN SETTLEMENT PATTERNS

As already noted, the Circum-Caribbean cultures are limited to Period IV and to three widely separated regions: the Greater Antilles, central Venezuela, and the Santa Marta region of northeastern Colombia (Rouse, 1953, Fig. 2; Reichel-Dolmatoff, 1954c, Table 15, Tairona). These will be discussed separately, since there seems to be a different pattern in each region.

The development of Circum-Caribbean culture in the Greater Antilles was apparently marked by a shift in population center from the coasts to the interiors of the islands. This has been noted in both eastern Cuba (Harrington, 1921, II, 389) and Puerto Rico (Rouse, 1952, Part 4, pp. 569–70). It is probably to be correlated with a greater emphasis on agriculture at the expense of fishing, which in turn may be due to improvements in agricultural techniques, such as the reported development of irrigation in Haiti (Rouse, 1948, p. 522). The vulnerability of the coast to raids by the Carib, who seem to have entered the Antilles about this time, may have been another factor (Rouse, 1952, Part 4, p. 570).

In Puerto Rico our survey indicates that the population fell off during Period IV, and this, too, may be the result of the Carib raids (ibid.). One would expect a rise of population in the islands farther west, which were not so exposed to the raids, but the evidence is not at hand.

The same kinds of burial and dwelling remains are found as in the Tropical Forest sites. Grave objects are more common in some places (e.g., Herrera Fritot and Youmans, 1946). Another difference is that separate middens, each apparently representing a house site, are occasionally arranged around a central plaza (e.g., Rainey, 1941, Fig. 6). This corresponds to the settlement pattern described in the historic sources, where it is said that each village contained one or more dance plazas or ball courts, with the chief's house alongside (Lovén, 1935, pp. 94–96, 336–38).

The dance plazas or ball courts are rectangular or oval in shape. On flat land some consist simply of refuse-free areas, but in hilly country they have been made level by excavating the uphill side and piling the dirt on the downhill side. Many were lined with stone slabs, set upright and occasionally carved with petroglyphs, and several are accompanied by stone-paved or embankment-lined roads. Stone idols were set up in some of them, and carved amulets, as well as other evidences of ceremonialism, abound (e.g., Mason, 1941; Rouse, 1952, Part 4, Figs. 3, 5, 10; Boyrie Moya, 1955). Caves were also commonly used as shrines and have yielded numerous idols and petroglyphs (Lovén, 1935, pp. 125–34).

A difference of opinion has arisen as to whether the ball courts and dance grounds, like the cave shrines, were simply places of worship, to which the Indians went from surrounding villages, or whether they themselves formed parts of villages, as implied by the statements in the historic sources cited previously (cf. Alegría, 1951; Rouse, 1952, Part 4, p. 478). We suspect that both forms of settlement may have been present in the areas of greatest ceremonial development, i.e., in Puerto Rico and the Dominican Republic.

Turning to Venezuela, we may note the occurrence of mounds and earthworks in a rather restricted area extending from Lake Valencia in the Maritime Andes south and west through the Llanos to the base of the Andes proper in the state of Barinas (Osgood and Howard, 1943, p. 134). Around Lake Valencia these consist of domiciliary and burial mounds, and there is also evidence of pile dwellings (Bennett, 1937). Burial practices include primary and secondary inhumation, as well as urn burial; and grave objects are common, including numerous clay figurines. In the absence of detailed surveys, little else can be said about the settlement pattern, but Osgood (1943, p. 51) has commented that "the occupation of mounds as living sites suggests a multiplicity of groups, each perhaps under a person of some authority."

On the Llanos to the south and west are other, larger mounds; and these are frequently connected by causeways of earth, known as *calzadas*, which measure as much as 1–3 meters in height, 6–25 meters in width, and several kilometers in length (Osgood and Howard, 1943, pp. 50–52). It is assumed that they were constructed to raise the land above flood level. Cruxent (1952, p. 286) has suggested that they may have served the multiple function of thoroughfares, house platforms, agricultural terraces, and hunting preserves. Once again, they imply a fairly large population and a certain complexity of political and social organization (Osgood and Howard, 1943, p. 52).

The third group of Circum-Caribbean structures is situated in the mountains of the Sierra Nevada de Santa Marta in northeastern Colombia. It consists of house foundations and platforms; agricultural terraces; roads, bridges, and steps; and water reservoirs, all constructed of rough or dressed stone slabs and blocks. In addition, there are ceremonial courts, lined with earthworks; mounds of earth with stone sides, which seem to be burial or ceremonial sites; stone-lined graves; and urn burials (Mason, 1931–39; Bennett, 1944, pp. 92–95; Reichel-Dolmatoff, 1954a, b). All these are grouped together in villages, of which "there are several hundred . . . some of them of great extension and covering many square kilometers of terrain" (Reichel-Dolmatoff, 1954c, p. 361). Thus the population must have been unusually large.

Reichel-Dolmatoff (1954b, p. 164) assumes that each house was occupied by a single family. He notes that there are marked differences in the material found in the various structures, which suggest "social stratification, or at least a certain specialization of the owners." The political and religious organization, too, must have been complex.

SUMMARY

Of the various aspects of the concept of settlement patterns, the one to which the most attention has been paid in the Caribbean is that of relationship to the environment. It has been shown that the Marginal Indians (at least in the Greater Antilles) lived primarily along the shore and favored marshy regions, in which the fishing was best. The Tropical Forest people also lived primarily along the coast or on rivers but in areas suitable for agriculture as well as fishing. The Circum-Caribbean Indians, on the contrary, seem to have concentrated in the interior, where they must have had to place greater emphasis on agriculture.

The information on population is incomplete, but there would seem to have been a gradual increase in the number and size of the settlements from Period I, with its Marginal people, through Periods II and III, in which Tropical Forest sites predominate, and (at least on the islands) into Period IV, when the Circum-Caribbean remains make their appearance.

Relatively little can be said about the nature of the settlements themselves. It has been suggested that the Marginal sites were camps, occupied by small, independent bands of Indians. The Tropical Forest and Circum-Caribbean settlements can instead be considered villages, and the latter were probably linked together by relatively elaborate forms of social and ceremonial organization, of which there are traces in the form of ball courts, ceremonial plazas, mounds, and earthworks of various kinds. Some inferences have been presented as to the nature of the houses themselves and of the social groups which occupied them, but these are purely speculative.

AN APPRAISAL OF "PREHISTORIC SETTLEMENT PATTERNS IN THE NEW WORLD"

By EVON Z. VOGT

THE development and increasing use of the concept of "settlement pattern" in archeology is an aspect of a wide-ranging theoretical interest in "territoriality" as a critical feature in the study of animal and human life. Serious study of the phenomena is being currently pursued on many fronts. Biologists are concerned with territoriality as an aspect of the social behavior of wild vertebrates. The large literature on the subject with regard to birds has been reviewed by Margaret Nice (1941), and its status in mammals has recently been discussed by W. H. Burt (1943). The work of biologists like Konrad Lorenz with various species of fishes and birds is providing exciting results, and Lorenz' recent semipopular book, *King Solomon's Ring* (1952), is being widely read. Even more recently, Bartholomew and Birdsell (1953) have discussed the problem of territoriality with reference to protohominids. Ethnologists have long had a deep interest in discovering the nature of local groups and consider "locality" or "territoriality" as one of two major factors in the study of the basic principles of organization in primitive societies, the other being kinship groupings. In our social-anthropological studies of value systems on our southwestern project we have considered the question of the extent to which settlement patterns influence cultural values and vice versa as one of our primary research problems (see Vogt and O'Dea, 1953).

Through all these types of research there runs the common empirical concern of discovering in what patterned manner the members of a species are spread over a given territory and the common theoretical concern of interpreting what implications these facts about the size, composition, and arrangement of local groupings have for the social behavior of the species under consideration.

In my judgment, however, the concept of "settlement pattern" is a key one for the archeologist not only because the factor of "territoriality" is significant in many fields of inquiry but also because it provides an approach to inferences about physical environmental relationships, on the one hand, and to sociopolitical (and perhaps also religious) relationships, on the other. Use of the concept immediately gives the geographer, the archeologist, and the ethnologist a point of departure for talking about common problems concerning the ecological determinants of human settlement patterns and the interrelationships between settlement patterns and other features of cultures.

With these general comments as a background, I should like to raise three questions: (1) What is meant by the concept of "settlement pattern"? (2) Judging from the materials presented in this volume, how far can archeologists confidently go in making interpretations about settlement patterns and their interrelationships with other features of culture? And (3), assuming that the approach is a useful one, what are some of the primary research needs for the future?

I raise the question about the content and limits of the concept at the outset, for it is evident in the papers in this volume and others in the recent literature that there is some difference in the range of phenomena included. For example, some include consideration of the individual domestic house type, whereas others begin with analysis of the spatial arrangements of two or more dwellings. At the other end of the scale, some archeologists include the settlement arrangements of several communities over a fairly wide geographical area; others are inclined to limit the analysis to a single village or community plan.

Looking at the problems from the point of view of an ethnologist, I would definitely favor an analysis of settlement patterns which included the whole range. As I see it, this would include a description of (1) the nature of the individual domestic house type or types; (2) the spatial arrangement of these domestic house types with respect to one another within the village or community unit; (3) the relationship of domestic house types to other special architectural features, such as temples, palaces, ball courts, kivas, and so on; (4) the over-all village or community plan; and (5) the spatial relationships of the villages or communities to one another over as large an area as is feasible.

I include this whole range because of the importance of knowing as much as we can about the individual nuclear family or extended-family living arrangements, on the one hand, and about the larger intervillage relationships, on the other, which may give clues for inferences about political structure that would be missed if the analysis were limited to one village or community.

If the concept of settlement pattern is focused upon the patterned manner in which household and community units are arranged spatially over the landscape, one may raise the question as to whether the concept should or should not include an ecological dimension. There is perhaps a certain logical neatness in restricting the use of the concept to sheer spatial arrangements and then proceeding to make three kinds of analysis: one which explores the relationships of living arrangements to geographical features, such as topography, soils, vegetation types, or rainfall zones; a second which focuses upon the social structural inferences that can be made about sociopolitical and ceremonial organization; and a third which concentrates upon the study of change through time with a view to providing materials for generalizing about cultural processes. However, I would not seriously quarrel with the view that the concept of settlement pattern should include the ecological dimension at the outset and thereby provide the basis for the other two types of analysis.

Turning, now, to the second question, I should like to state that I have found it difficult in these brief comments to do justice to each individual paper, since each is incredibly rich in detail and highly suggestive of more general relationships that might be studied. Each clearly represents a careful and insightful codification of years of research that has gone on in various archeological regions in the New World.

In a general way, however, one can state that the interpretation of the relationships of prehistoric settlement patterns to ecology and to sociopolitical and ceremonial organization proceeds on the basis of two kinds of inference: (1) from living peoples of an area who are presumed to be cultural descendants and hence provide living models of what went before and (2) from universal properties of culture that are applied to a particular case. In this connection it is important to bear in mind that when an archeologist labels a certain object an arrow point or a metate, he has already made an inference about its use, based upon an observation of how these objects are used either by particular living peoples or by cultural groups in general. He has not observed firsthand the artifact being used in such a manner, and the fact that archeologists can write meaningful reports at all is based upon a confidence in the continuity and regularity of culture and not upon cold, empirical fact. It then becomes a matter of varying degree of probability as to whether the inferences he goes on to make about settlement patterns and their ecological and cultural contexts are correct or incorrect.

In general, the confidence with which an archeologist can proceed in his inferential interpretations depends upon the amount and nature of archeological data that remain to be studied and upon the closeness in time and in basic patterns that a specific historic or living culture bears to the prehistoric remains. These two requirements are most closely fulfilled in the case of the Southwest, and the competent papers by Haury, Reed, Wendorf, and Schwartz show us not only that it is possible to go quite far in convincing interpretations of settlement pattern in this area but also that we may begin to raise new questions and break exciting new ground by using this approach. I am particularly interested in Haury's analysis of the ecological factors involved in the location and permanence of southwestern settlements and in the development of pueblo-type domestic architecture; in the suggested relationships between settlements and kinship and ceremonial organization; and in his ideas about the development and use of distant farmhouses. The Hohokam case is more difficult, not because the archeological remains are scant, but because there is not the same kind of direct linkage to living cultural models. Even here, however, the implications of Hohokam irrigation canals for inferences about social organization and for their role in emancipating settlements from naturally occurring water are leads that merit further research.

I am also intrigued by the differences which Erik Reed sees in the village-plan layouts in the Southwest, and I agree with him that these differences must undoubtedly reflect basic variations in social organization and culture pattern. At the moment, I have no improvements to suggest over the correlations advanced by Schroeder, which I believe are well worth entertaining as working hypotheses. Fred Wendorf complements the contributions of Haury and Reed by tracing out settlement-pattern relationships in more detail in the Chaco Anasazi and the Tularosa Mogollon. The contrasts and similarities are brought into sharp focus on these smaller canvases. Finally, Schwartz's paper on the Cohonina takes off in a different direction with a focus upon demographic change. Settlement pattern per se is used as a starting point for inferences concerning changes in population. Taken together, the four papers form an impressive addition to our knowledge of prehistoric southwestern settlement patterns and their relationships to ecology, demography, and socioreligious patterns. In the future it would be interesting to take a close look at Athabascan settlement patterns. In connection with the Navaho Tribal Claims case it has become apparent from the work of Richard Van Valkenburgh, Malcolm Farmer, and others that it is easily possible to link Navaho archeological sites (with a complex that includes forked-pole hogan, sheep corral, and sweathouse) to living cultural units. We may learn much from this direct and more recent linkage from archeology to ethnology.

An opposite kind of case is presented in the stimulating Meggers and Evans paper on the Tropical Forest area of South America. I once spent some time on Marajó Island and surrounding regions of the lower Amazon and can well appreciate their general point about the necessity of employing interpretation to arrive at a description of the house type and village plan represented in the archeological remains. This is a case where the prehistoric data are scant but where the living presence of Tropical Forest tribes permits important inferences about settlement patterns and their ecological and cultural contexts. I was especially interested in the changes through time of settlement location on Marajó Island and in the suggested typology of settlement types: several single-family houses, single communal houses, and several communal houses.

A third kind of situation is presented in the cases of Peru, Middle America, northern Mexico, the Caribbean, the eastern United States, and California. In Peru and Middle America the archeological remains are rich, in fact, so rich in some respects that research into such mundane matters as settlement pattern has been pursued systematically only quite recently. On the other hand, while living Indian populations still occupy the areas involved, they have been vastly changed by centuries of Spanish political control, and many critical features of the aboriginal cultures must be teased out of ethnohistorical sources of variable value. In the other areas (northern Mexico, West Indies, eastern United States, and California) the prehistoric remains are also relatively good, but most of the living Indian populations have either been concentrated on reservations under conditions that have markedly changed their aboriginal settlement patterns or have long since disappeared or been removed from their pre-Columbian habitats.

In the case of Peru, the most remarkable research development, as Kidder has so ably discussed in his paper, has been the extent to which settlement patterns through time can be convincingly interpreted by intensive study of one coastal valley. We have a depth of knowledge about the Virú Valley through the combined use of aerial photography, mapping, site surveys, and excavations that far surpasses what we know about the rest of Peru. It is evident that the Virú Valley methods need to be applied to other sections of Peru; they could also provide a model for research in other comparable geographic areas. I am also impressed by how much the study of prehistoric Peruvian culture through time can tell us about long-range cultural process and development.

The four interesting Middle American papers bring us up to date on the settlement-pattern situation in the Maya area and the Valley of Mexico; they also take us into some frontier areas of research in raising new questions and exploring relationships between settlement pattern and other cultural features. The paper by Shook and Proskouriakoff provides us with at least three important research findings. There is, first, the definition of the basic settlement pattern of the area, one of town settlement, with its core of civic and religious buildings. This pattern is found to be dominant in all periods and in all but the most remote localities. This generalization certainly raises again the fundamental question as to why we do not find earlier non-town settlements in nuclear Meso-America, as we do, for example, in Peru, the Southwest, and the Southeast. Second, the assumption of a general trend toward increasingly dense centers of population is called into question. And, finally, we are provided with a careful analysis of changing settlement types in the region of Guatemala City. Each of these research findings has obvious implications for our study of cultural development in the New World.

The paper by Stephan F. de Borhegyi on the settlement patterns in the Guatemalan highlands is unique in the present series in the extent to which the archeological materials on settlement patterns are utilized as a point of departure for an ethnohistorical inquiry as to the degree of continuity existing between the pre-Columbian past and contemporary communities in this region. His method of analysis is convincing as he sets up a typology of settlement patterns and then raises alternative hypotheses which might be advanced to account for the differences. His conclusions to the effect that contemporary settlement patterns stem from old pre-Columbian types (rather than from differences in economic pattern, linguistic groupings, ethnic composition, geography, or religious activities in the present cultural scene) make a genuine contribution to our ethnological knowledge of highland Guatemala.

The situation in the Maya lowlands is cogently summarized by Gordon R. Willey. It is evident that a number of knotty problems exist in this area which are still being debated by the specialists. These problems are unlikely to be resolved until more actual data on the settlement patterns of the prehistoric Maya community are somehow teased out of the lowland jungle regions of the Petén and adjacent areas. Meanwhile, I like Willey's formulation of three ideal types which can serve as working hypotheses to guide research in this difficult archeological region. As research proceeds on the archeological problems, we should be able to look forward to illuminating connections with the ethnographic present and to more systematic comparisons with highland Guatemala and with the southeastern United States, where some of the settlement types may have been quite similar.

The Sanders contribution on the central Mexican region also breaks some new ground both in its temporal scope (it is the only paper in the series which carries the analysis through from prehistory to ethnohistory to the modern, urbanized metropolis) and in the ideas he presents concerning the importance of a "symbiotic region" in forming a prerequisite for the development of large, mass populations and complex civilizations. I hope he continues his thinking along these lines; within the next decade or so we should know enough about the Valley of Mexico for a full-scale monograph to appear which will trace through cultural developments from prehistory to the modern scene and translate this cultural history into statements of cultural process along the lines that Sanders has sketched in this paper.

The two papers on northern Mexico by Kelley and MacNeish take us into an exciting region for the exploration both of historical problems concerning interconnections between nuclear Meso-America and the Southwest and the Southeast and of ecological problems concerning the relations of settlement pattern to environment. Systematic work in this zone has been long overdue, and it is gratifying to discover that the work of Kelley, Mac-Neish, and others is beginning to yield real results. The Kelley paper is noteworthy in two respects: (*a*) the demonstration of the correspondence between ecology and culture in the northward extension of Meso-American culture along a narrow ecological zone of the eastern foothills of the Sierra Madre Occidental *ca.* A.D. 900–1350 and (*b*) the discovery that this northward extension of Meso-American culture mingled with a southward extension into the Chihuahua Desert of a basic southwestern pattern. As Kelley points out, this gives us a picture of a virtual continuum of sedentary cultures from central Mexico to the southwestern United States, and we should no longer think of a cultural hiatus separating these two centers of cultural development at this time level. Earlier in time, the problem of a hiatus still exists, since evidence to date suggests that both these developments in north-central Mexico and the northward spread of Meso-American patterns on the Pacific Coast are too late to account for the earlier historical connections that are presumed to have existed. I have discussed this problem with Kelley, Robert Lister, and others, and we are in substantial agreement that the next place to look for these earlier connections is in the Sierra Madre Occidental itself, especially near the crest or just to the east of where the sierra breaks off westward into its rugged barrancas leading down to the Pacific Coast.

The work of MacNeish on the northeastern periphery is notable not only because of the discovery of early maize in this region but also because of the extent to which it has been possible to sketch in a long developmental sequence (of the type that is still conspicuously absent in the archeology of nuclear Meso-America) for the Tamaulipas region. Why we do not get these earlier developmental levels in Mexico and Guatemala is certainly still something of a mystery, but it is evident that we are coming closer to the core in this able research of MacNeish's, and I hope it will be pursued with vigor.

The five stimulating papers on the eastern United States (including for the moment the Plains in these considerations) have much in common, in that each of the writers concerns himself with developmental shifts in settlement pattern over a long time span, and it is clear that we are now reaching the point in control of eastern archeological data where impressive syntheses along these lines are possible. Sears addresses himself to the basic problem of constructing a typology of settlement patterns in terms of "unit patterns" which run the gamut from camps, through villages, towns, and ceremonial units; and in terms of "complex patterns," which include ceremonial, village, and town clusters and a combination town and ceremonial unit. He then goes on to plot the over-all cultural development through time in terms of greater settlement-pattern complexity.

Ritchie's paper on the Northeast is also concerned with development of settlement patterns, which he interprets as a more or less continuous process of amplification in size and complexity. He also goes a long way in this area to infer the type of social and religious organization that probably accompanied these settlement-pattern changes over time. It is evident that both Sears and Ritchie are attempting to move from statements of cultural history to statements of developmental process, and, as tentative formulations along these lines, their hypotheses will serve as guide lines for the gathering of crucial data and the refinement of concepts as research proceeds in the eastern United States.

Griffin and Williams, writing on the Mississippi Valley situation, are more cautious. They play their archeological cards closer to their chests and attempt more modest interpretive syntheses, which properly warn us that, along with the broader interpretations, we must also move to fill in gaps in our present data. Griffin, in particular, feels strongly that we do not know enough yet about the northern Mississippi Valley and upper Great Lakes area to attempt a workable classification of settlement patterns. But his competent delineation of the problems concerning the appearance of burial mounds and the later more extensive and complex earthworks in Ohio Hopewell provides a challenge for further thought and research by both archeologists and ethnologists, especially since there is apparently a complete hiatus between these developments and almost anything we can discover on the later ethnographic time levels in this region.

Although Williams also deals with change over time, I am especially interested in the results which are appearing in the relationships between physiography and culture when the lower Mississippi Valley is subjected to close scrutiny. These connections are emerging with considerable clarity and promise to add importantly to our knowledge of culture-environment relations.

Wedel's paper on settlement patterns in the Great Plains adds another important chapter to our accumulating knowledge of the interaction between nature and culture in this region of North America. Although gaps in the data still certainly exist, Wedel's interpretation through ten thousand years or so of time is convincing and exciting. I wish that he had extended the analysis (if only briefly) to include some consideration of more recent historic and modern settlement patterns, which would then have provided an interesting comparison with Sanders' treatment of central Mexican patterns. But this can be done in the future, and, when it is done, the Plains should provide another region in which we can delineate a set of dynamic, interactive processes involving natural environment, human cultures, and historical forces operating from earliest settlement to the present.

Two major contributions stand out in the Heizer and Baumhoff paper on California settlement patterns. The first is the useful working division of California into nine archeological areas with some internal cultural coherence; the second is the able summary they provide of the settlement patterns, ecological adjustments, and population densities that can be inferred for each area. It is evident that this step had to be taken before further analysis was possible. As gaps in the data are filled in, we can look forward to solutions to some intriguing general problems, such as the question as to how far back in time the apparent regional isolation and diversity run and what their ecological and cultural determinants are.

Rouse's interesting contribution on the Caribbean area focuses on the problem of the relationship of settlement pattern to natural environment as he connects the Marginal Indians primarily with littoral habitats, Tropical Forest people with sites along the coast or on rivers where there were also agricultural possibilities, and the Circum-Caribbean peoples with mainly interior locations. The differences clearly indicate variations in subsistence running from fishing to fishing and agriculture to a focus upon agriculture. With this shift over time came a gradual increase in the number and size of settlements and probably a correlated development in degree of complexity of social and religious organization. Again we see the outlines of a series of long-range cultural developments that will be rewarding to compare not only with developmental sequences on the mainlands of North and South America but also with sequences in Micronesia and Polynesia when the work of Alex Spoehr and others provides the requisite data from the Pacific.

This brings me to my final question about research needs for the future. I mention, first, the need for a typology of settlement patterns. Not only is such a typology needed for analysis in any given area, but it is probable that interested archeologists and ethnologists might soon be thinking of working out a typology that could apply cross-culturally. I recognize, however, that the development and application of a cross-cultural typology of settlement patterns raise the important question as to the level of interpretation that should be reached in any given area or any given culture before comparisons are made in terms of such a typology. While we may be ready for a typology in ethnology, it may well be that more preliminary work should be done on the archeology of settlement patterns before the typology is attempted.

In addition, I should like to stress a couple of points at which I believe recent ethnological studies have often failed to provide the kind of data that would be most useful in relating our materials to prehistoric settlement patterns. The most obvious lack is the complete absence of precise settlement-pattern data in many monographs—an understandable omission, perhaps, when one is dealing with a great range of fact about a living culture. But it is usually a relatively simple matter to add a chart or map giving the exact representation of the relation of houses to one another and the over-all village or community plan. More frequent use of aerial photographs could provide the basis for this information, and I, for one, do not plan to undertake another field trip without utilizing this technique at the outset.

We obviously also need more precise information about the relationships of sheer spatial living arrangements to sociopolitical structure, both in general and in the case of particular cultures. We can say something about the general limits imposed by particular living arrangements, but we ethnologists are often embarrassed when the archeologist turns to us for more specific information along these lines.

Finally, I would raise a general theoretical question which I do not believe has been resolved on the basis of existing research. This question concerns the extent to which cultural beliefs and values (features which are difficult to infer from archeological remains) may affect settlement patterns in a manner that appears to override considerations of ecological and economic adjustment. We know that certain obvious limits are imposed by ecological and economic patterns; yet within these limits certain religious beliefs, for example, may affect the situation one way or another. Haury makes reference to this possibility when he mentions that banding together on the part of the Pueblos may in part have been influenced by the requirements of the religious system in promoting rain-making ceremonies. Kidder also refers to a religious force which seems to be operating to draw the Chavín population together periodically. Some kinds of cultural values, i.e., traditional conceptions of what is the most desirable type of settlement arrangement, seem to have persisted from the pre-Columbian past in highland Guatemala and still affect the settlement patterns described by Borhegyi—at least, no contemporary factors seem to explain the present variations. To provide another example, it has often been assumed that the clustering in a Mormon village in Utah grew out of the requirements of irrigation agriculture; yet we know that the village plan of the Mormons was invented as a suitable plat for the City of Zion when the Mormons were still living in the Middle West (Vogt and O'Dea, 1953). Or, again, it would be difficult to explain on purely ecological-economic or defense grounds why the Hopis still continue to live compactly in inconvenient mesa-top pueblos. This is also a problem area of archeological and ethnological research that merits a great deal of additional attention as we pursue our work on settlement patterns.

BIBLIOGRAPHY

ALEGRÍA, RICARDO E.
1951 "The Ball Game Played by the Aborigines of the Antilles," *American Antiquity*, XVI, 348–52.

ANONYMOUS CONQUEROR
1917 *Narrative of Some Things of New Spain and Great City of Temestitan, Mexico.* Translated into English by MARSHALL H. SAVILLE. ("Documents and Narratives concerning the Discovery and Conquest of Latin America," No. 1.) New York: Cortes Society.

ANTEVS, E.
1948 "Climatic Changes and Pre-white Man," *Bulletin of the University of Utah* ("Biological Series," Vol. X, No. 7), XXXVIII, 168–91.
1951 *Climatic History and the Antiquity of Man in California*, pp. 23–31. ("University of California Archaeological Survey, Reports," No. 16.)

ARMILLAS, PEDRO
1950 "Teotihuacán, Tula, y los Toltecas. Las culturas post-Arcaicas y pre-Aztecas del centro de Mexico: excavaciones y estudios, 1922–50," *Runa*, III, 37–70.

BARRETT, S. A.
1908 *The Ethnogeography of the Pomo and Neighboring Indians.* ("University of California Publications in American Archaeology and Ethnology," Vol. VI, No. 1.)

BARRETT, S. A., and GIFFORD, E. W.
1933 *Miwok Material Culture.* (Bulletin of the Public Museum of the City of Milwaukee, Vol. II, No. 4.)

BARTHOLOMEW, GEORGE A., JR., and BIRDSELL, JOSEPH B.
1953 "Ecology and the Protohominids," *American Anthropologist*, LV, No. 4, 481–98.

BATRES, LEOPOLDO
1903 *Visita a los monumentos arqueológicos de La Quemada, Zacatecas.* Mexico, D.F.

BEARDSLEY, RICHARD K.
1948 Culture Sequences in Central California Archaeology," *American Antiquity*, XIV, 1–28.
1954 *Temporal and Areal Relationships in Central California Archaeology.* ("University of California Archaeological Survey, Reports," Nos. 24, 25.)

BELL, EARL H., and CAPE, ROBERT E.
1936 *The Rock Shelters of Western Nebraska in the Vicinity of Dalton, Nebraska.* ("Chapters in Nebraska Archeology," No. 5.) Lincoln.

BENNETT, WENDELL C.
1936 *Excavations in Bolivia.* ("Anthropological Papers of the American Museum of Natural History," Vol. XXXV, Part 4.) New York: The Museum.
1937 *Excavations at La Mata, Maracay, Venezuela.* ("Anthropological Papers of the American Museum of Natural History," Vol. XXXV, Part 2.) New York: The Museum.
1944 *Archeological Regions of Colombia: A Ceramic Survey.* ("Yale University Publications in Anthropology," No. 30.) New Haven: Yale University Press.
1948 "The Peruvian Co-tradition," *American Antiquity*, XIII, No. 4, Part 2.
1950 *The Gallinazo Group, Virú Valley, Peru.* ("Yale University Publications in Anthropology," No. 43.) New Haven: Yale University Press.

BENNETT, WENDELL C.
    1953   *Excavations at Wari, Ayacucho, Peru.* ("Yale University Publications in An-
            thropology," No. 49.) New Haven: Yale University Press.
BENNETT, WENDELL C., and BIRD, JUNIUS B.
    1949   *Andean Culture History.* ("American Museum of Natural History Handbook
            Series," No. 15.) New York: The Museum.
BENNYHOFF, J. A.
    1953   "High Altitude Occupation in the Yosemite Park Region." In HEIZER, R. F.,
            and ELSASSER, A. B., *Some Archaeological Sites and Cultures of the Central
            Sierra Nevada*, Appendix B. ("University of California Archaeological Survey,
            Reports," No. 21.)
    1956   *An Appraisal of the Archaeological Resources of Yosemite National Park.*
            ("University of California Archaeological Survey, Reports," No. 34.)
BORHEGYI, STEPHAN F. DE
    1954a   "The Evolution of a Landscape," *Landscape, Magazine of Human Geography*,
            IV, No. 1, 24–30. Santa Fe, New Mexico.
    1954b   "The Cult of Our Lord of Esquipulas in Middle America and New Mexico,"
            El Palacio, LXI, No. 12, 387–401. Santa Fe, New Mexico.
BOYRIE MOYA, EMILE DE
    1955   *Monumento megalítico y petroglifos de Chacuey, República Dominicana.* ("Pu-
            blicaciones de la Universidad de Santo Domingo," ser. 7, Vol. XCVII, No. 1.)
            Ciudad Trujillo.
BRAINERD, G. W.
    1951   "Early Ceramic Horizons in Yucatan." In TAX, SOL (ed.), *Selected Papers of
            the XXIXth International Congress of Americanists*, Vol. I: *The Civilizations
            of Ancient America*, pp. 72–78. Chicago: University of Chicago Press.
    1954   *The Maya Civilization.* Los Angeles: Southwest Museum.
BRAND, D. D.
    1935   "The Distribution of Pottery Types in Northwest Mexico," *American An-
            thropologist*, XXXVII, No. 2, 287–305.
    1936   "Notes To Accompany a Vegetation Map of Northwest Mexico," *University
            of New Mexico Bulletin*. ("Biological Series," No. 4.)
    1939   "Notes on the Geography and Archaeology of Zape, Durango." In BRAND,
            D. D., and HARVEY, F. E. (eds.), *So Live the Works of Men: 70th Anniver-
            sary Volume Honoring Edgar Lee Hewett*, pp. 75–105. Albuquerque: Uni-
            versity of New Mexico.
    1943   "The Chihuahua Culture Area," *New Mexico Anthropologist*, Vols. VI–VII.
BREW, J. O.
    1946   *Archaeology of Alkali Ridge, Southeastern Utah.* ("Papers of the Peabody
            Museum of Archaeology and Ethnology, Harvard University," Vol. XXI.)
BROWER, J. V.
    1898   *Quivira.* ("Memoirs of Explorations in the Basin of the Mississippi," Vol. I.)
BRYAN, LT. F. T.
    1857   "Explorations for Road from Fort Riley to Bridger's Pass, 1856," Appendix H,
            Rept. of the Chief Topog. Eng., Ann. Rept. War Dept., 1857. (35th Cong., 1st
            sess., Exec. Doc. No. 2, Vol. II.) Washington, D.C.: Government Printing
            Office.
BULLEN, RIPLEY P.
    1949   *Excavations in Northeastern Massachusetts.* ("Papers of the Robert S. Peabody
            Foundation for Archaeology," Vol. I, No. 3.) Andover, Mass.
BURT, W. H.
    1943   "Territoriality and Home Range Concepts as Applied to Mammals," *Journal
            of Mammalogy*, XXIV, 346–52.
BYERS, DOUGLAS S.
    1954   "Bull Brook—a Fluted Point Site in Ipswich, Massachusetts," *American An-
            tiquity*, XIX, No. 4, 343–51.

1955 "Additional Information on the Bull Brook Site, Massachusetts," *ibid.*, XX, No. 3, 274–76.

CAMPBELL, E. W. C.
1931 *An Archaeological Survey of the Twenty-nine Palms Region*, pp. 1–93. ("Southwest Museum Papers," No. 7.) Los Angeles: The Museum.
1936 "Archaeological Problems in the Southern California Deserts," *American Antiquity*, I, 295–300.

CAMPBELL, E. W. C., *et al.*
1937 *The Archaeology of Pleistocene Lake Mohave*. ("Southwest Museum Papers," No. 11.) Los Angeles: The Museum.

CAREY, H. A.
1931 "An Analysis of the Northwestern Chihuahua Culture," *American Anthropologist*, XXXIII, 325–74.

CARTER, G. F.
1941 "Archaeological Notes on a Midden at Point Sal," *American Antiquity*, VI, 214–26.

CASON, JOE E.
1952 "Report on Archaeological Salvages in Falcon Reservoir, Season of 1952," *Bulletin of the Texas Archaeological and Paleontological Society*, Vol. XXIII.

CHAMPE, JOHN L.
1946 *Ash Hollow Cave*. ("University of Nebraska Studies," n.s., No. 1.) Lincoln: University of Nebraska Press.
1949 "White Cat Village," *American Antiquity*, XIV, No. 4, Part 1, 285–92.

COLE, FAY-COOPER, and DEUEL, THORNE
1937 *Rediscovering Illinois: Archaeological Explorations in and around Fulton County*. Chicago: University of Chicago Press.

COLTON, HAROLD S.
1932 "Sunset Crater," *Geographical Review*, XXII, No. 4, 582–90.
1936 "The Rise and Fall of the Prehistoric Population of Northern Arizona," *Science*, Vol. LXXXIV, No. 2181.
1939 *Prehistoric Culture Units and Their Relationships in Northern Arizona*. (Museum of Northern Arizona Bull. 17.) Flagstaff: The Museum.
1946 *The Sinagua*. (Museum of Northern Arizona Bull. 22.) Flagstaff: The Museum.

COOK, S. F.
1943 "The Conflict between the California Indians and White Civilization. I," *Ibero-Americana*, No. 21.
1946 "A Reconsideration of Shellmounds with Respect to Population and Nutrition," *American Antiquity*, XII, 51–53.
1950 *Physical Analysis as a Method for Investigating Prehistoric Habitation Sites*, pp. 2–5. ("University of California Archaeological Survey, Reports," No. 7.)

COOK, S. F., and HEIZER, R. F.
1951 *The Physical Analysis of Nine Indian Mounds of the Lower Sacramento Valley*. ("University of California Publications in American Archaeology and Ethnology," Vol. XL, No. 7.)

COOK, S. F., and TREGANZA, A. E.
1947 "The Quantitative Investigation of Aboriginal Sites: Comparative Physical and Chemical Analysis of Two California Indian Mounds," *American Antiquity*, XIII, 135–41.
1950 *The Quantitative Investigation of Indian Mounds*. ("University of California Publications in American Archaeology and Ethnology," Vol. XL, No. 5.)

COOPER, JOHN M.
1946 "The Culture of the Northeastern Indian Hunters: A Reconstructive Interpretation." In JOHNSON, FREDERICK (ed.), *Man in Northeastern North America*, pp. 272–305. ("Papers of the Robert S. Peabody Foundation for Archaeology," Vol. III.) Andover, Mass.

COOPER, PAUL
    1936 *Archeology of Certain Sites in Cedar County, Nebraska.* ("Chapters in Ne-
          braska Archeology," No. 1.) Lincoln: University of Nebraska Press.
    1940 "Report of Explorations (1938)," *Nebraska History,* XX, No. 2, 94–151.
COSCULLUELA, J. A.
    1951 "Cuatro años en la Cienaga de Zapata," *Revista de arqueología y etnología,*
          época 2, No. 12, pp. 31–168.
CRUXENT, J. M.
    1952 "Notes on Venezuelan Archeology." In TAX, SOL (ed.), *Selected Papers of the
          XXIXth International Congress of Americanists,* Vol. III: *Indian Tribes of Ab-
          original America,* pp. 280–94. Chicago: University of Chicago Press.
DAVIS, JAMES THOMAS
    n.d. "The Patterson Mound: A Comparative Analysis of Site Alameda 328."
          (Thesis for the Master's degree deposited in the University of California
          Library, Berkeley, 1954.)
DUNLEVY, MARION L.
    1936 *A Comparison of the Cultural Manifestations of the Burkett (Nance County)
          and the Gray-Wolfe (Colfax County) Sites,* pp. 147–247. ("Chapters in Ne-
          braska Archeology," No. 2.) Lincoln: University of Nebraska Press.
EGGAN, FRED
    1950 *Social Organization of the Western Pueblos.* Chicago: University of Chicago
          Press.
EKHOLM, GORDON F.
    1940 "The Archaeology of Northern and Western Mexico." In HAY, C. L. (ed.),
          The Maya and Their Neighbors, pp. 320–30. New York: D. Appleton–Cen-
          tury Co.
    1944 *Excavation at Tampico and Pánuco in the Huasteca, Mexico.* ("Anthropologi-
          cal Papers of the American Museum of Natural History," Vol. XXXVIII, Part
          1.) New York: The Museum.
EWERS, JOHN C.
    1955 *The Horse in Blackfoot Indian Culture.* (Bureau of American Ethnology
          Bull. 159.) Washington, D.C.: Smithsonian Institution.
FARABEE, W. C.
    1914 "Mounds of Marajó, Fortaleza." (Field notebook on file at University Mu-
          seum, Philadelphia.)
FENTON, WILLIAM N.
    1951 "Locality as a Basic Factor in the Development of Iroquois Social Structure."
          In FENTON, W. N. (ed.), *Symposium on Local Diversity in Iroquois Culture,*
          pp. 39–54. (Bureau of American Ethnology Bull. 149.) Washington, D.C.:
          Smithsonian Institution.
FERDON, EDWIN N., JR.
    1955 *A Trial Survey of Mexican-southwestern Architectural Parallels.* ("Mono-
          graphs of the School of American Research," No. 21.) Santa Fe, N.M.
FEWKES, J. W.
    1900 "Tusayan Migration Traditions," *Nineteenth Annual Report of the Bureau of
          American Ethnology.* Washington, D.C.: Smithsonian Institution.
    1914 "Relations of Aboriginal Culture and Environment in the Lesser Antilles,"
          Bulletin of the American Geographical Society, XLVI, 662–78.
FISK, HAROLD N.
    1944 *Geological Investigation of the Alluvial Valley of the Lower Mississippi River.*
          ("Mississippi River Commission Publications," No. 52.)
FLANNERY, REGINA
    1946 "The Culture of the Northeastern Indian Hunters: A Descriptive Survey."
          In JOHNSON, FREDERICK (ed.), *Man in Northeastern North America,* pp. 263–
          71. ("Papers of the Robert S. Peabody Foundation for Archaeology," Vol.
          III.) Andover, Mass.

FORD, JAMES A.
 1951 *Greenhouse: A Troyville–Coles Creek Period Site in Avoyelles Parish, Louisiana.* ("American Museum of Natural History Anthropological Papers," Vol. XLIV, Part 1.)
 1954 "Additional Notes on the Poverty Point Site in Northern Louisiana," *American Antiquity*, XIX, No. 3, 282–85.
FORD, JAMES A., PHILLIPS, PHILIP, and HAAG, WILLIAM G.
 1955 *The Jaketown Site in West-central Mississippi.* ("American Museum of Natural History Anthropological Papers," Vol. XLV, Part 1.)
FORD, JAMES A., and QUIMBY, GEORGE I., JR.
 1945 *The Tchefuncte Culture: An Early Occupation of the Lower Mississippi Valley.* ("Memoirs of the Society for American Archaeology," No. 2.)
FORD, JAMES A., and WILLEY, GORDON R.
 1940 *Crooks Site: A Marksville Period Burial Mound in La Salle Parish, Louisiana.* (Louisiana Geological Survey, "Anthropological Studies," No. 3.)
 1941 "An Interpretation of the Prehistory of the Eastern United States," *American Anthropologist*, XLIII, No. 3, Part 1, 325–63.
FORDE, C. DARYLL
 1931 *Yuma Ethnography.* ("University of California Publications in American Archaeology and Ethnology," Vol. XXVIII, No. 4.)
FOSTER, GEORGE M.
 1944 *A Summary of Yuki Culture.* ("University of California Anthropological Records," Vol. V, No. 3.)
 1951 "Report on an Ethnological Reconnaissance of Spain," *American Anthropologist*, LIII, No. 3, 311–25.
GAMIO, MANUEL
 1910 "Los Monumentos arqueológicos de las immediaciones de Chalchihuites," *Anales del Museo Nacional de Arquelogía, Historia, y Etnografía*, Tercera época, II, 469–92. Mexico, D.F.
GARCÍA VALDES, PEDRO
 1948 "The Ethnography of the Ciboney." In STEWARD, JULIAN (ed.), *Handbook of South American Indians*, IV, 503–5. (Bureau of American Ethnology Bull. 143.) Washington, D.C.: Smithsonian Institution.
GIFFORD, E. W.
 1916 *Composition of California Shellmounds.* ("University of California Publications in American Archaeology and Ethnology," Vol. XII, No. 1.)
 1923 *Pomo Lands on Clear Lake*, pp. 56–77. ("University of California Publications in American Archaeology and Ethnology," Vol. XX.)
 1931 *The Kamia of Imperial Valley.* (Bureau of American Ethnology Bull. 97.) Washington, D.C.: Smithsonian Institution.
GODDARD, P. E.
 1923 *The Habitat of the Wailaki*, pp. 95–109. ("University of California Publications in Archaeology and Ethnology," Vol. XX.)
GOLDMAN, EDWARD A.
 1951 *Biological Investigations in Mexico.* ("Smithsonian Miscellaneous Collections," Vol. CXV.) Washington, D.C.: Smithsonian Institution.
GOUBAUD CARRERA, ANTONIO
 1946 "La Población de habla indígena en Guatemala," *Boletín del Instituto Indigenista Nacional*, I, No. 4, 17–22.
 1947 "Mercados regionales guatemaltecos," *ibid.*, II, Nos. 3–4, 139–70.
GRASSMANN, THOMAS
 1952 "The Mohawk-Caughnawaga Excavation," *Pennsylvania Archaeologist*, XXII, No. 1, 33–36.
GREENGO, ROBERT C.
 1951 *Molluscan Species in California Shell Middens.* ("University of California Archaeological Survey, Reports," No. 13.)

GRIFFIN, JAMES B.
1946   *Cultural Change and Continuity in Eastern United States Archaeology*, pp.
       37–95. ("Papers of the Robert S. Peabody Foundation for Archaeology," Vol.
       III.)
1952   "Prehistoric Cultures of the Central Mississippi Valley." In GRIFFIN, J. B.
       (ed.), *Archeology of Eastern United States*, pp. 226–38. Chicago: University
       of Chicago Press.
GRIFFIN, JAMES B., and SPAULDING, ALBERT C.
1952   "The Central Mississippi Valley Archeological Survey, Season 1950," *Prehis-
       toric Pottery of the Eastern United States*, II, 1–7. Ann Arbor: University of
       Michigan Press.
GRIFFIN, JOHN W.
1945   "New Evidence from the Fisher Site," *Transactions of the Illinois Academy
       of Science*, XXXVII, 37–40.
HACK, JOHN T.
1942   *The Changing Physical Environment of the Hopi Indians*. ("Papers of the
       Peabody Museum of Archaeology and Ethnology, Harvard University," Vol.
       XXXV, No. 1.) Cambridge: Harvard University Press.
HALL, E. T., JR.
1942   *Archeological Survey of the Walhalla Glades*. (Museum of Northern Arizona
       Bull. 20.) Flagstaff: The Museum.
HARGRAVE, L. L.
1938   "Results of a Study of the Cohonina Branch of the Patayan Culture in 1938,"
       Museum Notes, XI, 43–55.
HARRINGTON, M. R.
1921   "Cuba before Columbus." In *Indian Notes and Monographs, Museum of the
       American Indian, Heye Foundation*. 2 vols. New York: Heye Foundation.
1924   *An Ancient Village Site of the Shinnecock Indians*. ("Anthropological Papers
       of the American Museum of Natural History," Vol. XXII, Part 5.) New York:
       The Museum.
1948   An Ancient Site at Borax Lake, California. ("Southwest Museum Papers,"
       No. 16.) Los Angeles: The Museum.
HAURY, E. W.
1945   *The Excavations of Los Muertos and Neighboring Ruins of the Salt River
       Valley, Southern Arizona*. ("Papers of the Peabody Museum of Archaeology
       and Ethnology, Harvard University," Vol. XXIV, No. 1.) Cambridge: Har-
       vard University Press.
HAWLEY, F. M.
1937   "Pueblo Social Organization as a Lead to Pueblo History," *American Anthro-
       pologist*, XXXIX, 504–22.
HEIZER, ROBERT F.
1941   "The Direct Historical Approach in California Archaeology," *American An-
       tiquity*, VII, 98–122.
1942   *Massacre Lake Cave, Tule Lake Cave, and Shore Sites*, pp. 121–34. ("Carnegie
       Institution of Washington Publications," No. 538.) Washington, D.C.: The In-
       stitution.
1949   *The Archaeology of Central California. I. The Early Horizon*. ("University
       of California Anthropological Records," Vol. XII, No. 1.)
1951a *An Assessment of Certain Nevada, California, and Oregon Radiocarbon Dates*,
       pp. 23–25. ("Memoirs of the Society for American Archaeology," No. 8.)
1951b *A Review of Problems in the Antiquity of Man in California*, pp. 3–17.
       ("University of California Archaeological Survey, Reports," No. 16.)
1952   *A Survey of Cave Archaeology in California*, pp. 1–12. ("University of Cali-
       fornia Archaeological Survey, Reports," No. 15.)

HEIZER, ROBERT F. (ed.)
1953 *The Archaeology of the Napa Region.* ("University of California Anthropological Records," Vol. XII, No. 6.)
HEIZER, ROBERT F., and ELSASSER, ALBERT B.
1953 *Some Archaeological Sites and Cultures of the Central Sierra Nevada.* ("University of California Archaeological Survey, Reports," No. 21.)
HEIZER, ROBERT F., and FENENGA, FRANKLIN
1939 "Archaeological Horizons in Central California," *American Anthropologist,* XLI, 378–99.
HEIZER, ROBERT F., and LEMERT, EDWIN M.
1947 *Observations on Archaeological Sites in Topanga Canyon, California.* ("University of California Publications in American Archaeology and Ethnology," Vol. XLIV, No. 2.)
HEIZER, ROBERT F., and MILLS, JOHN E.
1952 *The Four Ages of Tsurai.* Berkeley: University of California Press.
HERRERA FRITOT, RENÉ, and YOUMANS, CHARLES L.
1946 *La Caleta: joya arqueológica antillana.* Havana.
HEWES, G. W.
1941 "Archaeological Reconnaissance of the Southern San Joaquin Valley," *American Antiquity,* VII, 123–33.
HEWETT, EDGAR L.
1936 *The Chaco Canyon and Its Monuments.* ("Handbooks of Archaeological History.") Albuquerque: University of New Mexico Press.
HILL, A. T., and KIVETT, M. F.
1941 "Woodland-like Manifestations in Nebraska," *Nebraska History,* XXI, No. 3, 147–243.
HILL, A. T., and METCALF, GEORGE
1942 "A Site of the Dismal River Aspect in Chase County, Nebraska," *Nebraska History,* XXII, No. 2, 158–226.
HILL, A. T., and WEDEL, WALDO R.
1936 "Excavations at the Leary Indian Village and Burial Site, Richardson County, Nebraska," *Nebraska History,* XVII, No. 1, 2–73.
HOLDER, PRESTON, and WIKE, JOYCE
1949 "The Frontier Culture Complex: A Preliminary Report on a Prehistoric Hunters' Camp in Southwestern Nebraska," *American Antiquity,* XIV, No. 4, 260–66.
HOOVER, J. W.
1941 "Corros de trincheras of the Arizona Papagueria," *Geographical Review,* XXXI, No. 2, 228–39.
HOSTOS, ADOLFO DE
1941 "Notes on West Indian Hydrography in Its Relation to Prehistoric Migrations." In his *Anthropological Papers,* pp. 30–53.
HOWARD, H.
1929 *The Avifauna of Emeryville Shellmound,* pp. 301–94. ("University of California Publications in Zoölogy," Vol. XXXII.)
HOWE, HENRY F.
1943 *Prologue to New England.* New York.
HRDLICKA, ALES
1903 "The Region of the Ancient Chichimecs, with Notes on the Tepecanos and the Ruin of La Quemada, Mexico," *American Anthropologist,* V, 340–85.
HUGHES, JACK T.
1949 "Investigations in Western South Dakota and Northeastern Wyoming," *American Antiquity,* XIV, No. 4, 266–77.
HURT, WESLEY R., JR.
1952 *Report of the Investigations of the Scalp Creek Site 39GR1 and the Ellis Creek Site 39GR2, Gregory County, South Dakota.* (South Dakota Archeological

Commission, "Archeological Studies Circulars," No. 4.) Pierre: The Commission.

HYDE, GEORGE E.
1951   *Pawnee Indians*. Denver: University of Denver Press.

JAMES, EDWIN
1823   *Account of an Expedition from Pittsburgh to the Rocky Mountains, Performed in the Years 1819–20 . . . under the Command of Major Stephen H. Long*. 2 vols. Philadelphia.

JENNINGS, JESSE D.
1952   "Prehistory of the Lower Mississippi Valley." In GRIFFIN, J. B. (ed.), *Archeology of Eastern United States*, pp. 256–71. Chicago: University of Chicago Press.

JEPSON, WILLIS LINN
1923   *A Manual of the Flowering Plants of California*. Berkeley: Associated Students Store.

JOHNSON, FREDERICK, *et al.*
1942   *The Boylston Street Fishweir*. ("Papers of the Robert S. Peabody Foundation for Archaeology," Vol. II.) Andover, Mass.

JOHNSON, FREDERICK, and RAUP, HUGH M.
1947   *Grassy Island*. ("Papers of the Robert S. Peabody Foundation for Archaeology," Vol. I, No. 2.) Andover, Mass.

JONES, M. R.
1952   *Map of the Ruins of Mayapan, Yucatan, Mexico*. ("Carnegie Institution of Washington Current Reports," Vol. I, No. 1.) Washington, D.C.: Carnegie Institution.

JUDD, NEIL M.
1954   *The Material Culture of Pueblo Bonito*. ("Smithsonian Miscellaneous Collections," Vol. CXXIV.) Washington, D.C.: Smithsonian Institution.

KELLEY, J. CHARLES
1939   "Archaeological Notes on the Excavation of a Pithouse near Presidio, Texas," *El Palacio*, Vol. XLIV, No. 10.
1949   "Archaeological Notes on Two Excavated House Structures in Western Texas," *Bulletin of the Texas Archaeological and Paleontological Society*, Vol. XX.
1951   "A Bravo Valley Aspect Component of the Lower Rio Conchos Valley, Chihuahua, Mexico," *American Antiquity*, XVII, No. 2, 114–19.
1952   "Factors Involved in the Abandonment of Certain Peripheral Southwestern Settlements," *American Anthropologist*, LIV, No. 3, 356–87.
1952–53   "The Historic Indian Pueblos of La Junta de Los Ríos," *New Mexico Historical Review*, XXVII, No. 4, 257–95, and XXVIII, No. 1, 21–51.
1953   "Reconnaissance and Excavation in Durango and Southern Chihuahua, Mexico," *Yearbook of the American Philosophical Society*, pp. 172–76.

KELLEY, J. CHARLES, CAMPBELL, T. N., and LEHMER, D. J.
1940   "The Association of Archaeological Materials with Geological Deposits in the Big Bend Region of Texas," *Sul Ross State Teachers College Bulletin*, XXI, No. 3, 31–38 and 73–81.

KELLEY, J. CHARLES, and SHACKELFORD, W. J.
1954   "Preliminary Notes on the Weicker Site, Durango, Mexico," *El Palacio*, LXI, No. 5, 145–60.

KELLY, I. J.
1938   "Band Organization of the Southern Paiute," *American Anthropologist*, XL, 633–34.

KIDDER, A. V.
1916   "The Pottery of the Casas Grandes District, Chihuahua," *Holmes Anniversary Volume, Anthropological Essays*, pp. 252–68. Washington, D.C.: J. W. Bryan Press.

KIMBALL, FISKE
  1922 *Domestic Architecture of the American Colonies and of the Early Republic.*
         New York.
KINIETZ, VERNON W.
  1940 *Indians of the Western Great Lakes, 1615–1760.* ("Occasional Contributions
         from the Museum of Anthropology of the University of Michigan.") Ann
         Arbor: University of Michigan Press.
KIRCHHOFF, PAUL
  1952 "Meso-America." In TAX, SOL (ed.), *Heritage of Conquest,* pp. 17–30. Glen-
         coe, Ill.: Free Press.
KIVETT, M. F.
  1949 "Archeological Investigations in Medicine Creek Reservoir, Nebraska," *Amer-
         ican Antiquity,* XIV, No. 4, 278–84.
  1952 *Woodland Sites in Nebraska.* ("Nebraska State Historical Society Publications
         in Anthropology," No. 1.) Lincoln: The Society.
KNEBERG, MADELINE
  1952 "The Tennessee Area." In GRIFFIN, J. B. (ed.), *Archeology of Eastern United
         States,* pp. 190–98. Chicago: University of Chicago Press.
KNIFFEN, FRED B.
  1928 *Achomawi Geography.* ("University of California Publications in American
         Archaeology and Ethnology," Vol. XXIII, No. 5.)
  1939 *Pomo Geography.* ("University of California Publications in American Ar-
         chaeology and Ethnology," Vol. XXXVI, No. 6.)
KROEBER, A. L.
  1909 "The Archaeology of California." In BOAS, F. (ed.), *Putnam Anniversary
         Volume,* pp. 1–42. New York: G. E. Stechert & Co.
  1917 *Zuñi Kin and Clan.* ("Anthropological Papers of the American Museum of
         Natural History," Vol. XVIII, Part II.) New York: The Museum.
  1925 *Handbook of the Indians of California.* (Bureau of American Ethnology Bull.
         78.) Washington, D.C.: Smithsonian Institution.
  1932 *The Patwin and Their Neighbors.* ("University of California Publications in
         American Archaeology and Ethnology," Vol. XXIX, No. 4.)
  1934 "Native American Population," *American Anthropologist,* XXXVI, 1–25.
  1936 *Culture Element Distributions.* III. *Area and Climax,* pp. 101–16. ("University
         of California Publications in American Archaeology and Ethnology," Vol.
         XXXVII.)
  1939 *Natural and Cultural Areas of Native North America.* ("University of Cali-
         fornia Publications in American Archaeology and Ethnology," Vol. XXXVIII.)
KUBLER, GEORGE
  1947 "Mexican Urbanism in the Sixteenth Century," *Art Bulletin,* XXIV, No. 2,
         160–71.
LARCO HOYLE, R.
  1948 *Cronología arqueológica del Norte del Peru.* Trujillo, Peru.
LEACOCK, ELEANOR
  1954 *The Montagnais "Hunting Territory" and the Fur Trade.* ("American An-
         thropologist Memoirs," No. 78.)
LEHMER, DONALD J.
  1938 "The Jornada Branch of the Mogollon," *University of Arizona Social Science
         Bulletin,* No. 1.
  1954 "The Sedentary Horizon of the Northern Plains," *Southwestern Journal of
         Anthropology,* X, No. 2, 139–59.
LEWIS, T. M. N.
  1954 "The Paleo-Indian Problem in Tennessee." In *Ten Years of the Tennessee
         Archaeologist, Selected Subjects,* pp. 248–50. Chattanooga, Tenn.: Tennessee
         Archaeological Society.

LILLARD, J. B., HEIZER, R. F., and FENENGA, F.
1939 *An Introduction to the Archaeology of Central California.* (Sacramento Junior College, Department of Anthropology, Bull. 2.)

LINNÉ, SIGVALD
1934 *Archaeological Researches at Teotihuacán, Mexico.* ("Publications of the Ethnographical Museum of Sweden," No. 1.) Stockholm.
1942 *Mexican Highland Cultures: Archaeological Researches at Teotihuacán, Calpulalpan, and Chalchicomula in 1934–35.* ("Publications of the Ethnographical Museum of Sweden," No. 7.) Stockholm.

LINTON, RALPH
1940 "Crops, Soils, and Culture in America." In HAY, C. L. (ed.), *The Maya and Their Neighbors*, pp. 32–40. New York: D. Appleton–Century Co.

LORENZ, K. Z.
1952 *King Solomon's Ring: New Light on Animal Ways.* London: Methuen Press.

LOTHROP, S. K.
1924 *Tulum.* ("Carnegie Institution of Washington Publications," No. 335.) Washington, D.C.: Carnegie Institution.

LOUD, LLEWELLYN L.
1918 *Ethnogeography and Archaeology of the Wiyot Territory.* ("University of California Publications in American Archaeology and Ethnology," Vol. XIV, No. 3.)
1924 *The Stege Mounds at Richmond, California.* ("University of California Publications in American Archaeology and Ethnology," Vol. XVII, No. 6.)

LOUGEE, RICHARD J.
1953 "A Chronology of Postglacial Time in Eastern North America," *Scientific Monthly*, LXXVI, No. 5, 259–76.

LOVÉN, SVEN
1935 *Origins of the Tainan Culture, West Indies.* Göteborg: Elanders Boktryckeri Aktiebolag.

McBRIDE, GEORGE McCUTCHEN, and McBRIDE, MERLE A.
1942 "Highland Guatemala and Its Maya Communities," *Geographical Review*, XXXII, No. 2, 252–68.

McCOWN, B. E.
1945 "An Archaeological Survey of the San Vicente Lake Bed, San Diego County, California," *American Antiquity*, X, 255–64.

McGREGOR, JOHN C.
1952 "The Havana Site." In DEUEL, THORNE (ed.), *Hopewell Communities in Illinois*, pp. 45–91. ("Scientific Papers," Vol. V.) Springfield: Illinois State Museum.

McGREGOR, JOHN C., et al.
1951 *The Cohonina Culture of Northwestern Arizona.* Urbana: University of Illinois Press.

McINTIRE, WILLIAM G.
1954 *Correlation of Prehistoric Settlements and Delta Development: Trafficability and Navigability of Delta-Type Coasts.* ("Technical Reports of the U.S. Mississippi River Commission," No. 5.)

MacNEISH, R. S.
1947 "A Preliminary Report on Coastal Tamaulipas, Mexico," *American Antiquity*, Vol. XIII, No. 1.
1948 "Prehistoric Relationships between the Cultures of the Southwestern United States and Mexico in Light of an Archaeological Survey in the State of Tamaulipas, Mexico." (Doctoral dissertation, Department of Anthropology, University of Chicago.)
1950 "A Synopsis of the Archaeological Sequence in the Sierra de Tamaulipas," *Revista mexicana de estudios antropológicos*, Vol. XI.

1954 "An Early Archaeological Site near Panuco, Vera Cruz," *Transactions of the American Philosophical Society*, XLIV, Part 5, 539–641.

1955 "The Third Tamaulipas Archaeological Expedition," *American Philosophical Yearbook for 1954.*

n.d. "An Introduction to the Archaeology of the Sierra de Tamaulipas, Mexico." (MS.)

MARTIN, PAUL S., and RINALDO, JOHN B.

1950 *Sites of the Reserve Phase, Pine Lawn Valley, Western New Mexico.* ("Fieldiana: Anthropology," Vol. XXXVIII, No. 3.) Chicago: Chicago Natural History Museum.

MASON, JOHN ALDEN

1931–39 *Archaeology of Santa Marta, Colombia: The Tairona Culture.* ("Field Museum of Natural History Anthropological Series," Vol. XX, Nos. 1–3.) Chicago: The Museum.

1937 "Late Archaeological Sites in Durango, Mexico, from Chalchihuites to Zape." In DAVIDSON, D. S. (ed.), *25th Anniversary Studies.* ("Publications of the Philadelphia Anthropological Society.")

1941 *A Large Archaeological Site at Capá, Utuado, with Notes on Other Porto Rico Sites Visited in 1914–15.* ("New York Academy of Sciences, Scientific Survey of Porto Rico and the Virgin Islands," Vol. XVIII, Part 2.) New York: The Academy.

MAYER-OAKES, WILLIAM J.

1955 *Prehistory of the Upper Ohio Valley: An Introductory Archeological Study.* ("Anthropological Series," No. 2; "Annals of the Carnegie Museum," Vol. XXXIV.)

MEGGERS, BETTY J., and EVANS, CLIFFORD, JR.

1957 *Archeological Investigations at the Mouth of the Amazon.* Washington, D.C.: Smithsonian Institution (in press).

MEIGHAN, CLEMENT W.

1953 *The Coville Rock Shelter, Inyo County, California.* ("University of California Anthropological Records," Vol. XII, No. 5.)

1954 "A Late Complex in Southern California Prehistory," *Southwestern Journal of Anthropology*, X, 215–27.

1955a *Notes on the Archaeology of Mono County*, pp. 6–28. ("University of California Archaeological Survey, Reports," No. 28.)

1955b *Archaeology of the North Coast Ranges, California*, pp. 1–39. ("University of California Archaeological Survey, Reports," No. 30.)

1955c *Excavation of Isabella Meadows Cave, Monterey County, California*, pp. 1–30. ("University of California Archaeological Survey, Reports," No. 29.)

MEIGHAN, CLEMENT W., and EBERHART, HAL

1953 "Archaeological Resources of San Nicolas Island, California," *American Antiquity*, XIX, 109–25.

MILLS, JOHN E.

1950 *Recent Developments in the Study of Northwestern California Archaeology*, pp. 21–25. ("University of California Archaeological Survey, Reports," No. 7.)

MINDELEFF, COSMOS

1900 "Localization of Tusayan Clans," *Nineteenth Annual Report of the Bureau of American Ethnology.* Washington, D.C.: Smithsonian Institution.

MINDELEFF, VICTOR

1891 "A Study of Pueblo Architecture," *Eighth Annual Report of the Bureau of American Ethnology.* Washington, D.C.: Smithsonian Institution.

MOOREHEAD, WARREN K.

1922 *Archaeology of Maine.* Phillips Academy, Andover, Mass.: Andover Press.

MORLEY, S. G.

1946 *The Ancient Maya.* Stanford, Calif.: Stanford University Press.

MULLOY, WILLIAM

1952 "The Northern Plains." In GRIFFIN, J. B. (ed.), *Archeology of Eastern United States*, pp. 124–38. Chicago: University of Chicago Press.

1954a "Archeological Investigations in the Shoshone Basin of Wyoming," *University of Wyoming Publications*, XVIII, No. 1, 1–70.

1954b "The McKean Site in Northeastern Wyoming," *Southwestern Journal of Anthropology*, X, No. 4, 432–60.

MURPHY, HENRY C.

1875 *The Voyage of Verrazano: A Chapter in the Early History of Maritime Discovery in America.* New York.

MURPHY, HENRY C. (ed.)

1867 *Journal of a Voyage to New York and a Tour in Several of the American Colonies in 1679–80, by Jaspar Dankers and Peter Sluyter of Wiewerd in Friesland.* ("Memoirs of the Long Island Historical Society," Vol. I.) Brooklyn, N.Y.

NELSON, N. C.

1909 *Shellmounds of the San Francisco Bay Region.* ("University of California Publications in American Archaeology and Ethnology," Vol. VII, No. 4.)

1910 *The Ellis Landing Shellmound.* ("University of California Publications in American Archaeology and Ethnology," Vol. VII, No. 5.)

NICE, MARGARET M.

1941 "The Role of Territory in Bird Life," *American Midland Naturalist*, XXVI, 441–87.

NOGUERA, EDUARDO

1930 *Ruinas arqueológicas del Norte del Mexico, Casas Grandes (Chihuahua), La Quemada, Chalchihuites (Zacatecas).* ("Publicaciones de la Secretaria de Educación pública.") Mexico, D.F.

NOMLAND, GLADYS AYER, and KROEBER, A. L.

1936 *Wiyot Towns.* ("University of California Publications in American Archaeology and Ethnology," Vol. XXXV, No. 5.)

O'BRYAN, DERIC

1952 "The Abandonment of the Northern Pueblos in the Thirteenth Century." In TAX, SOL (ed.), *The Indian Tribes of Aboriginal America: Selected Papers of the XXIXth International Congress of Americanists.* Chicago: University of Chicago Press.

OEHLER, GOTTLIEB F., and SMITH, D. Z.

1851 *Description of a Journey and Visit to the Pawnee Indians, April 22–May 18, 1851.* ("Moravian Church Miscellany, 1851–52.")

OLSON, R. L.

1930 *Chumash Prehistory.* ("University of California Publications in American Archaeology and Ethnology," Vol. XXVIII, No. 1.)

ORR, P. C.

1951 "Ancient Population Centers of Santa Rosa Island," *American Antiquity*, XVI, 221–26.

OSGOOD, CORNELIUS

1943 *Excavations at Tocorón, Venezuela.* ("Yale University Publications in Anthropology," No. 29.) New Haven: Yale University Press.

OSGOOD, CORNELIUS, and HOWARD, GEORGE D.

1943 *An Archeological Survey of Venezuela.* ("Yale University Publications in Anthropology," No. 27.) New Haven: Yale University Press.

PARSONS, E. C.

1939 *Pueblo Indian Religion.* 2 vols. Chicago: University of Chicago Press.

PEABODY, CHARLES

1904 *Exploration of Mounds, Coahoma County, Mississippi.* ("Papers of the Peabody Museum of Archaeology and Ethnology, Harvard University," Vol. III, No. 2.)

PHILLIPS, PHILIP
    n.d.   "The Lower Yazoo Basin." (MS in preparation.)
PHILLIPS, PHILIP, FORD, JAMES A., and GRIFFIN, JAMES B.
    1951   *Archaeological Survey in the Lower Mississippi Alluvial Valley, 1940–1947.*
            ("Papers of the Peabody Museum of Archaeology and Ethnology, Harvard
            University," Vol. XXV.)
PICHARDO MOYA, FELIPE
    1945   *Caverna, costa y meseta.* Havana.
PIMENTEL, LUIS GARCÍA (ed.)
    1897   *Descripción del Arzobispado de México hecha en 1570.* Mexico, D.F.
QUIMBY, GEORGE I.
    1942   "The Natchezan Culture Type," *American Antiquity,* VII, No. 3, 225–75.
    1951   *The Medora Site, West Baton Rouge Parish, Louisiana,* pp. 79–135. ("Field
            Museum of Natural History Anthropological Series," Vol. XXIV, No. 2.)
    1954   "Cultural and Natural Areas before Kroeber," *American Antiquity,* XIX,
            No. 4, 317–31.
RAINEY, FROELICH G.
    1940   *Porto Rican Archaeology.* ("New York Academy of Sciences, Scientific Sur-
            vey of Porto Rico and the Virgin Islands," Vol. XVIII, Part 1.) New York:
            The Academy.
    1941   *Excavations in the Ft. Liberté Region, Haiti.* ("Yale University Publications
            in Anthropology," No. 23.) New Haven: Yale University Press.
REED, ERIK K.
    1942   "Implications of the Mogollon Concept," *American Antiquity,* VIII, No. 1,
            27–32.
    1946   "The Distinctive Features and Distribution of the San Juan Anasazi Culture,"
            Southwestern Journal of Anthropology, II, No. 3, 295–305.
    1948   "The Western Pueblo Archaeological Complex," *El Palacio,* LV, No. 1, 9–15.
    1949a   "The Significance of Skull Deformation in the Southwest," *ibid.,* LVI, No. 4,
            106–19.
    1949b   "Sources of Upper Rio Grande Pueblo Culture and Population," *ibid.,* No. 6,
            pp. 163–84.
    1950   "Eastern-central Arizona Archaeology in Relation to the Western Pueblos,"
            Southwestern Journal of Anthropology, VI, No. 2, 120–38.
    1951a   "Turkeys in Southwestern Archaeology," *El Palacio,* LVIII, No. 7, 195–205.
    1951b   "Types of Stone Axes in the Southwest," *Southwestern Lore,* XVII, No. 3,
            45–51.
    1951c   "Cultural Areas of the Pre-Spanish Southwest," *New Mexico Quarterly,* XXI,
            No. 4, 428–39.
REICHEL-DOLMATOFF, GERARDO
    1954a   "Investigaciones arqueológicas en la Sierra Nevada de Santa Marta. 1, 2,"
            Revista colombiana de antropología, II, No. 2, 174–202.
    1954b   "Investigaciones arqueológicas en la Sierra Nevada de Santa Marta. 3," *ibid.,*
            III, 139–70.
    1954c   "A Preliminary Study of Space and Time Perspective in Northern Colombia,"
            American Antiquity, XIX, 352–66.
RICKETSON, O. G., JR.
    1929   *Excavations at Baking Pot, British Honduras.* ("Carnegie Institution of Wash-
            ington Publications," No. 403; "Contributions to American Archaeology,"
            Vol. I, No. 1.) Washington, D.C.: Carnegie Institution.
RICKETSON, O. G., JR., and RICKETSON, E. B.
    1937   *Uaxactun, Guatemala, Group E, 1926–1931.* ("Carnegie Institution of Wash-
            ington Publications," No. 477.) Washington, D.C.: Carnegie Institution.
RIDDELL, H. S.
    1951   *The Archaeology of a Paiute Village Site,* pp. 14–28. ("University of Cali-
            fornia Archaeological Survey, Reports," No. 12.)

RITCHIE, WILLIAM A.
1932 *The Lamoka Lake Site.* ("Researches and Transactions of the New York State Archeological Association," Vol. VII, No. 4.) Rochester: The Association.
1936 *A Prehistoric Fortified Village Site at Canandaigua, Ontario County, New York.* ("Research Records of the Rochester Museum of Arts and Sciences," No. 3.) Rochester: The Museum.
1938 *Certain Recently Explored New York Mounds and Their Probable Relation to the Hopewell Culture.* ("Research Records of the Rochester Museum of Arts and Sciences," No. 4.) Rochester: The Museum.
1940 *Two Prehistoric Village Sites at Brewerton, New York.* ("Research Records of the Rochester Museum of Arts and Sciences," No. 5.) Rochester: The Museum.
1944 *The Pre-Iroquoian Occupations of New York State.* ("Rochester Museum Memoirs," No. 1.) Rochester: The Museum.
1945 *An Early Site in Cayuga County, New York.* ("Research Records of the Rochester Museum of Arts and Sciences," No. 7.) Rochester: The Museum.
1946 *A Stratified Prehistoric Site at Brewerton, New York.* ("Researches and Transactions of the New York State Archeological Association," Vol. XI, No. 1.) Rochester: The Association.
1947 *Archaeological Evidence for Ceremonialism in the Owasco Culture.* ("Researches and Transactions of the New York State Archeological Association," Vol. XI, No. 2.) Rochester: The Association.
1950 "Another Probable Case of Prehistoric Bear Ceremonialism in New York," *American Antiquity,* XV, No. 3, 247–49.
1953a "A Probable Paleo-Indian Site in Vermont," *ibid.,* XVIII, No. 3, 249–58.
1953b *An Early Owasco Sequence in Eastern New York.* ("New York State Museum Circular," No. 32.) Albany: The Museum.
1955 *Recent Discoveries Suggesting an Early Woodland Burial Cult in the Northeast.* ("New York State Museum and Science Service Circulars," No. 40.) Albany: The Museum.
RITCHIE, WILLIAM A., and MACNEISH, RICHARD S.
1949 "The Pre-Iroquoian Pottery of New York State," *American Antiquity,* XV, No. 2, 97–124.
ROBERTS, FRANK H. H., JR.
1929 *Shabik'eshchee Village.* (Bureau of American Ethnology Bull. 92.) Washington, D.C.: Smithsonian Institution.
1940 *Developments in the Problem of the North American Paleo-Indian,* pp. 51–116. ("Smithsonian Miscellaneous Collections," Vol. C.) Washington, D.C.: Smithsonian Institution.
1953 "Earliest Men in America," *Cahiers d'histoire mondiale,* Vol. I, No. 2.
ROGERS, DAVID BANKS
1929 *Prehistoric Man of the Santa Barbara Coast.* Santa Barbara, Calif.: Santa Barbara Museum of Natural History.
ROGERS, EDWARD H.
1943 "The Indian River Village Site," *Bulletin of the Archaeological Society of Connecticut,* No. 15, pp. 3–78.
ROGERS, M. J.
1929 "Stone Art of the San Dieguito Plateau," *American Anthropologist,* XXX, 454–67.
1939 *Early Lithic Industries of the Lower Basin of the Colorado River and Adjacent Desert Areas.* ("San Diego Museum Papers," No. 3.)
ROUSE, IRVING
1941 *Culture of the Ft. Liberté Region, Haiti.* ("Yale University Publications in Anthropology," No. 24.) New Haven: Yale University Press.
1942 *Archeology of the Maniabón Hills, Cuba.* ("Yale University Publications in Anthropology," No. 26.) New Haven: Yale University Press.

1947   "Ceramic Traditions and Sequences in Connecticut," *Bulletin of the Archaeological Society of Connecticut*, No. 21, pp. 10–25.

1948   "The West Indies." In Steward, Julian (ed.), *Handbook of South American Indians*, IV, 495–566. (Bureau of American Ethnology Bull. 143.) Washington, D.C.: Smithsonian Institution.

1949   "The Southeast and the West Indies." In Griffin, John W. (ed.), *The Florida Indian and His Neighbors*, pp. 117–37. Winter Park, Fla.: Rollins College.

1951   *A Survey of Indian River Archeology, Florida.* ("Yale University Publications in Anthropology," No. 44.) New Haven: Yale University Press.

1952   *Porto Rican Prehistory.* ("New York Academy of Sciences, Scientific Survey of Porto Rico and the Virgin Islands," Vol. XVIII, Parts 3–4.) New York: The Academy.

1953a   "The Circum-Caribbean Theory: An Archeological Test," *American Anthropologist*, LV, 188–200.

1953b   *Guianas.* ("Program of the History of America," Vol. I, No. 7; "Instituto Panamericano de Geografía e Historia Publicación," No. 157.) Mexico, D.F.

Rowe, John H.
1944   *An Introduction to the Archaeology of Cuzco.* ("Papers of the Peabody Museum of American Archaeology and Ethnology, Harvard University," Vol. XXVII, No. 2.)

1946   "Inca Culture at the Time of the Spanish Conquest." In Steward, Julian (ed.), *Handbook of South American Indians*, Vol. II. (Bureau of American Ethnology Bull. 143.) Washington, D.C.: Smithsonian Institution.

Roys, L. Ralph
1952   *Conquest Sites and the Subsequent Destruction of Maya Architecture in the Interior of Northern Yucatan*, pp. 129–82. ("Carnegie Institution of Washington Publications," No. 596; "Contributions to American Anthropology and History," Vol. XI, No. 54.) Washington, D.C.: Carnegie Institution.

Russell, R. J.
1932   *Dry Climates of the United States.* ("University of California Publications in Geography," Vol. V, Nos. 4 and 5.) Berkeley: University of California Press.

Ruttenber, E. M.
1872   *History of the Indian Tribes of Hudson's River.* Albany, N.Y.

Sanders, William T.
n.d.   "The Urban Revolution in Central Mexico." (MS in Peabody Museum Library, Harvard University.)

Sargent, Howard R.
1952   "A Preliminary Report on the Excavations at Grannis Island," *Bulletin of the Archaeological Society of Connecticut*, No. 26, pp. 30–50.

Sauer, Carl O.
1944   "A Geographic Sketch of Early Man in America," *Geographical Review*, XXXIV, No. 4, 529–73.

Sayles, E. B.
1936a   *Some Southwestern Pottery Types, Series V.* ("Medallion Papers," No. 21.) Globe, Ariz.: Gila Pueblo.

1936b   *An Archaeological Survey of Chihuahua, Mexico.* ("Medallion Papers," No. 22.) Globe, Ariz.: Gila Pueblo.

Schaedel, Richard P.
1951   "Major Ceremonial and Population Centers in Northern Peru." In Tax, Sol (ed.), *The Civilizations of Ancient America: Selected Papers of the XXIXth International Congress of Americanists*, Vol. I. Chicago: University of Chicago Press.

Schenck, W. Egbert, and Dawson, Elmer J.
1929   *Archaeology of the Northern San Joaquin Valley.* ("University of California Publications in American Archaeology and Ethnology," Vol. XXV, No. 4.)

SCHOLES, F. V., and MERA, H. P.
   1940   *Some Aspects of the Jumano Problem,* pp. 265–99. ("Carnegie Institution of Washington Publications," No. 523; "Contributions to American Anthropology and History," No. 34.) Washington, D.C.: Carnegie Institution.

SCHULTZ, C. B., and FRANKFORTER, W. D.
   1948   "Preliminary Report on the Lime Creek Sites: New Evidence of Early Man in Southwestern Nebraska," *Bulletin of the University of Nebraska State Museum,* III, No. 4, Part 2, 43–62.

SCULLY, EDWARD G.
   1951   "Some Central Mississippi Valley Projectile Point Types." (Mimeographed MS in Museum of Anthropology, University of Michigan, Ann Arbor.)

SEARS, PAUL B.
   1942   "Xerothermic Theory," *Botanical Review,* VIII, No. 10, 708–36.

SEARS, WILLIAM H.
   1954   "The Sociopolitical Organization of Pre-Columbian Cultures on the Gulf Coastal Plain," *American Anthropologist,* LVI, No. 3, 339–46.

SELLARDS, E. H.
   1952   *Early Man in America.* Austin: University of Texas Press.
   1950   *Sexto censo general de población, abril 18 de 1950.* Guatemala City: Dirección General de Estadística, Oficina Permanente del Censo.

SHACKELFORD, W. J.
   1955   "Excavations at the Polvo Site in Western Texas," *American Antiquity,* XX, No. 3, 256–62.

SHETRONE, HENRY C.
   1926   "Exploration of the Ginther Mound: The Miesse Mound." In MILLS, W. C. (ed.), *Certain Mounds and Village Sites in Ohio: Transactions of the Ohio State Archaeological and Historical Society,* IV, Part 3, 59–75. Columbus.

SHOOK, EDWIN M.
   1952   "Lugares arqueológicos del altiplano meridional central de Guatemala," *Antropología e historia de Guatemala,* IV, No. 2, 3–40.

SHOOK, EDWIN M., and KIDDER, A. V.
   1952   *Mound E-III-3, Kaminaljuyu, Guatemala.* ("Carnegie Institution of Washington Contributions to American Anthropology and History," Vol. XI, No. 53.) Washington, D.C.: Carnegie Institution.

SIMPSON, L. B.
   1934   "Studies in the Administration of the Indians in New Spain. 2. The Civil Congregation," *Ibero-Americana,* VII, 29–129.

SMITH, A. L.
   1950   *Uaxactun, Guatemala: Excavations of 1931–1937.* ("Carnegie Institution of Washington Publications," No. 588.) Washington, D.C.: Carnegie Institution.

SMITH, BENJAMIN L.
   1948   "An Analysis of the Maine Cemetery Complex," *Bulletin of the Massachusetts Archaeological Society,* Vol. IX, Nos. 2–3.

SMITH, C. E., and WEYMOUTH, W. D.
   1952   *Archaeology of the Shasta Dam Area, California.* ("University of California Archaeological Survey, Reports," No. 18.)

SMITH, CARLYLE SHREEVE
   1950   *The Archaeology of Coastal New York.* ("Anthropological Papers of the American Museum of Natural History," Vol. XLIII, Part 2.) New York: The Museum.

SNYDERMAN, GEORGE S.
   1951   "Concepts of Land Ownership among the Iroquois and Their Neighbors." In FENTON, W. N. (ed.), *Symposium on Local Diversity in Iroquois Culture,* pp. 15–34. (Bureau of American Ethnology Bull. 149.) Washington, D.C.: Smithsonian Institution.

SPECK, FRANK G.
1935 *Naskapi: The Savage Hunters of the Labrador Peninsula.* Norman: University of Oklahoma Press.

SQUIER, ROBERT J., and GROSSCUP, GORDON L.
n.d. "Preliminary Report of Archaeological Investigations in Lower Klamath Basin, California: 1954." (Mimeographed report to the U.S. National Park Service.)

STANISLAWSKI, DAN
1947 "Early Spanish Town Planning in the New World," *Geographical Review,* XXXVII, No. 1, 94–105.
1950 *The Anatomy of Eleven Towns in Michoacán.* ("Institute of Latin American Studies, Latin American Studies," No. 10.) Austin: University of Texas Press.

STEPHENSON, ROBERT L.
1951 *Archaeological Excavations at the Falcon Reservoir, Starr County, Texas.* ("River Basin Surveys: An Appraisal of the Archaeological Resources," No. 52.) (Mimeographed report at the Smithsonian Institution.)

STEWARD, JULIAN H.
1933 *Ethnography of the Owens Valley Paiute.* ("University of California Publications in American Archaeology and Ethnology," Vol. XXXIII, No. 3.)
1936 "The Economic and Social Basis of Primitive Bands." In *Essays in Anthropology Presented to A. L. Kroeber,* pp. 331–50. Berkeley: University of California Press.
1937 "Ecological Aspects of Southwestern Society," *Anthropos,* XXXII, 87–104.
1938 *Basin-Plateau Aboriginal Sociopolitical Groups.* (Bureau of American Ethnology Bull. 120.) Washington, D.C.: Smithsonian Institution.
1947 "American Culture History in the Light of South America," *Southwestern Journal of Anthropology,* III, No. 2, 85–107.
1948 "The Circum-Caribbean Tribes: An Introduction." In his *Handbook of South American Indians,* IV, 1–41. (Bureau of American Ethnology Bull. 143.) Washington, D.C.: Smithsonian Institution.
1949 "Cultural Causality and Law: A Trial Formulation of the Development of Early Civilizations," *American Anthropologist,* LI, No. 1, 1–27.

STEWART, O. C.
1943 *Notes on Pomo Ethnogeography.* ("University of California Publications in American Archaeology and Ethnology," Vol. XL, No. 2.)

STRONG, W. D.
1927 "An Analysis of Southwestern Society," *American Anthropologist,* XXIX, 1–61.
1935 *An Introduction to Nebraska Archeology.* ("Smithsonian Miscellaneous Collections," Vol. XCIII, No. 10.) Washington, D.C.: Smithsonian Institution.
1954 "Recent Archaeological Discoveries in South Coastal Peru," *Transactions of the New York Academy of Sciences,* Ser. II, Vol. XVI, No. 4.

STRONG, W. D., and EVANS, CLIFFORD, JR.
1952 *Cultural Stratigraphy in the Virú Valley, Northern Peru: The Formative and Florescent Epochs.* ("Columbia Studies in Archaeology and Ethnology," Vol. IV.) New York: Columbia University Press.

STUMER, LOUIS M.
1954 "Population Centers of the Rimac Valley of Peru," *American Antiquity,* Vol. XX, No. 2.

SWANTON, JOHN R.
1942 *Source Material on the History and Ethnology of the Caddo Indians.* (Bureau of American Ethnology Bull. 132.) Washington, D.C.: Smithsonian Institution.

TAX, SOL
1937 "The Municipios of the Midwestern Highlands of Guatemala," *American Anthropologist,* XXXIX, No. 3, 423–44.

TAYLOR, W. W.
 1948 *A Study of Archaeology*. ("American Anthropological Association Memoirs,"
 No. 69.) Menasha, Wis.: Banta Press.

THOMPSON, J. E. S.
 1940 *Late Ceramic Horizons at Benque Viejo, British Honduras*. ("Carnegie Institution of Washington Contributions to American Anthropology and History,"
 No. 35.)
 1954 *The Rise and Fall of Maya Civilization*. Norman: University of Oklahoma
 Press.

TOUSSAINT, M., GÓMEZ DE OROZCO, FEDERICO, and FERNÁNDEZ, JUSTINO
 1938 *Planos de la ciudad de México, siglos XVI and XVII*. Mexico, D.F.: Instituto
 de Investigaciones Estéticas de la Universidad de México.

TREGANZA, A. E., and MALAMUD, C. G.
 1950 *The Topanga Culture: Second Season's Excavation of the Tank Site, 1947*.
 ("University of California Anthropological Records," Vol. XII, No. 4.)

TREGANZA, A. E., SMITH, C. E., and WEYMOUTH, W. D.
 1950 *An Archaeological Survey of the Yuki Area*. ("University of California Anthropological Records," Vol. XII, No. 3.)

TSCHOPIK, HARRY, JR.
 1946 "Some Notes on Rock Shelter Sites near Huancayo, Peru," *American Antiquity*, Vol. XVII, No. 2.

TURNEY, OMAR A.
 1929 *Prehistoric Irrigation in Arizona*. Phoenix: Arizona State Historian.

UHLE, MAX
 1907 *The Emeryville Shellmound*. ("University of California Publications in American Archaeology and Ethnology," Vol. VII, No. 1.)

VOGT, EVON Z., and O'DEA, THOMAS F.
 1953 "A Comparative Study of the Role of Values in Social Action in Two Southwestern Communities," *American Sociological Review*, XVIII, No. 6, 645–54.

WALLACE, W. J.
 1951 "The Mortuary Caves of Calaveras County, California," *Archaeology*, IV,
 199–203.

WATERMAN, T. T.
 1920 *Yurok Geography*. ("University of California Publications in American
 Archaeology and Ethnology," Vol. XVI, No. 5.)

WAUCHOPE, ROBERT
 1934 *House Mounds of Uaxactun, Guatemala*. ("Carnegie Institution of Washington Publications," No. 436; "Contributions to American Archaeology," Vol. I,
 No. 7.)
 1950 *A Tentative Sequence of Pre-Classic Ceramics in Middle America*. ("Middle
 American Research Records," Middle American Research Institute, Tulane
 University, Vol. I, No. 14.)

WEBB, WILLIAM S.
 1942 *The C. and O. Mounds at Paintsville, Sites JO 2 and JO 9, Johnson County,
 Kentucky*. ("University of Kentucky Reports in Anthropology and Archaeology," Vol. V, No. 4.) Lexington: University of Kentucky.
 1943 *The Riley Mound Site Be 15 and the Landing Mound Site Be 17, Boone
 County, Kentucky*. ("University of Kentucky Reports in Anthropology and
 Archaeology," Vol. V, No. 7.) Lexington: University of Kentucky.
 1946 *Indian Knoll, Site Oh 2, Ohio County, Kentucky*. ("University of Kentucky
 Reports in Anthropology and Archaeology," Vol. IV, No. 3, Part 1.) Lexington: University of Kentucky.

WEBB, WILLIAM S., and SNOW, CHARLES E.
 1947 *The Adena People*. ("University of Kentucky Reports in Anthropology and
 Archaeology," Vol. VI.) Lexington: University of Kentucky.

WEDEL, WALDO R.

1935 "Minneapolis I, a Prehistoric Village Site in Ottawa County, Kansas," *Nebraska Historical Magazine*, XV, No. 3, 210–37.

1938 *The Direct-historical Approach in Pawnee Archeology.* ("Smithsonian Miscellaneous Collections," Vol. XCVII, No. 7.) Washington, D.C.: Smithsonian Institution.

1941 *Environment and Native Subsistence Economies in the Central Great Plains.* ("Smithsonian Miscellaneous Collections," CI, No. 3.) Washington, D.C.: Smithsonian Institution.

1942 *Archeological Remains in Central Kansas and Their Possible Bearing on the Location of Quivira.* ("Smithsonian Miscellaneous Collections," CI, No. 7.) Washington, D.C.: Smithsonian Institution.

1949 "Some Provisional Correlations in Missouri Basin Archeology," *American Antiquity*, XIV, No. 4, 328–39.

1953 "Some Aspects of Human Ecology in the Central Plains," *American Anthropologist*, LV, No. 4, 499–514.

WENDORF, FRED

1954 "A Reconstruction of Northern Rio Grande Prehistory," *American Anthropologist*, LVI, No. 2, 200–227.

WENDORF, FRED (ed.)

1953 *Salvage Archaeology in the Chama Valley, New Mexico.* ("Monographs of the School of American Research," No. 17.) Santa Fe: The School.

WENDORF, FRED, and REED, ERIK

1955 "An Alternative Reconstruction of Northern Rio Grande Prehistory," *El Palacio*, LXII, Nos. 5–6, 131–73.

WILL, G. F., and SPINDEN, H. J.

1906 *The Mandans.* ("Papers of the Peabody Museum of American Archaeology and Ethnology, Harvard University," Vol. III, No. 4.)

WILLEY, GORDON R.

1949 *Archaeology of the Florida Gulf Coast.* ("Smithsonian Miscellaneous Collections," Vol. CXIII.) Washington, D.C.: Smithsonian Institution.

1953 *Prehistoric Settlement Patterns in the Virú Valley, Peru.* (Bureau of American Ethnology Bull. 155.) Washington, D.C.: Smithsonian Institution.

WILLEY, GORDON R., and BULLARD, W. R., JR.

1956 "The Melhado Site: A Prehistoric Maya House Mound Group near El Cayo, British Honduras," *American Antiquity*, Vol. XXII, No. 1.

WILLEY, GORDON R., BULLARD, W. R., and GLASS, J. B.

1955 "The Maya Community of Prehistoric Times," *Archaeology*, VIII, No. 1, 18–25.

WILLIAMS, STEPHEN

1954 "An Archeological Study of the Mississippian Culture in Southeast Missouri." (Unpublished Ph.D. thesis, Department of Anthropology, Yale University.)

n.d. "The Nodena Report." (MS in preparation.)

WILLOUGHBY, CHARLES C.

1898 *Prehistoric Burial Places in Maine.* ("Papers of the Peabody Museum of Archaeology and Ethnology, Harvard University," Vol. I, No. 6.) Cambridge, Mass.: Harvard University Press.

WITHERS, ARNOLD M.

1954 "University of Denver Archeological Fieldwork, 1952–1953," *Southwestern Lore*, XIX, No. 4, 1–3.

WITTFOGEL, K., and GOLDFRANK, E. S.

1943 "Some Aspects of Pueblo Mythology and Society," *Journal of American Folklore*, LVI, 17–30.

WITTHOFT, JOHN
  1952 "A Paleo-Indian Site in Eastern Pennsylvania: An Early Hunting Culture,"
         Proceedings of the American Philosophical Society, XCVI, No. 4, 464–95.
WORMINGTON, H. M.
  1949 *Ancient Man in North America*. (Denver Museum of Natural History, "Popu-
         lar Series," No. 4.) 3d ed., revised. Denver: The Museum.